W9-ABM-516

BALBOA: CONQUISTADOR

BALBOA: CONQUISTADOR

The Soul-Odyssey of Vasco Núñez,
Discoverer of the Pacific 〰〰〰

OMAR V. GARRISON

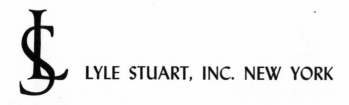
LYLE STUART, INC. NEW YORK

TO MARTHA, MY MOTHER

In Memoriam

If the world is a miracle, the history of life is a dream; we know not whither it goes, nor do we know its beginning and end. All humanity plays to a certain extent a blind game, and is kept together less by clear knowledge than by the instinctive dream-pole. An internal, hidden poet leads them by a secure thread through the labyrinths of time and space. Hidden in the breast of man lie the everlasting messengers of Heaven and Hell, who step forth, now as glorified spirits to console, now as terrific monsters on his path. Hegel said somewhere, "All History is a book of dreams, a collection of dreams"; and if the dreams had been collected which men had dreamt during a certain period, a true picture of the spirit of the time would have been given.

—Joseph Ennemoser

Gentlemen, this is no tale of Amadis the Gaul, but a true account of Vasco Núñez de Balboa, that man who was our Captain and adelantado of the Austral Sea, called by the Indians of those regions, Tibá or Great Lord.

It was he who by much labor and all the tragical affairs of the sea, first discovered and gained to the crown of Castile that great sea of the south. So he gave meaning to the shapeless maps and thereby cast and imaged all those enterprises that were brought to pass afterward.

Prologue ~~~~~~

I am the man called Juan of Toledo: born an hidalgo and of pure blood: a voyager to the Indies: and I marched with the adelantado Vasco Núñez even to the sea of the south.

As one who has discovered some of the secrets and diversities of the country and witnessed the high things done in these parts, I must make known who he was and all that happened to him and to the company who resorted to him.

Consider how he passed over to these shores with nothing of his own save his sword and his honor (for he was a man of good cape, his blood enriched by kinship with the royal house of León). Yet such were his qualities and valor that the Catholic King, of glorious memory, raised him to noble estate and bestowed on him the pre-eminences and favors of adelantado.

As for these spite-weavers and Judases who evilly conspired his death: they are devils and the sons of devils (and in the life hereafter, let their balls turn to brimstone, sunk in everlasting fire). Our Captain judges them still—a terrible look, *señores!*—from the eye-holes of that once noble head, raised high on a pole above the plaza of this town: for it was he who brought us hither and built it with his own hands and the hands of honorable men.

We were the first of our kind to inhabit this country: men of desperate boldness: the first to nourish its soil with the blood of Castile, León, Aragon, Venice. And how many thus perished: they who rot in the alien glebe, and some have fed the wild beasts, and

11

some lie in their seaweed coffins, dreamless . . . lost . . . as though they had never lived. And none of us, the living, knows in his heart if the time between life and death be of a season or an hour.

Tyranny and injustice rule now, and these dapper-jacks come newly from Spain with their bright and unused armor, their untempered stomachs: they are well lodged, visited, and served, their fat rumps velveted with our losses.

But it was we who took this land and our lives forfeit. Ours was the soldier's fare and the fighting. Valderrábano, Botello, Muñoz, Argüello! I marched with those men: *baquianos* who knew the miseries of the country.

I remember the voyages, loud with storms: troubled sleep in strange places: the bad food, the hard labor, how evening would come with the plum-blue dusk and the slow drift of smoke over the Indian villages: the fire-images by night: the endless pelting rain from those skies and the bitter nidor of marshes, rusting our armor and rotting our clothes: the sound of thudding feet and the lost cries of battle. . . .

And over and through these things the sound of our austral sea, locked in my heart as in a shell. . . . As we saw it for the first time through a golden net of sunlight, where the small leaves quivered like fishes: the nostril-opening smell of its airs that lifted the hair with coolness . . . and beyond, where it rolled and glittered in the distant sun.

Holy Mother! Let those in the time to come remember that hour of our glory. Theirs will be the memoried names upon new houses: for them the lasting uplands, the plowed earth with good seed in it, and children born under the strong rooftree of the enduring abode.

Yet the life of this our Captain has in it such letters of good credit as in the days hereafter may easily dispose the lies here empowered with malice: the evil deeds here done.

Chapter I ~~~~~~~~~~~~~~~~~~~~~~~~~~~~~~~~~~~~

On the nones of March in the year 1501, there put forth from Cadiz, a port of the Ocean Sea, two ships which set their course for the Indies on a voyage of traffic and discovery.

The said ships were a nao, *Santa Maria de Gracia*, of some eighty tons' burden, and a caravel, *San Antón*, smaller in size, but sturdy of build and newly rigged for the outward passage.

Commanding that enterprise was Rodrigo de Bastidas, a notary of Seville, and a man well-favored as to good behavior and courtesy. As a consequence of the good name he carried, namely that he exercised great care and diligence in all his undertakings, the Bishop Fonseca, in charge of discoveries, had received his petition for an *asiento* with open ears.

The notary had spoken with great eloquence, shaping his speech into such apt remarks as might assure Fonseca that we would countervail our charges with much gain. That above all, at no point in those pagan lands where we shoaled ship or dropped anchor would we forget that message of the Holy Faith and to make baptisms: that this would redound to the temporal glory of him, of Bishop Fonseca, who to that end sent with us two priests.

As reports of this enterprise were quickly spread abroad, three score officers and men of great merit gladly left the security of their accustomed condition to enlist in the voyage. Among the valorous company thus enrolled and willing to do what was laid upon them, was Vasco Núñez de Balboa, a man skilled with the

13

use of the sword and who had fought against the Moors as a dependent of the deaf Lord of Moguer.

He was fair and tall: of gallant mien: his face handsome and full of sentiment. His voice likewise drew attention, and in his words we perceived a man of clear understanding and without guile in him.

But as for *nombradía*, he was little honored or renowned in that day, being counted a common soldier who lived by his blade. Yet, of all of us who that day went forth in those ships, the greatest honors and triumphs were to be his.

We sailed first to the Canaries, where we took aboard such supplies as were there provided and which had not been laden in Spain. These were mainly fresh meat, cheeses, sweet water, and certain medicinal herbs.

Being thus provisioned and ready in all respects to take our voyage by sea while the wind served us, we departed those islands exercised with lively thoughts of what we might bring to pass in our great enterprise.

We stood to the West by South, sailing before the wind like voyaging clouds.

I deem it a matter unnecessary to remember the full diurnal of our course thither, save for mention of the storms which rose (to our great trouble) but which we passed through, thus arming us with great faith for all that was to follow afterward, even unto being cast away.

On the twelfth morning out from the Grand Canary, the wind hauled North and was a loom gale, loud in the riggings. So they luffed her, while the order came:

"Off with the bonnets!"

And all that day was a gloom, with a scud on the sky and the mariners at the halyards. And I heard the helmsman's cry faint on the wind: "*Guarda! Guarda!*"

Such as were of the ship's company, men of the sea, walked with ease on the ship, their legs familiar to the tilting decks. But we who had followed our fortunes on land were cast about and felt ourselves at the edge of illness.

The cook, a big Portuguese with heavy rings of fat around his

14

neck and a look of insolence in his eyes, roared forth in his bull's basso, as he stood in the cuddy, preparing food.

He sang a chanty of the sea, the refrain of which was caught up by some of the mariners at their tasks.

> "O, what have you done with the master
> That he walks the decks no more:
> With the foamy wake behind him
> And the whistling shrouds before?
>
> *In a scuttle-butt we chunked him:*
> *Ah! Ah! And haul away!*
> *That night the Devil bunked him:*
> *Ah! Ah! And haul away!"*

There was no sunset that day, and night fell black upon us. A thin veil of rain slanted across the ship and the sails were wet with it. The wind rose and with it the sea. So the mariners took in the mainsail, doing it quietly this time and by the feel of it, for little was visible in that heavy pall.

There was much fear of fire among the seafarers: thus no lamps were lighted for the darkness, save the small helmsman's light, the ship's lantern at the stern, and a small signal aloft for the *San Antón* to follow.

Through a cloud-rift overhead, a lone star appeared, vapory and distant: the only thing in that world of heaving darkness that did not move, but remained steadfast and sure. We marked it as a good omen, and a gromet sang out, his steadfast choir-boy treble unwinding like the tremulous song of a bird lost over the waters.

"O star, guide us in the dark night of this our world. Amen."

The wind increased and shrilled in the rigging aloft. They struck all sail except enough to lend her steerage-way. And all that night we tossed about in a squall. We who took shelter in the sterncastle heard from below the heavy trampling of the horses and their terrified whinnys as they were thrown about in the rolling nao.

Then, as it were in an instant, the wind veered, dropped, and a lull came. The gale through which we had been plunging fell to a soft breeze: the great sierras of water smoothed themselves into long troughs in which we rocked.

15

The boatswain went quickly forward and uncovered the hatchway. To those within he bellowed: "*Ha de proa!* Hie you for a vow! Bring light!"

The mariners gathered on deck with a hoarse babble of talk. From their words we learned that the calm which had fallen was to be of brief duration and would be followed by yet another tempest. As it was their wont, they assembled on deck to cast lots as to which of them would make a pledge to the Holy Virgin, in the name of all, seeking her protection and salvation for the nao.

All who were aboard therefore joined in the said divination. Bastidas and those of the afterguard came, one at a time, and with a look haggard of the sea in that faint light.

The Notary carried a small ship's lantern, which he passed over to a gromet to hold.

"The peas?" asked the master then. "Where are the peas?"

"Floriano has gone for them," the boatswain answered him.

And even at that moment, the Portuguese came swiftly from the bodega carrying a quantity of chickpeas in a gourd.

"How many souls aboard?" Master Boriol then asked Bastidas.

The Notary gave thought and replied, "Thirty-two."

The master thereupon counted out that number into the cupped hands of the first mate, who transferred them into a red woolen cap of the kind worn by the mariners. All had fallen silent and followed the master's movements as though he had been a priest occupied with a holy service.

The master drew forth a single chickpea from the cap and, holding it between the thumb and forefinger of his left hand, took from Floriano a sliver of charcoal with his right. On the pea thus held he traced a small black cross.

"For the blessing, Fray Antonio."

And so to the monk, who took it gently into the hollow of his hand and held it as it were a consecrated host. He was a thin, tall man, slightly bowed. He had the lean and austere face of his order's founder, and his eyes gleamed darkly in the pale light beneath his cowl. He was of my city, of Toledo, and was a man of some honor, having served the Queen as counsellor and chronicler.

"*In nomine patri, filii et spiritus sanctus.*"

He returned the pea to Boriol, who dropped it into the cap with

16

the others. As the peas were shaken together, the master asked: "What shall be the vow, Don Rodrigo?"

"That, and we come safely through the tempest, the bearer of the vow shall go and keep vigil all night in the Church of Santa Maria del Antigua in Seville, there to have said a Mass of thanksgiving at our common expense. And he shall carry as testimony to the loving mercy of Our Lady a taper of one *vara*'s length."

The cap was passed from hand to hand, beginning with Bastidas, the master, the first mate, and so on. I was myself about to draw forth a pea when the *veedor*, peering closely at the pea he had pulled out, exclaimed: "It has fallen to me!"

He signed himself with the cross, kissed the consecrated pea, and cast it into the sea with the motion of one sowing a seed.

In lusty chorus and great familiarity, the ship's complement sang their *Salve Regina*. For my part, I kept silence, believing as I did, that the ceremony was a sailor's superstition.

The second tempest, which followed closely upon the first as the mariners had said it would do, blew itself out before dawn. There was much fear among us that the *San Antón* had been lost to the tempest we had survived. She was a smaller craft than our *capitana*. Still, her sailing qualities were of the first mark. And Juan de la Cosa, under whose hand she sailed, was a skilled navigator and pilot.

Our concern was given dignity shortly before midday when the lookout sighted what seemed to be a piece of wreckage floating in the sea. It was, however, too far away to identify or to bring aboard the flagship for closer inspection.

Even as we spoke among ourselves of this solemn portent, the lookout shouted from the roundtop: "A ship! A ship!"

"Where passing?" Boriol called back, trumpeting through his cupped hands.

"On the port quarter," came the faint and wind-ravaged answer.

Looking in that direction, I could dimly descry a misty shape, perchance a sail. It rose and then disappeared with the movement of the sea.

But as we sailed nearer, it took the familiar shape of a caravel. She was hove-to, awaiting our approach. A cry of rejoicing went up from all our company. And for us landsmen it was a sight worth

17

seeing, how the skilled mariners aboard both barks worked them alongside each other.

"By my Patron!" cried Bastidas across to Juan de la Cosa. "You seem to be in a single piece. We feared you lost."

"Lost? In so mild a tempest?" he answered him, laughing easily as was his way. "Our bugler, Simón Llorente, can whistle a stronger wind than that."

"Fine words for a man with a dry foot," Bastidas nodded. "How do you make out our position?"

"Yesterday my reckoning was four hundred and ten leagues from the Canary. Admiral Columbus found signs of islands in this region, and that was a good log. At daybreak today a pelican came to our ship, and later a river bird. These betoken land."

"You have not sighted one of those isles?"

"No, I believe they lie some leagues southward."

"Then, with fair winds, perhaps in two more sabbaths we will fall with land?"

"With good sailing, yes."

So did we stretch sail and fill away, following our course westward: and for the rest of that voyage the weather favored us. On the morning of the twenty-ninth day, while the sun was yet only a halberd's length above the horizon, the lookout cried: "Land! Land!"

Scanning the sea to starboard, I discerned a smoky blur along the horizon. It might easily have passed for a bank of low clouds. But the veteran mariners were certain it was land. For the past three days we had seen good signs: floating green rush, some ducks, and many gray gulls.

The master gave the order to shorten sail: and we altered our course, steering toward that dark shape on the distant water.

Thus it rose out of the sea, with gray-green foliage forming a great mound of the water.

As the shipmates of our nao pressed along the sides of the vessel and hung from the rigging, joyous with the sight, Fray Antonio suddenly began to chant the *Gloria in Excelsis Deo*. They all took it up, their unschooled voices rumbling like a rattle of stones across the decks.

A Lombardy was discharged to make known to the *San Antón*, some leagues astern, that we had sighted land.

Keeping good watch and bearing but slack sail, we moved toward that green island in the sun. And after a cautious search of the unknown waters, we found safe anchorage in six fathoms of clear water.

Chapter 2 ∿∿∿∿∿∿∿∿∿∿∿∿∿∿∿∿∿∿∿∿∿∿∿∿∿∿∿

On the third day after we had raised that island which we named Isla Verde, and during the second watch of the night, we once more sighted land.

For the remainder of that night, the two ships stood off and on, fearing shoals along the shore. But with the coming of the first light, we made sail and moved slowly toward land until we found ourselves in water which soundings showed to be of anchorage depth.

Both Bastidas in our ship and Cosa in the *San Antón* ordered boats to be got ready, and with a company of eleven men, they coasted along the shore.

I was not a member of the landing party, and I watched them from the poop until they disappeared from view around a point. The sky had begun to clear, but the stars were still bright overhead. And I stood regarding them, like a *romancero* (so do all men, but speak not of it to each other). And I saw them, as it were, silver bells which for many ages had remained silent over this land, waiting for some moment of great discovery, whereat their thronging sweet notes would fill heaven and earth with the annunciation.

A cold wind blew across the deck, with a blade-sharp edge on it, and such did not favor my dreaming. The air began to pierce the quilting of my doublet with the sharp needles of present truth: I looked toward the land, and saw mountains beyond, rising through the thin light, dark and unknown.

There, I thought, at last is Tierra Firme. Faith, and there's a backbone to it.

The pinnaces returned at noon, with Bastidas in a state of excitement.

"Tierra Firme," he announced as he climbed aboard. "Cosa has so declared. A few leagues down shore is a small village, the smoke of whose fires we have already seen rising. Make ready the articles of trade."

The men complied with wondrous speed. The fever of greed had already taken hold of them. From almost every niche and container in the ship, they brought forth a sudden profusion of hawk's bells, glass beads, lace points, red caps, and other baubles that could be exchanged for gold and pearls.

Bastidas assembled us all on deck with final instructions as to behavior and traffic with the Indians of this land. How the writ he carried gave us the right to barter for "gold ornaments, silver, copper, lead, tin, quicksilver, and any other metal whatsoever."

The document likewise granted license to acquire *aljofar*, pearls, precious stones and gems; slaves, Negroes, and mixed breeds; and monstrosities, serpents, fishes, and birds; also spices and drugs and every other thing of whatsoever name or quality or value it might carry.

But nothing was to be taken by violence.

"We have not come over to these Indies to plunder villages, commit hostile acts, or to carry away women." So said Bastidas, his voice loud as a horn: and I heard them laugh behind their hands like boys.

"Such is not the will of our great and just sovereigns," he told us with a frown (but he was young: not yet thirty): "and such, certainly, is not the desire of Rodrigo de Bastidas.

"Therefore, beware of God's wrath if you wantonly ravage the innocent of these lands. But even more beware the anger of your Captain General.

"I proclaim to you now: any man found engaged in unlawful acts or evil commerce shall forfeit all his avails, here and in Castile.

22

"Now, gentlemen of Spain, go with luck, and look to it that you bait your hooks delicately."

We clambered into the boats and rowed toward shore. Rounding a point, we found ourselves entering a calm-watered voe. The shoreline there met the edge of a dark-green forest, from which rushed forth a deep-channelled river.

Cosa, who was in the leading boat, now called back to those of us who followed: "Bear hard upon it, you *marineros*. There's a strong current here."

So they worked hard on the oars: they fought the swiftness of that stream which would bear us back from our desired course. They also had difficulty in steering the boats, for the strong current turned us about, this way and that.

After thus struggling against the powerful issue of that great river, we put in where the banks were less steep and the thickets sparse (the first landing party having landed here before us).

Bastidas climbed to the top of a small hill. From that point he descried once more the village he had seen before.

"I see a well-trodden trail," he called to us below. "When all are arrived from the ships, we will proceed."

But as he spoke, there was a threshing in the riparian brushwood, and, as we looked in wonder, a score of Indians sprang out of hiding. They swiftly surrounded us, their bowstrings drawn, their arrows pointed at us.

Beholding for the first time the indigenes of those lands, I saw that they were well-formed and had smooth and gentle faces. Though completely naked, save for a breechclout, their bodies were finely painted over-all with figures of birds, beasts, and foliage. The lace-like designs were done in blue, red, and yellow.

There was silence withal: we were taken in ambush and none durst move for fear that they would let fly with their arrows. For their part, the Indians held a doubt whether to discharge at once and have done with us or to wait until they learned more of us.

While we stood thus in fearful suspense, Juan de la Cosa softly made known to us that he would speak to the Indians a few words he had learned in those lands when he had come thither with the Admiral. And so he did, turning the strange words slowly from his tongue.

23

"*Bidema soqua rupo*," he said, and his meaning plain: "Brothers, we salute you."

They relaxed their bowstrings in wonder and stared at the Biscayan in silence. Then one of them, who was a Captain, came forward and spoke to Cosa in their tongue, his words running after each other in confusion, like frightened mice. He also made signs with his arms, sweeping toward the sea, gesturing us to return to our boats, to go back into the sea whence we had come.

Cosa answered him slowly and with great difficulty in their tongue, using also gestures for words. So he would have them know that we were not set for conquest in their country: that we were friends and wished to traffic and to teach them the True Faith.

To seal the truth of his words, Cosa opened his own pouch and brought forth a few articles of commerce. He offered their Captain a copper bracelet. The Indian took the gift with great caution and murmured some words over it, and slipping it over his wrist. When some of his men put out their hands to touch it, he spoke quickly to them in anger.

As for the Holy Cross which Cosa then held before him, he gave it but a glance as though it were a thing of no value. But wishing to make trade, he commanded the Indians with him and they lay aside their weapons. Gathering about us, they spoke excitedly like small children and their speech was such as we could not understand, but its meaning was clear: they would see and touch what the white strangers had brought to their shores.

Bastidas, with much relief at the turn taken by our adventure, came down the hillside: and to allure the Captain of the Indians, made him a gift of a hawk's bell, which he thought well of, making signs of joy.

Barter began at once. Many of the Indians wore an ornament to their faces: oval plates of gold or silver, resembling small crescent moons. The tips of the said moons curved sharply to pinch the wearer's nose, from which they depended to cover his mouth from corner to corner.

These ornaments being the only gold in sight, we made offers of the trinkets we carried in exchange for them. The Indians were not of a mind to let go these cherished pieces: but the wonder of our pinchbecks and spangles could not long be denied.

24

"Inquire of them," Bastidas told Cosa, "if there be gold in any quantity among the people of these lands, or whether they have pearls."

The Biscayan stumbled through the interrogation, pointing to one of the ornaments to show that he spoke of gold.

The Indian Captain answered him rapidly, his own golden crescent bobbing before his mouth as he spoke. He raised one arm above his head as though to indicate a crown or diadem. And he clapped his hands four times, repeating some word of their tongue.

Then Cosa said: "He makes known to us that a great King lives farther to the South. He says this monarch has many pearls and much gold, the which men of those regions take pleasure in. They wear the gold in bands about their heads and in their ears. They wear also fine plumes from a great bird. Let us remember those, *compañeros*, when we go into the towns. If we have an eye only for gold, while blowing ourselves flat for a grist of it, we may say a windy '*adios*' to some better gains."

"Will they take us to their towns?" asked Bastidas.

"Yes, if we avoid offense, they will bed us in their own houses."

"Then let us put a foot to the trail. These hares are too small for our bows."

Cosa once more spoke several words to the principal Indian and made further signs of friendship, which the indigene understood. He picked up his bow and called to his warriors. These also reclaimed their weapons, which they had dropped upon the ground in the friendly embracings and trafficking.

By signs, they made clear to us that we were to follow them, showing with gestures such inducements as eating, sleeping, and lying with women.

So we marched toward the village, our nostrils dilated to the strange and bitter scent of bushes along the riverside and bursting big flowers that hung in the thickets like roses in a girl's hair.

Our hearts were glad with the felicity and welcome rest on land after the long voyage; and with the ministering friendship of the people of that land.

We came to their town: it was clean-swept and smelled of fragrant wood. Their houses, which they opened freely to us, were cane and mud-walled structures, very irregular in shape and scattered in random disorder along the river's edge. The roofs were made of simple ridgepoles, over which had been laid palm leaves and river grasses. The chimney was unknown: and wayward smoke of their fires was allowed to escape as it could, through a small opening in the roof, or thin crevices in the walls.

At such times as the fires were lighted, a heavy smoke pall filled the house, a matter of which the Indians took little heed. When it fell out that the fire had been lighted while one of us was asleep inside (we of Castile), we would awake then with hoarse and choking outcries, stumbling blindly to the doorway, cursing and coughing.

In appearance, the women were less well-favored than their men, though often well formed in their youth: their skin smooth and fragrant with crushed flowers: their hair shining black, tied with a colored hempen band at the back of the head.

And they received us as though we were bridegrooms: and they gladly served all our needs. And to me was appointed a tall and beautiful girl with straight thighs and a proud mien. And when I was come into her house, she caused me to sit in a hammock and to drink of their wine, which they call *chiti*: and afterward she took off my clothes and washed them and dried them for me. She did not know the modesty of Christian women, and with childlike innocence caressed me, readily clasping even my shameful parts.

Thus we were entertained with much love and bounty. Thus we continued in that town, wherein we learned many secrets and planned many discoveries. So Cosa had said it, out of earshot of Fray Antonio: "Timid cartographers call this the 'Region of Mysteries,' *joven*. Look to it that you explore them all, even to the omega."

Chapter 3 ~~~~~~~~~~~~~~~~~~~~~~~~~~~~~~~~~~~~~

We left those friendly shores and filled away with a fair wind at dawn: left the torch-lit feasts, with the wild and naked dances, the young girls shaping blue *enaguas* about their bellies, with flowers sprouting from their waists: the spilled wine, the loud quarrels, and the thrown knife quivering in the wood: left the sun-laced shelter of the thatched dwellings, where we had smelled the mornings: and the cane altar, where we had set up the True Cross and made many baptisms.

The Indians came after us in little boats, and with loud voices beseeched us to stay, their words vanishing on the wind.

And we sailed for five months more in new waters, setting our course West, South, and Southwest along Tierra Firme.

We felt our way slowly like sea crabs along the foreign shores, putting into many good harbors. And, giving upon the land, we discovered many villages, from which Indians came forth to meet us, to accept us, and to do us honor.

Navigating thus, we passed from Coquibacoa and continued on our course past mountains higher than those of Spain, shading our sun-dazzled eyes to stare in wonder at the dark sierra against the sky.

At that place called Gaira, we found a people fearless and warlike, who came like demons out of those strange forests, releasing upon us a swift torment of arrows.

We did not tarry, therefore, but set sail, calling upon our Saints to steer our ships upon their way and to bring our great enterprise to a reasonable finish.

But the morning was against us and turned dark in the sky. Great thunder, like a distant roll of drums, brought rain. So they shortened sail and for two days we stood, as the mariners said it, *"a la corda,"* beating about in the unfamiliar sea.

On the third day, the weather cleared and we discovered a pleasant bight, which we named Santa Marta. There the native men shaved their heads and were tonsured like monks, and we called them *"los coronados."* Yet they were not friars and were hostile, receiving our words in silence, for they were unused to traffic.

After gathering dyewood and certain apothecary drugs, we weighed anchor and passed once more into unknown seas, running with the tides. In the quick-rising storms of August, we beat our way among the islands and along the mainland shores, held clear of shoals by the grace of the Blessed Mother and the seamanship of Cosa, Boriol, and the pilots Rodriguez and Morales.

We entered a great bay, which Bastidas named Cartagena, and anchored there for three Sabbaths. We were eager for trade, but the Indians were savage and would not have speech or make peace. They had no god, were unclean, and ate their own kind, not from grievous hunger, but from odious custom and because, as Cosa said it, they were fiends out of hell.

We saw with horror how they would butcher a man as he had been a goat, roasting his members over their fires on raised poles which they called *barbacoas*. The head was given to their children as a plaything.

Seeing this, Bastidas was angry, and he ordered a landing party armed with arquebuses and crossbows under the charge of Vasco Núñez. And his command was: "Give them no favors but death!"

So they burned and plundered a village and returned to the ships with a small quantity of gold, a certain number of Indians taken for slaves, and an *arroba* of fine salt for our stores.

We sailed from Cartagena and made war among the islands, where we found a people following the barbaric customs of the mainland. In those waters, we coasted the silent shores, keeping good watch and bearing slack sail. Through the green light of sum-

28

mer we saw the trees stooping to the burden of a fair wind: and I remember the smell blown seaward of many good and sweet herbs.

In this way, we explored and named the islands of San Bernardo, Baru, and the islets called Arenas.

We continued West by South, where the river called Cenú was brought to view. In the wide mouth of that passage we came to anchors and, giving upon a village inland by a league, we were received in friendship by the Indians, who entertained us: and their lord commanded us to be well-feasted with suckling boar, roasted *maiz*, and other such victuals as the country yields.

Afterward they desired to have a sight of some of our wares, the sacks and cornets whereof we had set in their midst during the banquet. And now it was that we greatly increased the fruits and gains of our enterprise.

For a small mirror, these people would give a good quantity of excellent dyewood: for a hawk's bell, an *almud* of cassaba meal: for a comb, a fardel of fine plumage: for a knife, a small ornament of gold.

They wondered marvelously at the trinkets we brought: and, by divers signs and allurements, we entreated them into trade.

Juan de la Cosa, having the tongue of the people by reason of his voyage hither with the Admiral, proceeded with great diligence to traffic with the cacique or ruler of those regions, turning many good words. And the manner of his enterprise was this:

He brought forth a page's cap of scarlet velvet and set it upon his head with much reverence as it had been an imperial crown. All of our company could see how the matter stood then: the Indian lord murmured some word and reached out as if to touch so royal an article of apparel, but Cosa stayed his hand.

And so they had speech together in the language of that country and with the help of gestures: and Cosa made known to him that the cap was a thing of great worth and not to be reckoned as an article of trade except for the price of the sun-metal, which was their name for gold.

The cacique, therefore, burning with desire, willed his servants to bring certain pieces of wrought gold, some in the form of leg bands and others in the likenesses of fish and of long, slender bees.

29

Whereat a tremor passed among the Castilians and they drew in their breath through their teeth as it were the sound of the surf hissing upon the sand. And the voice of Luis Camacho:

"*Hijo!* There you have five hundred pesos of gold for a velvet cap that values a hundred *maravedies*. Let this fool exchange with me and I will give him half my stores as well as a *cuartilla* of wine that will sing in his guts like a hundred nightingales."

Ledesma answered him: "Give the wine first and perchance he will have an ear for your colting."

Being thus inflamed at the sight of gold, the Castilians gathered round about the Indian lord, thrusting sundry articles of trade toward him with loud cries (shouting altogether), which gave him much displeasure.

He waved them aside, and his words were for Cosa, rising as the sound of mourning on the evening wind. And the pilot, a man of his purpose, with his face set, but laughter gnawing inside his belly, gave us the cacique's speech:

"He entreats me to make the trade. If I go away with the cap, he will ever weep when he remembers it. Heaven will denounce his doings and he will be no lord, but a dweller in the barrows of the ash-gods. Will I not show pity to an old man, blind as a mountain owl with age, and slow with the weight of death?"

And striking his head and breast, he made all signs of misery and grief: and he spoke again: "No gold remains. This was not a ripened year, and we have bartered for *maiz* from the people of Chiapo. The plantains have gone with the summer feasts and beetles feed over the land. We are poor. The *chikaly-chickalees* have flown and lodge near the distant rivers. Soon death will be among us."

When he had spoken thus, he sighed as one in sorrow. Cosa did not answer him, but presently stood up to take his leave. Whereupon, with a howl of woe, the cacique prayed him to remain, and made known to him that he would have further truck.

And he sent one of his vassals, who brought from his house on the hill a small punnet, covered with a blue cloth of their weaving, and carried in his open hands as it had been an offering or a sacrament. He placed it at the feet of his lord, who then exposed to view what it held.

Dios y Santo! There were pearls orient and round that had not their like in Spain, nor indeed, in any Christian kingdom of the world. Dropping to his knees Cosa lifted them in his hand: and they were of the bigness of peas, and like great tears clouded over with hoar frost. The compañeros were dumb with wonder at the sight of them.

Cosa used his best policy to gain as many of the most lustrous pearls as he could. It was thus that, after further corsing with the cacique, he pouched fifteen of the finest gems and delivered to him the red cap, who, receiving it, set it with great dignity upon his head.

The pilot gathered all of his avails, with the words: "I must be away with all speed before this donkey swallows his fodder and begins to bray," and so departed, taking the direction toward the sea.

Then Muñoz told our men: "Now is this bargaining jackass for us to traffic with." Whereat all of them started up with a wild clamor and encircled the Indian lord, dangling their trinkets before his eyes and seeking to persuade him in smooth sort, and with many words and signs.

But all their labor was to no purpose. Now that he possessed the greatly desired cap, he would brook no further exchange. And to their cries, he answered never a word, but closed his eyes and rocked gently back and forth, nodding and nodding as do the Jews when they recite their prayers.

We committed ourselves again to the seas, putting forth at evening, laden with our goods from a year's trading in those lands. A heavy twilight wind blew up suddenly, shaking in the sails as a token of storm to ensue. And so it came, with the waves perilous: and they fumbled her on the larboard tack, heaving sideways in the bubbling green torrents.

"In the name of God our maker," cried Vasco Núñez to Martín Boriol, master of our *capitana*, "why do we weigh anchor with the coming of darkness, and the weather contrary?"

And his answer was a sentence of death passed upon our hopes, we who had devoutly wished a quiet voyage home without further misadventure and malice of the sea:

"God defend us through this heavy chance, for both our ships have many leaks. Cosa has thought it good to flee in demand of a safe harbor where we may find pitch and other things expedient for their redress."

In this distress, we beat up and down in those seas all that night, fearful that we would lose both our treasure and our lives. We kept a vigilant eye unto the *San Antón* (Cosa having taken the lead because he was the better pilot): but she vanished from our sight in the tempest, her flickering sternlight drowned in a black gulf of water.

The mariners worked the pumps with their prayers, and others (I among them) turned to with the buckets. We labored thus in the heaving darkness, while the gale brought the waves aboard of us upon our backs. We took scanty rest as best we could between our terms.

So we fought the great sea's will: and the helmsman swung on the tiller's haft as a hanged man on a gibbet. And the word came: new leaks! water to the horses' bellies. And those whose fortunes had held them upon the land (never having known such extremities) began to cry that we were lost and to prepare themselves for drowning. But the mariners, and men of the best valor (among whom Vasco Núñez was counted as one), took counsel as to how we might best save ourselves. And they sought, with new devices and incredible labor, to overcome the brunt of the outrageous tempest.

Mary, Mary, Stella maris: we prayed then for your grace as in the hour of our death: but the screaming wind in the shrouds gave us a stern answer!

Still, in the second watch we heard strange voices over the billows, as it had been a choir or a religious company singing together. And with the coming of those blessed sounds, we knew that we were delivered.

And thus it fell out: with the first light of day, the waves lessened and the winds turned reasonable and soft.

About midday, the lookout espied afar off a ship which we took to be our lost consort, the *San Antón*, whereat there was much rejoicing. At the order, the helmsman altered our course, and we made toward the said ship. As we approached, we perceived that it was in truth the *San Antón*, hove-to and abiding for our coming.

"Ho there on board!" cried our lookout.

32

And an answering hail came brokenly over the waters: "Ho there, *Santa Maria!*"

As we rode close aboard her, we saw that the crew of the *San Antón* worked as diligently as our own company to keep their vessel afloat, for they had also met with the same extremity. So they had laid hands to their buckets, to the soldiers' targets and to divers other containers with which they bailed out both forward and astern.

Juan de la Cosa came over to us to have words with our Master Boriol, and his voice carried like a spindrift across the decks: "By the Mass! You are also with your neck in the halter. Well, I have learned the cause of it, but too late. We left our wits at Cape de la Vela, not looking to the hulls in these months."

And Boriol: "What plague is this: what passes with these ships?"

"The *broma,* that creature of the Devil."

"Which is that creature?"

"A ravening shipworm that lives in these waters. They bore through the walls of our ships and in great numbers attack, devouring them from stem to stern. Saints! Mine is the Turk's head and no mistake. The Indians spoke of this thing to me: that it destroyed their war craft. And I thought only of canoes, not of caravels and naos. What a donkey without the ears!"

"Is there a remedy, then, for this dangerous mischief?"

"Remedy? God's love, all speed to shore and quick arms on the ladle. Follow your course North by East, and you will bring up the island of Jamaica. There we will find certain trees that put out a thick resin which may serve as well as pitch for our bottoms. But we lose time: all sail to the wind!"

Thus by brave necessity they sailed our ships to Jamaica. And finding insufficient pitch on those shores, thence to that small island called Isla del Contramaestre, a few leagues offshore from Española.

We found on that island an abundance of a gummy resin, which we took out by incision of certain trees, they being of reasonable greatness. This gum, which was strong of smell and very oily, changed in the boiling of it, having then in manner and strength the virtue of tar.

The nao and caravel were careened and the leaks repaired as

best we could accomplish it. And after this redress, we continued there a month, while Cosa scanned the unfriendly skies, hoping for fair weather.

And in that wait was our doom, for the *broma* were again at work in our ships, like enemies of hell. Nevertheless, when a clearing came, we put off once again, standing toward New Isabella.

We had sailed but few leagues when new leaks began to appear in all parts of both ships: and it was Cosa's will that we put about and make swift return to the island from which we had sailed.

Even as this commandment was made known, great black clouds appeared without warning, like hidden enemies, over the far rim of the sea: and for the space of two days and nights we ran before a mighty storm. With our weary and weakened arms, we worked at the buckets and pumps to the uttermost of our power, but the water continued slowly to rise within our ships.

On the third day, through the shadowy blur of twilight, we descried land. Not knowing how the coast lay and being in sore distress, we struck our sails and lay adrift, where we sounded and found eighteen fathoms.

There was an order taken then to hoist out the boats and to store therein our armament and all our avails of true worth. So it was done. And the slaves were released out of their fetters.

Thus in the most miserable calamity, with the fury of a tempest at our backs and the land swallowed up in darkness before our eyes, we sought the shore.

(I remember the sounds and sorrow of that night: the rise and fall of the sea and all of us kneeling in those lurching barks as though at some holy service: and there is a sickening weakness in my stomach, with my breath gasping in my throat. I see the hooded form of the friar, spectral and dim in the bow of our boat, holding the cross before them to give them courage as they pull at the oars, chanting together:

"*O clemens, O pia*
O dulcis Maria!")

They beached the boats at last, the mariners working them strong and skillfully through the heavy surf and onto the soft seasands.

We lept on land with shouts of joy: and it was a thing worth seeing that Bartolomé Sanchez the hooper was so strengthened by the felicity of his salvation that he lifted on shore a chest weighing two *quintales*, which had required two men to load.

When all our goods, provisions, and armament had been set upon the land, Cosa assembled us in good order: and Bastidas by exhortation desired that we should all kneel and with one voice give dutiful thanks for our deliverance from the perilous sea.

This accomplished, the company of both ships repaired to a sloping upland above the beach. We built fires of small logs and stalks in order to dry our clothing and to keep at bay the wild beasts from the forests beyond.

There Cosa addressed us, and when he spoke his voice was grave: "Santo Domingo lies many days' march to the East, and no welcome for us there, I ween. For we have no right nor writ to touch these shores: and even though we come by no desire of our own, but only God's will as castaways, the governor of this territory (that greedy hog!) will give us little succor.

"The nature of the country I know not, though it is said to be chiefly of swampy shaws and mountains, wherewith there is great contending in order to cross. Of the natives, I have heard that they are well disposed and much given to traffic, though at first they flee if it be a large number of strangers approaching. For this reason, and because the villages are small and in no wise could provide victuals and lodging for a band of our count, I would, if Don Rodrigo so commands, that we divide ourselves into three companies of smaller size."

Bastidas speedily gave his sign of consent, and Cosa continued: "At tomorrow's first light then, *compañeros*, we march. Go carefully: drink only of moving waters: avoid as much as possible the naked sunlight, which in these regions begets calentures. Three of us will conduct and lead: Don Rodrigo, Master Boriol, and I, Juan de la Cosa. Join yourselves to which of us you will, but look to it that the division be equal."

So we resorted each man to the Captain of his choosing: I, Juan of Toledo, to Cosa (and Vasco Núñez also was of our company). With the first light of day we marched: and having no beasts of burden, we carried only the gains and commodities growing out of our enterprise and such things as would serve us in our need, for as Cosa had said it: "Our weapons, alas, we must destroy. If they are left, they will surely be discovered by the Indians, who may then set upon us with our own crossbows. It is more to our need that we carry articles of traffic to provide victuals, for the land is poor.

"Two crossbows, then: one arquebus, every man's sword, bucklers for all: five halberds—these go with each company. You, Zamudio, look to the worthiness of these weapons that are taken, and to the destruction of those we leave."

At the first village, we found Indian guides who, being allured with shiny coins, fishhooks, and sundry other articles, made ready to conduct us to Santo Domingo.

We took our journey by three separate ways: Don Rodrigo and his company through the valley called Del Nido: Boriol and his men by Azua: and we (with Cosa) by Ozama.

We left the sea, which had so cruelly used us, and we climbed the trails upward through the mountain passes with the heavy burden of our armor and our goods on our backs. We marched in the netted shadows under the leaves, avoiding the sun. On the moist slopes among the thick tree ferns and in the grass savannahs we saw birds of brilliant plumage and in the forests owls of snowy white. The hot air hummed with harmful insects: flies, black gnats, and mosquitoes and they swarmed out to attack us in clouds and were a great torment to the point of madness. Some were of the bigness of wasps, and their stings had in them the burning fire of poisoned darts. Many of our men were fevered from their hurts and all suffered greatly, our faces swollen shapeless to deformity: and we could find no relief day or night.

But by good providence and needful commodities provided by Indians along our way, we came to the city of Santo Domingo on March 21, 1501, though our bodies were near death.

And the Governor's guard which came out to us while we were yet a bow-shot from the town, gave us such greeting as we had been savages or infidels, rather than Christians who stood in need of succor.

Some of those of the better sort among the escort made known to us that Bastidas and his company had arrived three days before us: and that they were charged with unlawful entry and illegal traffic with the indigenes of the country.

We were further informed that our own necks were in the same halter: and that our goods would be seized and the order was for us to be taken and stayed until our cause was tried with all legal form.

"Such is the charity of our countrymen, one to another," said Juan de la Cosa, who was greatly angered at our being thus ill-used by the Castilians.

And Vasco Núñez, who marched beside him, also complained heavily, and said: "It is a certain truth that they belong to the Devil, who rules over all who are greedy of gain. The god they worship is a one-eyed yellow idol." Then, to the chief Constable: "When will our cause be heard?"

To which the Constable (a lusty fellow with one ear struck from his head) answered him: "When frogs grow hair, if the Governor keeps the straight jaw he now has."

Cosa replied hotly he would then be called to answer to the Royal Council and to our Sovereigns: that we were upon this island by no will of our own, but by a very act of God. "And it is our desire only to board the next ship taking departure for Spain."

Whereat, the Constable laughed very hollowly and deep in his throat, answering him: "And so, perchance, you will, Captain—in chains. It makes less than a year that the Governor sent the very Admiral of the Ocean Sea to Castile in the gyves. What good color does he need to arrest a notary and his band of dunghill beetles?"

Being come to the town, when they had taken all that we had (which was, by estimation, three hundred *marcos* of gold) we were mewed up in the dungeons, where we remained in miserable state for the space of five days.

The Governor of Española that year was Don Francisco de Bobadilla, officer of the royal household of Castile: Comendador of the Religious and Military Order, Calatrava: and, in short, a man of high estate.

He had been sent out to the Indies to ascertain what persons had raised themselves against justice in the island of Española and to proceed against them according to law.

The said persons, if they must be named, were the illustrious discoverer, Christopher Columbus, together with his two brothers, Bartolomé and Diego: and others he had placed in authority.

The writ, signed by both Sovereigns, was the victory of the Admiral's enemies, who had poisoned the Queen's ears against him.

And certain enterprisers and worthy gentlemen of the Court and country (whose principal purposes the Admiral had opposed) conveyed into Her Majesty's presence a number of Indian women who (they said) had been cruelly taken from their homes and separated from their young children at the Admiral's command.

Then our Illustrious and Compassionate Queen, perceiving the great fear and misery in the eyes of the women who squatted before her, was moved to anger. And striking her open hand with her fist, she cried: "What right has the Admiral to give away my vassals?"

To add further merit to their arguments, the aforesaid Cavaliers also brought to Her Majesty an *información* which made known divers acts of cruelty, and abuses committed against the Indians. And one of the said excesses was in manner thus:

A small number of Indians refused to genuflect before the Holy Sacrament or to honor Our Lord in any of the prescribed acts of faith, or to acknowledge the Church as the mistress and superior of the world universe. The Admiral ordered, therefore, that they be put to the sword. He was at that time in the fortress and, their execution being hard by, the cries of two of them who did not expire straightway but lay groaning in the sun, disturbed his rest.

He summoned the guard and commanded that they were to be dispatched at once, for their plaint disquieted him. In brief time, their lamentation ceased. But later that same night, it appeared that the soldier charged with the executions (who was severe with infidelity) had not done the will of the Admiral, but had stopped their mouths with wool that their cries would no longer molest him.

The wife of one of these Indians, who knew some words of Castilian, upon learning what had befallen her husband, came to the Admiral at sunset. And she informed him that her spouse had understood nothing of that which had been read to him and knew not what was required of him.

He was then brought out, still alive (such is the vigor of the people in these lands), and when it was told to him in his tongue, he bowed down and was baptized at once by one of the friars, though he died a short time afterward from so great a loss of blood.

As for that Genoese tyrant, Christopher Columbus, who ruled in her name, Her Majesty ordered that he be put in chains and sent back to Spain to answer for his excesses, betrayals, and bad faith.

And when he was come over to Española, Don Francisco made many arrests and committed to prison as many of the Admiral's partisans and retainers as he could find. His order was: throw the miscreants into the pits! If the dungeons be insufficient in number, then dig more.

But those men who had come hither with the governor's fleet, had in sight to go in search of purchase and spoils: and they were little disposed (as they said it then) to break their backs to build a *mazmorra* for the *Colonistas*. Why provide room for the spike-tail hinnies to take their ease? Let them be put into the festering holes they had procured for the good men who had so long been shut up therein!

And so it fell out that a multitude of prisoners (both Cavaliers and men of occupations) were forced into those miserable keeps which to that time had lodged half their number.

Thus pressed most grievously against each other in the cold darkness, they could scantly move their arms and legs: and until death had taken many of them, they could not lie down, even in dire sickness, but were constrained to shift for themselves as best they could.

And Bobadilla, a man whom it pleased to create discord between people, set over the prisoners the same men who had been confined in the dungeons before the arrival of the Governor on Española.

The said guards, who in truth were largely libertines, thieves, and men of low estate, and who had never known the meaning of honor or respect, now required of every prisoner that he salute them as officers and worthy men. Thus, they demanded that the hapless creatures in their charge reply to their revilings with answers such as "You speak with reason, Don Gonzalo": "Many thanks, Your Lordship": or, "I await your orders, Excellency."

Upon the sixth day after we were committed to the prison, all the while not knowing what should become of us, there came again the constable's men to fetch us out of the dungeons.

39

And they informed us that the Governor, acting from Christian charity, had ordered our liberty.

When, therefore, the iron door was unbolted and we stumbled forth into the blessed light of the sun as Lazarus from the tomb, we wept joyful tears and cried aloud our thanks to God.

Bobadilla was not moved by conscience to give us freedom (as we soon perceived) but by a desire to set all things in good order before he should be called to account. For letters had come to him from Spain, disclosing to him the will of the Sovereigns: that they were sending out a new Governor to establish a more just *gobernación*.

Further, Their Majesties had disposed that the aforesaid Governor, Fray Nicolás de Ovando, require a full account of Bobadilla's acts and methods during his rule in Española.

After being set free, it besteaded us to shift for ourselves, for we had not the means of buying victuals withal or of providing lodging for our bodies that were near death.

Some of our company desired to go to La Navidad and to other settlements upon the island, where (if God so willed it) they might enroll in some enterprise which could relieve them of their hard extremity. And the Governor giving his leave, they departed with all speed.

As for Vasco Núñez and Juan of Toledo, we sojourned in the house of the friars Dominican, who ministered to our wants from the slender provision allowed them by their order.

In October of the same year, Ovando came to that island with his armada: the ships in much splendor, fully dressed with flags: two score and nine of them standing in on a strong tide, with musicians on the bows—the sound of trumpets, flutes, and timbrels coming to us across the turning waves.

And that was the end of the tyranny practiced by that fat hog Bobadilla, who (for such was the will of Providence) perished in the sea on his homeward voyage. But to maintain a show of respect for Crown authority, Comendador Ovando allowed the charge against Bastidas to stand: but he remanded the case (and along with it, Don Rodrigo and Cosa) back to Spain for trial.

So they embarked: and the flotilla sailed from the port of Santo Domingo with a fair wind, but a great swell rolling. And the last tall and pennanted pole had barely quivered out of sight over the rim of the dark sea, when a great storm (which the Caribs call *huracan*) struck over those waters with the fury of hell.

As night drew on, the outrageous tempest fell also over the town with such marvelous vigor that walls and roofs availed nought: for these vanished in the terrible howling darkness. There was no house that escaped damage, save the church (wherein we sheltered) and the fortress, builded of stone. Had not the great goodness of God been miraculously shown us, we would have all perished.

With the coming of day, the people crowded into the muddy streets, homeless and in great distress. And the Governor resolved, after good deliberation, to rebuild the town on the opposite bank of the river, which he deemed a better place.

Touching upon the fleet which had put forth at so accursed a time, the pilots and mariners gave it as their opinion that no ship could strive against so boisterous a blast, and that all were of a certain cast away. Hearing which brought great heaviness to our hearts, so we were scarce able to speak for sorrow, remembering then the good days we had passed with Don Rodrigo and Juan the Biscayan. (Now, God be thanked for it, we know of their salvation: how their ship ran before the wind and passed through seas so high and ugly that never have eyes seen their like.)

As for the new city of Santo Domingo which the Governor had willed, the men who had come out to the Indies with his flotilla fell in dislike of such labor as was required to build it. So they secretly cried him down: if His Excellency wanted a new town (so they said) let them build it who would live in it. As for themselves, they had no dream of sandy graves in strange places, but would return to Castile when their work here was done (work, that is to say, of gathering loose nuggets of gold from the streams with nets, a kind of fishing in which they were certain they would be well practiced). So they took their departure by night, carrying with them little clothing, no tools, and scant victuals.

But the *vecinos* who had dwelt there (which were in number three hundred and twenty-three) and we who knew the pestilence and hardships of the country, tarried: for we had learned patience.

I, Juan of Toledo, sought me out a workmaster: and Vasco Núñez was with me. And compounding with certain carpenters to serve them, we cut the joints for the beams and ridgepoles, and we shaved the clean joists. We bent to our tasks in the needling heat with slowly increasing strength: and the smell of newly split wood was in the air and the odor of the smoking limepits.

Naked Indians toiled up and down the thong-lashed ladders, giant brown ants carrying buckets of mortar, pieces of timber, and (upon their heads) baskets of roof tile.

They tried the bells for the new church towers, and their clamor was muffled in the drowse of the noonday, like distant timbrels. And the rhythm of mallets beat hollowly through the morning and fell silent at the time of rest, as did the shovels, the ox-carts, the creaking wooden gear-wheels of the hoists, the shrill pulleys, the gavelocks.

So we raised that town: four streets running from South to North and five from East to West: two royal houses built of stone: the church, the cabildo, tribunal, and jail: a market with porticoes: the Convent of Santo Domingo and the Hermitage of Santa Ana: forty fine residences of wood covered with tile: nineteen small houses: and fifteen straw *bohios*.

Those men who had gone in search of easy and quick riches in divers parts of the Island began to return in small companies, ragged and in great want. And they stood amazed at what we had wrought, for they had gone on a fool's venture, whereas we had supplied our needs.

Their provision had been frittered away while they had learned that gold must be dug from the mines and in small quantities, which required both skill and knowledge. Whereupon they left off their pretence and sought for other means of maintaining themselves.

Many died of starvation: altogether, half their number perished. And those who remained lived as best they could, mainly through barter of their fine apparel and divers other things of value which they had brought hither from Spain.

The new town being finished and our work done, we called for our wages and bethought us how we might best use our avails as assurance to supply our future needs.

Vasco Núñez secured a concession of land along the southwest coast of the island at that place called Salvatierra de la Sabana, where the Governor had ordered new settlements to be founded, the soil there being more fertile and the Indians in those parts more numerous for labor.

There with great success he raised pigs, which fattened quickly on the rich palm cabbage that grew in abundance on his land. The good ground he had likewise furnished him with divers fruits and other natural increases such as grow in the good soil of that region, and all of them as well tasted as those of Spain or of any other part of the world.

There was great want of his abundance in Santo Domingo, for the stores which had been shipped from Spain had long since been consumed: and in the provinces the Indians would not plant crops, for (they said) what they sowed the white men would surely reap.

With the gains thus made from his diligent labor during the first two years that he dwelt in Salvatierra, Vasco Núñez purchased yet another seventy-five *fanegadas* of ground and received a *repartimiento* of fifty Indians to tend it: for he believed that the fruits of a larger plantation would be in proportion.

This faith in cultivation of the earth, alas, betrayed him at last to failure and debt. For, the common sort, unable to maintain themselves in any other way, now bought or were allotted small parcels of land and turned to cultivation. They soon brought about an abundance which, though it did not exceed the people's needs, exceeded their means.

Matters standing thus, prices were brought down until no profit was to be had: and there came whole weeks together when large quantities of plantain, tunas, dates, and melons lay rotting in the market, their bursting ripeness a banquet for clouds of black flies.

While these things were in doing, the Indians sat idly about, perched upon the drag-stone of the big arrastra where cassaba roots were ground to meal, or in the shade of their huts asleep. The rice-flails bleached bone-white in the fiery sun, where they had been dropped from the hands of the *naborias*. Each day brief rain of the tropics fell and left half-empty cacao querns floating with brown scum. The slow, creeping decay of the jungle, like the torpor of death, covered everything.

Howbeit, there was hunger in that city: and many who had been men of credit and accompt in Spain now marched through the streets and repaired to the marketplace in shameful state of half-nakedness, crying for food.

In the burial ground, the new graves daily increased in number until they reached the farthest confines of the cemetery. And still men died. They died of hunger, of fevers, and of all the diseases that come from famine. Beneath the hot blue skies of a foreign summer, the dark crosses were planted at divers angles: and they were inscribed with the noble and renowned names of Spain: Don Diego de Manzanedo: Don Carlos de Ayora: Don Francisco de la Sagra: Licenciado Alonso Barrantes: here rests Don Pedro de Córdova . . . y de Alcántara . . . thus perished . . . *In te Domine speravi*. . . .

And still their cries came to us from the streets: broken, faint, like a thing dreamed: like the whimper of a beaten dog.

"*Por Dios, señores*, a little bread. We starve! We starve!"

And on a certain evening I rode forth with Vasco Núñez on the trail. And a little without the town, upon a high place he stayed his horse (and so I mine): and with sorrowful countenance he looked back upon the city outstretched beneath us. There through the deepening shades of nightfall we saw the torches of beggars, orange and yellow through the palms, as the *pordioseros* passed from house to house, entreating orts and refuse.

And seeing it all, Vasco Núñez spoke softly as though at confession: "Consider the end, which is death. They came (they said) moved with a desire to advance God's glory and to seek the good of our Sovereign. Yet their love was not for man nor God, but for gold. So it has betrayed them all: surely their souls are beyond ransom."

I thought then: where is certainty for man? We may say with Boethius that he that has fallen never was secure. Yet they believed themselves so. Being rich, they sat at table in soft ease: and at their feasts and revels gave scant thought to the hungry, the sick, and those in extremity. They thought to hold as their own the pleasures of the world. Yet what can a man possess as his own? Nothing. Desire trolls him on: his lust is ever ahead in the distance. Yet in the end he holds a handful of dust. Even in the storied beehive of memory he can preserve nothing: for that abundance must also partake of the famine of death. *Omne meum: nihil meum*: it is all mine, yet none mine.

44

Caught in the quicksands of the years, Vasco Núñez turned to gambling. And for days together he would resort to the tables of chance, both those of cards and of dice, saying that every man played hazard with his life and that he but gave better speed to the game.

Unmoved by the passions and great tumults of the other players, he suffered the most grievous losses with a calm demeanor and a good face. Some therefore said he was bloodless and others that he was mad.

But I tell you that he was neither. It was his desire that with favoring Providence he might gather in a certain quantity of money which he could employ to countervail the charges for a voyage of discovery: for it was his principal purpose (as he told it to me) to discover the great secrets which are in these Indies and to grow into familiarity and friendship with the people thereof, that he might bring them to civility and good order.

How could such a man be still upon the earth: upon an island set in the timeless heartbeat of the sea?

Chapter 4 ~~~~~~~~~~~~~~~~~~~~~~~~~~~~~~~~~~~~~~~

I, Juan of Toledo, being then in the service of the *veedor*, enlisted in the enterprise of a certain lawyer called Bachelor Martín de Enciso, who held all things in readiness for a voyage to San Sebastián in the province of Urabá, three hundred leagues distant from Española.

The said Bachelor had agreed with Alonso de Ojeda, governor of New Andalucía (and with Juan de la Cosa, his lieutenant) that he would at his own charges furnish two ships—a nao and a bergantine—and sail over to them at San Sebastián, thereby relieving their needs.

On the day before embarking, as I sat in the portico of the Plaza Mayor in the company of Vasco Núñez and Bartolomé Hurtado (an hidalgo who had come to the Indies with Ovando), there came a Governor's man and posted a notice or edict. It was addressed to "such Cavaliers, Esquires, and other persons who are debtors on this island of Española," advertising them that reports had reached his, the Governor's, ears from reliable founts that a number of reckless persons who had debts and encumbrances planned to evade their just obligations by boarding secretly the vessels of Bachelor Martín Fernandez de Enciso.

And the Governor commanded and charged such persons to desist from all such pretense. It further informed them that an armed caravel of the Governor's armada would escort the aforesaid ships of Enciso two leagues clear of the harbor. Any miscreant

47

taken while thus trying to escape the island would be arrested and stayed in the dungeons of Santo Domingo.

And, having read the proclamation, Vasco Núñez said: "What choice here? If they attempt a leave-taking, they are thrown into the dungeons tomorrow: if they remain, they go the day after, because they cannot pay their debts. They, did I say? I am myself one of their black number, thanks to the sly business of the lawyers, who are devils all, and who have bubbled me out of my ultimate *maravedi*. Now this Bachelor Enciso is to stuff his holds with provisions from my land."

Then Hurtado asked of him: "You are beholden to Enciso?"

"For past a hundred ducats. By the Cross I swear it, I will victual half the company at San Sebastián and with never so small a word as *gracias*."

"You would enroll yourself in the exploit otherwise?"

"I would, man, and with all speed. But if my shadow should fall upon his decks, the death-bed louse would deliver me to the Governor's guard with his own writ of accusal about my neck."

The matter being well-pondered and the effect of Vasco Núñez's words being well digested, Hurtado inclined across to us and spoke gently: "Tell me, have the stores you provide been carried aboard Enciso's nao?"

"No: they lie ready at the embarcadero and will be laden to-night."

"Of what kind and number are those supplies?"

"Ah, that is easy to answer you. A score of times I have counted them with a finger of wrath and a plague on the sum of them each time around: two hundred pounds of bacon, seven *haldas* of rice, seven casks of cassaba flour—"

"Hold there! Of what size are these casks?"

"Of the bigness of a *bota*. Why do you ask me?"

"Why, indeed? Give the Bachelor six casks and save one for yourself. Understand me?"

Vasco Núñez pulled at his beard in perplexity. "You squeeze your jests too hard, Bartolo."

"Jest? I think Enciso will call it by another name. Listen, this thing is easy as a seaman's oath: When the casks are brought aboard, the orders are to place them head-up in good order. *Bueno.* One of these casks, vented at the bottom, does not carry cassaba meal. No: therein lie the armor of Vasco Núñez, the sword of Vasco Núñez, and the carcass of the said Vasco Núñez."

"But it is certain that this knavery will be discovered to Enciso by the mariners or by the Constable's sentry."

"It will not be so. Juan and I will engage their attention with other business during the freighting. Now: we have the loyalty of the boatswain's mate, with whose help you can convey yourself from the cask to the lateen mizzen, wherein you will find good comfort for the night. During the midwatch, with darkness to protect you from imminent danger, you will place yourself once again in the cask. When the nao is in the bosom of the sea, three strong raps on the lid will resurrect you."

"And I am seized and put in chains!"

"Again no. When Enciso is brought to a knowledge of your marvellous feat, he will cloud over with ire and heat your ears with words of law. But what can be done? He will not turn back. Also, you are a valiant soldier: he knows that. To feed you in irons brings him nothing. As a *baquiano* well practiced in all things pertaining to conquest, you can acquit yourself nobly. If a good wind is wanting for your course, we will blow in that direction, arguing your cause. The Bachelor wants peace to abide amongst us, the voyage being his heavy interest. To make no more words upon it, you will be enrolled as one of the company."

"You speak with great certainty, Bartolo. But will it not be more to his liking to have me thrown overboard or sell me as a slave to the Indians? Such is the justice of lawyers. But why flail the wind? We go not as we wish, but as we can. So I will leave my cape to the assassins."

And so it was done: and that man who by cunning and valor was to conduct us to the shining threshold of a new world, embarked upon his voyage stuffed in an empty flour-butt.

The nao *Concepción*, laden and dressed, stood out to sea with a fair and good wind upon the 13th of September in the year of our redemption 1510.

The Governor's caravel, having discovered no legal reason to stay the armada, came about and returned to Santo Domingo after our setting out two leagues to sea.

The Bachelor Enciso walked about the decks with a marvellous, springy step like that of a cock that has just come forth from the roost at the same early hour. And when we had lost Española and were past five leagues upon our course, he was of a mind to call assembly simply to crow a little and to flap his wings.

But while he yet pondered all that he would say to the whole company, there came to his ears the shouts and roaring laughter of men below. Looking down, he saw the men in a great press about a certain barrel: and presently they broke away enough to allow passage through their midst of the ship's carpenter, who carried a mallet and a bar. A big yellow dog was sniffing about the bottom of the butt.

So the Bachelor began to inquire diligently of the master and contramaestre what these actions might mean. And receiving from them no reply to his liking, he came down to them, crying: "What passes here? *Mande!*"

And the men parted ranks that he might approach the cask, as the shipwright removed the final peg that secured the lid.

"What does this mean, you mutinous ship rats?"

And, as it were in answer to his question, the lid of the cask rose up, followed by the head of Vasco Núñez. The big dog (who was his own beast, called Leoncico) leaped joyfully against the barrel. As for Enciso, he stared in wondrous unbelief at what he beheld.

Vasco Núñez blinked at the bright sunlight and, seeing the irate visage of the Bachelor confronting him, he rose to his feet and bowed from the open cask.

"Your pardon, Señor Alcalde—"

"I am not yet Alcalde!" Enciso answered him angrily.

"—for favoring you with my presence in this unwonted way."

"Favoring me! You impudent, wine-rotted Turk! Do you know the law in this case? No, I thought not. It is my privilege—no, my sworn duty—to put you ashore on the first land sighted by the lookout. And so it will be done, whether the shores are peopled or barren. Favoring me!" he howled again, his fury rising. "Carvajal, lay hold on this *llovido* . . . you are undone this time, *señor*."

As the Bachelor was speaking, Vasco Núñez climbed from the butt. When he stood on the deck, he stretched his cramped limbs and breathed deeply of the fresh breeze. And to Enciso he said: "But reason, Don Martín. Had I remained on that plaguey island, it would have profited none but the jailer. What redress would my

50

debtors (of whom you are one) find for their grievances in a starving prisoner? What you all want is not vengeance, but money, is it not so? Well, accept me as one of your company and all my creditors shall have their due. You first, for your patronage, then the others. Am I not a good soldier? Let Bastidas and my Lord of Moguer answer to that. And have you ever heard of any Captain in these new and savage lands who had one too many fighters? I hazard no. Here you gain one without enticements and promises. You lose nothing and you will avail yourself of much."

"A strange change of eyesight, Vasco Núñez," Enciso answered him in scorn. "When you were upon the island, it was little enough you spoke of payment to your creditors. And as for your debt to me, *Santísima!* have I ever received aught but mouldy cassaba and rotten pork to discharge it? So when you speak of your encumbrances in such sweet terms of honor, I bethink me of the proverb, 'When the fox predicates, let the chickens beware.' In one mode, you address me as Chief Judge and in the next petition me to aid an absconding debtor."

All Vasco Núñez's good words of persuasion did not serve, and after brief deliberation, Enciso said in the manner of a magistrate: "If I be Alcalde as you say it, let my first judgement be passed here: and it is this: You will be set on shore of the first land that appears."

And all of us there present knew that such a condemnation was a sentence of slow and painful death: for the islands we would raise first upon our course were known to be without habitants or water.

Some of the men therefore (and I was of their number) began to make a loud complaint and to speak against the Bachelor's injustice. And Hurtado also spoke for us: "This Vasco Núñez has reason. Has he fallen among savages or Christians? He has done no wrong except to fall into debt, a pit we are all in peril of, God protect us. Why wrestle with laws? They are for the peaceful countries and those who dwell with the world's ease. Here our law is mercy for Christians and the Devil take the rest."

There were shouts from the men of "Hear! Hear!" and "Give him his word!"

Enciso, then feeling the mutinous spirit of the company and not wishing to provoke their ill will so early in the voyage, made

51

show of yielding to their opinions. (But we knew that from that time forth he would carry a grudge against Vasco Núñez.)

Now he said: "I am persuaded. Let this Vasco Núñez, before you all as witnesses and the notary to set it down, swear his concordance and loyalty to my command during the present exploit and for a year to follow ashore."

To which Vasco Núñez made answer: "My many thanks, Bachelor; and my hand ready with my name and pledge."

"Look to it that you prove worthy of the mercy," Enciso told him and departed toward the ladderway aft.

Later he told his lieutenant, Luis de la Rua (in my presence): "That jackal's tongue wins the opinions of men too easily. With it he may yet divide my ranks from each other, but unite them in a cause against me. If I am half the intrigant I dress myself to be, he will be got rid of in brief and work my peace thereby. It is well said: 'One pig with the itch can upset the whole sty.'"

So we crossed those seas without hindrance or chance: and sailing between an island and the main, we came to anchor at nine fathoms in a good harbor, which our pilot gave out to be Cartagena.

Though no man of our company knew aught of it then, that was the place where in the year past the rash and sanguinary Alonso de Ojeda had ravaged the whole countryside with a great loss of his men, for the people of that region are very warlike and fight with poisoned arrows.

Francisco Pizarro, a soldier of mean birth but of great valor (by reason of his mighty lust for gold), marched with Ojeda in that *entrada*: and afterward he made known to me all the things that had happened there. And his relation was this:

Ojeda's armada arrived at these coasts on November 15th in the year 1509. Coming to anchor in the harbor and perceiving the seeming richness of the country, it was Ojeda's will that they establish there a fort and settlement. But Juan de la Cosa, who was Pilot major and a man of great experience and skill in sea causes, opposed it, saying the people of those parts were both fierce and cruel and that they dipped their arrows in deadly poison. He entreated Ojeda therefore to continue on their course to Urabá, where they would encounter indigenes of a more peaceable character.

But Ojeda would not give ear to his counsel: and he ordered two score well-appointed men to go ashore and to raid the Indian villages that were nearest the harbor.

So it was done: the sixty captives were taken and sent on board the ships, together with a number of plates of inferior gold called *guanin*.

Regarding the good success of this action, Ojeda commanded another march on a larger town called Turbaco some five leagues distant from the shore. For this exploit he mustered seventy of the best men to accompany him. Juan de la Cosa likewise went with the company, desiring to be of service, for he spoke against the venture and advertised Ojeda that he ought in conscience to consider the safety of his own life as well as that of his men.

When the Castilians were come to the town they found it empty of people: for the Indians had taken flight to the forests. But they had there disposed themselves in such a manner that they were in secret readiness to assault their enemies from every quarter.

Ojeda's men, greedy for spoils, divided their ranks in order to loot the *bohios* which were bestrewed among the trees. And in that sundering was their doom: for the Indians rushed forth in great numbers, both men and women, releasing their arrows, the poison whereof is of such force that any man struck by them will surely die.

In this way, they dispatched more than two score Christians before they could array themselves in good order to fight. Even thus, they had scant chance against so resolute and numerous an enemy. Most of them there perished without hope or remedy.

As for Ojeda, he and a small number of his men sought refuge in a large *bohio*, the roof whereof they threw off lest the Indians set it afire. But it was to scant purpose: and Ojeda on the sudden sprang forth from the cane shelter like a tiger, slashing on every side with his blade and flying as if on wings into the darkness of the forest.

Those who remained (Cosa among them) defended themselves as best they could. But it so fell out that all were killed save Cosa

53

and one other. And the Pilot major, perceiving that he had been struck with an envenomed arrow and would soon die, said to his companion: "Brother, since God has protected you from harm, sally forth and fly: and if ever again you see Alonso de Ojeda, tell him of my fate."

Ojeda (such was his marvelous strength and the power of the miraculous Virgin he carried) concealed himself in the jungle and, marching only at night, moved through those hideous swamps back toward his ships.

"And we who remained (so Pizarro affirmed it) went on shore to search for him. But as we marched, we heard Indian conches and drums and the noise they make beating upon their wooden shields, and Nicolás de Piña, the cooper, was struck with a poisoned arrow in his leg. *Santísima!* He writhed like a wounded serpent with the burning pain of it. We cut it off straightway and put to the wound herbs such as the surgeon carried, but he died the day following.

"After that we coasted the strand in boats and fired off signals. At last we came one day to a matted mangrove brake. Pedro Muñoz, who has the quick eye, suddenly cried out, 'Devil at confession!' as his oath was. 'A Castilian!' And he pointed with his finger into the thick of the tangled roots.

"There we saw a shadowed form like a man in the dimness of that stagnant swamp. *Hijo!* and those were strong roots twisted there. We hacked at them with cutlasses, and poled the boat in. There we found Ojeda. We believed him dead because he did not move. In one hand he still held his sword. And in his target we counted the dents of three hundred arrows. And he lived! We dragged him out to the shore and warmed him to life with a fire, and rubbed him with oil, for he was chill as the tomb itself.

"At the same time, we beheld an armada bearing in toward the harbor. And we perceived that they were ships of Diego de Nicuesa. As you may have heard it, Nicuesa and Ojeda were two sparrows on a single sprig of wheat. When they were last in España, Ojeda had told him, told Nicuesa, that (to give it the General's own words): 'Like a hog you are, Nicuesa: you will be behoof to nobody until you are dead. Look to it I don't give your nephews your fat.'

"Those were his last words to Nicuesa: now he felt no joy at

54

having his enemy discover him in that weak condition. So he ordered us back aboard our vessel and to leave him alone in a cove. 'Get rid of Nicuesa with all speed, but at no hand tell him where I am.'

"So we did as he commanded. But Nicuesa read it all in our eyes. 'Dogs!' he cried, shaking his sword over our heads. 'Are we Christians or ship rats that batten on one another? And this fume between your General and me, has it put out the eyes of brotherhood and begotten a baseness and vileness of heart? Take me to your General. If he lives, I pledge him my hand goods.'

"We brought him therefore to where Ojeda was hiding in shame and humiliation at his great defeat. And it was something worth seeing how they embraced on that lonely shore with tears.

"And we marched again. Faith, and we laid them a hellish siege that time. Four hundred souls of us with Nicuesa's men, and our orders were that no Indian was to be taken alive. We gave on the town at night and would have burned them all in their dungy hammocks, save that we passed through a wood where a multitude of parrots had taken roost. These noisy birds harkened to us and filled the night with their squawking cries. So they spread the alarm. Still, only a few of the Indians who woke thought timidly on the sounds, believing every Christian already dead by their cursed barbs.

"A Princess their sovereign was, called Matarap, and no dastard in battle. It was said afterward that she personally dispatched four Spaniards with a certain jack-spear they use, called *azagay*. Well, and she had her St. Martin's day. Ojeda pursued her back to her own house, for she had come out to us in full readiness to fight. The General called her to come forth, but she would not, so the *bohio* was fired. *Purísima!* It was her will to die rather than to be taken. And so she did: we could see her plainly in the flames, embraced with her household. Ah! I was giddy that night with the smell of roasted flesh and the new blood. My wrist ached with the sword and my throat smarted with the smoke of their thatched dwellings. And Ojeda like a leaping devil in the firelight, with his shouts of 'Lay it on! Lay on, I say!'

"Afterward we searched the smoking ruins for spoils. And while thus grubbing it was that I beheld the body of Juan de la Cosa. Blessed Jesus! I was blind with the sight of it! There he swung in a tree, as full of arrows as a hedgehog: bloated and blue with the rotting poison they use: and the play of our torches on the once-loved face of that friend, of Juan the Biscayan, now puffed and bigswoln like the carcass of a goat: and pocked with black flies, slow in the shuddering light. . . . So we wept for it, and our hearts shrank. . . ."

Ignorant of all that had thus passed and of Ojeda's terrible devastation of the region, at daybreak of the day following our arrival, the mariners hoised out the boat, wherein Enciso and ten of our company went on land to fetch fresh water.

And near the shore where they beached their boat, lay many Indians secretly hidden and ready to fall upon them. So they sortied forth with loud cries and assailed the Spaniards with arrows, stones, and jack spears.

The *compañeros* pushed out in the boat once more, their bucklers held over their heads. Then Vasco Núñez said to Enciso: "Let us hold. I know some words of this tongue. Let me speak."

"Do it then, and with few words."

So Vasco Núñez shouted to the swarming Indians, putting to careful use those words he had learned when he had trafficked on Tierra Firme with Bastidas. And at his first words, coming to their ears above the sound of the sea-fall, they held their bows and harkened to him.

"People of Veragua [so he said in their tongue]: we come as friends of you who dwell here. This earth will be a peace to our feet. See! By my tooth, I swear it. We take only water for our thirst. After one fire, we are gone from this country. With the sun, we go westward to the land of Tulan, where we were brought forth and begotten."

They pondered his words, pressing together, talking and blinking. Some bent one leg, lifting a foot like herded cattle.

Then an old man answered him: "You who know the speech of Veragua. We are avengers of our kith, who fell on the long spears and in the smoking thunder of your brothers who came before you. Our homes have blown away in flames from their torches. We that remain dwell like wild hares in the brushwood of the hills. So it was prophesied to our sires by the owls. Thus you have shown your magic and sorcery. Truly now it is fearful in the burnt

56

maiz-fields: truly the auguries are mostly dark and the sky fallen. Come, if your oath be upon your tooth, for by such swear the men of Coyba and their word is straight. Take water, but lie not in these crossings. Be gone. . . . Even so we will perish: for it has been told to us since a long time before. Our eyes will be dried up in their bowls, our flesh eaten by the unclean creatures. Woe! Woe!"

We took water from a sweet spring, and were in all readiness to weigh when the starboard watch espied a sail a league offshore. And Enciso ordered them to fire the Lombardy as a signal. This being done, the other vessel answered in the same sort and came to us in the harbor. Whereupon we found the ship to be the brigantine *Salvador*, which was one of Ojeda's armada. And when she fell aboard the *Concepción*, we beheld therein a company of Castilians all in hard extremity, ill-appareled, and seemingly dying of famine. They were under the leading and conduct of Francisco Pizarro and by estimation numbered thirty-five souls.

"Where is your General? Where is Ojeda?" Enciso asked in great suspicion. "Have you left him to the crows, you hopping fleas?"

Then Pizarro (in whom was a mortal malice for all lawyers and men of the court for the many injuries and injustices done upon him by them) answered him thus, a sneer hiding behind his words: "We are no deserters, *señor*, and do we look as such? Here, Bolanos. . . . Now, Bachelor, look at this man's belly, swollen with bark and roots we grubbed in that God-forgotten place: his humors foul as the latrines of an Arab's town: or Alonso de León with no more cloth to his bum than a heathen's clout. Or that lazarly Rodrigo de Villafuerte, with maggots at work in his wounds. Or I myself looking like some revenant from hell, with the bones pushing through my hide. Yes, we are deserters, Cavalier: deserters of plague, poison, and death. As for Governor Ojeda, he set sail aboard the nao fifty days past in demand of Santo Domingo to determine why you had not come with the provisions you had pledged for our salvation. And his orders were—"

"Pardon me! When Don Alonso departed from Santo Domingo, he went with a caravel and two small brigantines. The caravel returned to Española with your urgent message of distress and

57

is still there. Yet you say he sailed from you in San Sebastián aboard a nao. Pray tell me, Pizarro, how he came by a ship in these waters, begirt with heathen shores."

And Pizarro, to show his disrespect as well as his misliking of the present business, hobbled to the side and spat into the sea before he made answer.

"Your trust flatters us, Bachelor. But since our guts cry out in want while we have speech here, I will give you the thing in fine: While we yet waited in despair for your coming with supplies, meanwhile setting our teeth in the bitter larches we had sod in our empty pots, a nao one morning came to view. We cried 'Socorro!' and made out to it, weeping our thanks to God for mercy.

"But it was not you, Don Martín: that you will receive as truth. It was Bernardino de Talavera. Ha, I see you have knowledge of Señor Talavera. A lucky pirate, Bachelor: and his holds stuffed with provisions which he stole from Española, belikes from your own storehouse.

"He made a trade with Ojeda and a good one too, for our tongues were big in our mouths and gold will buy a dead man little else than a chiseled stone. Three thousand *castellanos*. But we fed on it, though we were hungry at the end of each meal, for Ojeda kept the supplies secure under his own lock and the chief portion for himself.

"When these supplies were gone, Ojeda set sail in the ship Talavera had stolen, with orders to us to wait fifty days for his return. The fifty days we waited, with famine and death our companions, while he no doubt fell privy to some black design of his excellent friend, the pirate Talavera. In short, of the three hundred men who came out with Ojeda on this cursed exploit, there remain these thirty-five fleshless specters. Here is Ojeda's own writ of commandment to us, signed by him."

Enciso, after the manner of a Crown prosecutor before a tribunal, gave close attention to the document and read every word thereof before he spoke.

"Very well: let your men pass over and they will be fed and their wounds dressed."

Enciso also ordered them to unite themselves to our company and so to make ready for return to San Sebastián. Whereupon Pizarro and all his men fell into great tumult, grumbling against the

58

commandment and threatening mutiny. And Pizarro boldly spoke their minds.

"Return to San Sebastián? The country barren, the waters polluted, the arrows poisoned. Even the fort is gone, for we beheld the flames of it before we were half a league from shore. You address the wrong men for such a return to hell, Don Martín."

"Address you, say? Know you, Pizarro, that I command you. You will not desert this armada with ease. One word more and you are in the wives. Understand?"

Pizarro then turned politic and subtle: and in a soft voice he said: "The thirty-five revenants before you, Bachelor, are no soldiers, but men long dead and ready for the crows. Why carry a crew of cadavers on your venture? There will be troubles enough with your own men and their fresh complaints, not to add the old miseries of these ghosts. Permit us to continue our course to Española, and secretly to your hand I will deliver all that we have garnered by our blood—two thousand pesos in fine gold."

But Enciso would not yield, intending (as the sequel proved) to seize the gold when the opportunity favored it. And Pizarro, having to mind the helpless state of his company, ordered his men to swear fealty to Ojeda's lieutenant.

Departing from Cartagena, we sailed in manner South by East, toward the Gulf of Urabá and the city of the lost, as the men of Ojeda called San Sebastián.

After we had sailed some three days (without a favorable wind) we were brought to that point called Caribana. And because it was drawing toward night, the pilot thought it good to lie off and on until morning before doubling the point. But presently we found ourselves in swift and dangerous currents. Fearing that we should be swept onto shoals, the master ordered enough sail to proceed, running at only two or three knots.

We had continued thus for two glasses when our ship suddenly lurched, staggered, and rolled to larboard. There came a splintering crash and she shuddered horribly in all her timbers.

"We have struck a shoal!" cried the watch.

And thus I remember it: the shouted orders rising over the stridor of the pigs and the piercing whinnies of the twelve mares: "Load provisions and launch the boats . . . *mande!*" And the mar-

59

iners stripped naked, running white as ghosts in the moonlight on the canted decks: and the loud cracking and groaning as the feral sea, like some roaring monster, devoured our ship.

A mad desire to throw everything overboard before she foundered and went down, worked in us all. Wherefore soon a litter of casks, apparel tied to planks, and pieces of wreckage (as well as other things of whatever kind that would float) rode on the waves of the dark sea around us.

With talk of the smooth sort and promise of recompense to come, Vasco Núñez procured that his dog would be put into one of the boats and his life thus preserved, for otherwise he would have perished.

As for Vasco Núñez and the rest of us, we had much ado to save ourselves: but with good Providence and strong arms we reached shore every man.

But while we could thus rejoice and give thanks for our lives, we had yet an earnest concern for our supplies. And all the day following, from sun-rising to the coming of darkness, we searched the sea (Pizarro and the men of Ojeda helping us in the undertaking) for what might still be found afloat.

And when we saw with what small fruit and commodity we had labored all that day, and to what extremity we had now been reduced, our hearts failed us. For, as Pizarro said it, we beheld the sad harvest of an evil season.

At Enciso's bidding, the boatswain gave the count of it, intoning it as a priest a requiem: "Twelve barrels of meal, nine cheeses, seventy-three swords, four halberds, fourteen bucklers, and one *quintal* (more or less) of ship's biscuit, damaged."

With these scant stores we went aboard the brigantines and weighed anchors and continued our voyage to San Sebastián, coasting the shore for a distance of three leagues before we had sight of the ruined settlement.

When we were yet a half league from shore, Pizarro (in whose brigantine we had taken passage) shaded his eyes and looked toward land. "Behold the city of death, *compañeros*. Not a pole stands where the fort was, built by the sick hands of those who perished . . . and by us! Look! Tell us what remains of the thirty houses, the church, the barricades, the True Cross that stood there. . . ."

60

In truth, nothing remained of the town save a mound of black, charred ruins. But Enciso kept a resolute countenance: and he ordered us all ashore and put us on small food: and we encamped in the ashes. He appointed sentries at the four corners: to the others his mandate was: "Clear the ruins. Mark the foundations for another fort. You, Barbosa, take a score of men and bring timber. Pizarro, muster a force of arms and give them good protection at their work. *Manos a la obra!*"

But they went as slaves under the lash, their heads down: without spirit, without hope. And Pizarro gave tongue to their thoughts:

"Here will our bones lie, picked clean by the crows. Here we will surely perish, for I warrant that the heathen lurk in waiting not more than a long bow-shot away, ready with their poisoned barbs. God defend us!"

They worked in a squall of rain, the skies dark, with strands of cloud blown up from the matted forests behind them like spun gray webs to snare the stranger. For tools they had only swords, mattocks, and cutlasses.

On the second day, as they labored in the jungle to cut certain small trees for a palisade, Pizarro's suspicion fell out accordingly: the Indians rushed forth from their places of concealment to give armed battle.

The Spaniards fought valorously, but were poorly armed: wherefore they withdrew step by step toward the encampment. Their adversaries, shouting wildly and leaping about from side to side, did not cease to harass them continually with round stones shot from slings, fire-hardened lances of jack palm, and arrows which they released in great numbers.

And when they perceived that the Castilians were fatigued to such an extent that they could but poorly defend themselves, they advanced on them and began (to the Christians' humiliation and disgust) to hurl great wads of human excrement, which they had moistened with water to make a stinking compost.

The *compañeros* were ill-prepared to receive this foul deluge, which splattered over their bucklers into their beards and faces.

"*Gran bestia!*" growled Barbosa to Vasco Núñez, as he squatted beside a rivulet to wash himself clean after the skirmish. "At

61

no hand would I face again that shower of ordure even though I march in my own blood forward." And so dashing another handful of water into his face, he howled again: "Will I ever soak off the reeky cling of it . . . ha! What stoats are these that fight with flyblown mixen? Do we battle an army or a mule's anus?"

Whereupon Vasco Núñez laughed. "In bad times a good face, as it is said."

And Barbosa answered: "Better a clean face!"

Two of the men who had gone with Pizarro into the forest to search for timber were struck with poisoned arrows: and these could not be helped, but died in terrible anguish, calling upon God to be eased in their great suffering.

And when this was seen, it bred among our men a marvellous fear: for we had not the armor to protect ourselves withal against the envenomed barbs which the Urabaes shot at us with great skill and cunning.

Nor had we any remedy for the strong and pestilential juice wherewith they anointed the points of their arrows. The said poison they compounded in this sort:

In large pots which they placed over very hot fires, far from their places of abode, they brewed together roots of the manzanillo tree, certain small apples of a fair red kind (but of which none dare eat), hairy worms, spiders, giant ants, bat wings, the head and tail of a very poisonous fish, toads, and the tails of serpents.

To attend and wait upon this Devil's broth, they appointed a slave girl of small account: for the fumes thereof killed the person with whose breath they were combined.

Our men being thus in dread of the poisoned arrows, and without the means of defending themselves against so many well-armed foes, thought it the better course to build a *barricada* of earth-works and butts filled with sand, which things were near at hand.

But the Bachelor Enciso, having put on his full armor and with a great show of valor, said to all: "Gentlemen, let us not quail before a few enemy bowmen because they have villainously empoisoned their shafts. As your lawful commander, I will lead and conduct you in a battle of fire and blood which will be a full recompense for our slain brothers and for the fatigues and travails we have endured: my life to it."

62

And the men received his words in silence. Yet, so proceeding in this determination, he led a company of one hundred men along that trail hewn out by those who had gone before. And they had no sooner lost sight of the settlement than they were assailed with a flight of arrows from an ambuscade.

Whereupon Enciso sought to save himself by flight, leading the men in a swift retreat. And (as it was afterward declared unto us) he was thus put to rout not by an army of a thousand soldiers armed with arquebuses and other artillery, but by three naked Indians.

Thus did Enciso lose his honor: and there was an ugly spirit of mutiny among the people who went about sullenly, discussing it with one another in the shadows of night: saying that he—the *alcalde mayor*—was plotting to take what stores remained and to flee with his friends, leaving the residue of the company to famine and death.

And some said that it stood upon us to seize the scant provisions before that devil laid hands upon them: and to take the ships and to use all diligence to sail away, leaving to Enciso the hell whereto he had led us.

In that time we stood in sore need of victuals: and each day our men lost strength and some died. All these circumstances being well-considered, Vasco Núñez asked leave to take his dog Leoncico (whom the Indians feared more than they feared a score of armed Christians) and to make an *entrada* in search of such natural increase as the country might yield.

And Enciso giving consent, he departed secretly at night that the Indians might not know of his exploit.

Exploring thus not far inland, he discovered a grove of date trees wherein a herd of wild boars were wont to root for the fallen fruit. Thither he led a troupe of our best crossbowmen, who were able to shoot ten of the animals.

These wild pigs (which are called peccaries) were smaller than the swine of Spain: and their tails were so short that some of our people believed them bobbed by the Indians. They differed also in that their hind feet were not cloven.

Thus, for the space of a week we fed greedily of the meat, together with dates and certain roots which (our hunger being so great) we found savory and sweet.

But as the herd of peccaries was depleted or moved away from the hunters, famine and sickness once again made us their captives: and we were reduced to a state of uttermost wretchedness.

Then the men began to speak openly of rebellion, declaring they would rather die in the dungeons of Santo Domingo than to abide any longer in this hell where they would surely expire of hunger or be slain every man by the fiendish heathen. And Gaspar de Mendoza, who gave tongue to their darkest thoughts, moved them to a great clamor and shouts of dissent, saying:

"What evil yet awaits? Of the green sickness, we perish: by the poisoned prickles of our enemies, we perish: by cursed wakefullness, we perish! We have shot wide of the bow hand. And did we article for a soldier's fare or a roach's famine? Ay! we have eaten rats, dogs, lice, beetles, beach grubs! Mother of God! Let us return, though our lives forfeit. Let us go back to Santo Domingo. That is my counsel, and there is no fee for it."

Then Vasco Núñez, who had given ear to Mendoza's plaint while occupied with plucking goose-grass from his red beard, now struck in: "Gaspar is a fine orator. But he dresses himself for mutiny. Bachelor Enciso has all things at commandment here, and he has no word for return."

"Let him command the indigenes!" cried Mendoza. "As for those who have the courage to follow me, we will have the mastery of two ships to carry us from this purgatory."

"Consider well, Mendoza," Vasco Núñez returned. "Enciso's power is that of the Crown: as loyal vassals of our Sovereign, you are sworn to obey. But you board and break sail against orders. You voyage without food. Many die. Those, if any, who remain alive against tempest and famine to reach Española, are there given the dungeons and quick death.

"Still, as you say with reason, here we live as men alive in their own graves. I have thought also upon this. Now I remember that in the years past, I came by these very coasts with Rodrigo de Bastidas. We entered this gulf, but we went ashore on the western side. There on the right hand, as it seems to me, we gave upon a village on the bank of a great river. There were fertile fields, for it was a land very cool and abundant for food. There the inhabitants do not poison their arrows and the river (which they call Darien, that being the name also of their kingdom) is rich in gold. Why do we not try for those shores?"

In answer to him, they began to shout all together: "To Darien! To Darien!"

And when their desire was made known to the Bachelor Enciso, he readily gave consent: for he divined the ugly spirit of the men and he stood in constant fear of their treachery.

With many shouts of rejoicing, we weighed and made sail: and held our course across that gulf to the western shore, which is Darien. And when we were yet a league off, all the people assembled on the decks to take knowledge of the land.

We forgot then our hurts, our hungers, and our troublesome affairs, now overpassed: and we stared in hope and rapture toward the hazy mounds upon the sea. The midday heat quivered in the air, shimmering in long waves about our ship: and the wind veered, and carried to us the hot, humid breath of the tropical forest. Heavy swells came out from shore to meet us and we drove in bow down, with water washing over the decks.

The lookout was silent in the rigging, pondering the appearance of things. And as we drew in nearer, he cried to the ragged, starved men below: "An abundant plain I see, like the land of Jerez, but more green. Trees are there: *palmeras de cocos*, a field of *maiz* . . . to the west, down from the hills come paths, deep-worn, walked over for a hundred years."

"And people?" Enciso shouted up to him. "What of people?"

"Of people, nothing. Nor one of them is seen. No movement, except of grasses and leaves."

Leoncico, the dog of Vasco Núñez, stretched his neck over the ship's side, sniffing toward shore. He bayed deeply, lifting his nose higher in the wind.

"He smells Indians," said Pizarro. "And every fiend of them ready to let fly with their cursed arrows."

In company with the brigantine *Santiago*, we came to anchor in a quiet road: and the two ships riding, we made ready to go on shore.

Whereupon the Bachelor Enciso procured that every man, both of our company and of Ojeda's following, swear never to retreat, however dangerous or desperate our plight.

So he spoke thus: "Lest some feel faint in the strong fighting that surely awaits us, or turn back with the temptation of longer life, let every man swear that at no hand will he retreat one step or give over before the heathen enemy. Vasco Núñez has said it: that there are no poisoned arrows among the people of this land. We fight in the service of our King and against the enemies of God. Remember that: and remember your oaths. Notary, lay down under our hands the truth of these proceedings: and let all sign."

When we had landed to the number of ninety in armor and were arranged in good order, Enciso again came before us and, removing his morion from his head, said: "Gentlemen, forasmuch as our Lord in His infinite mercy has delivered us from death, that we might extol His glory (and here exhort the pagans to do the same), let us with loud acclamation render unto Him our deepest thanks. And in His Presence and with you all as witnesses, I do swear that if ours be the victory in this land, I will send a pilgrimage to the shrine of Nuestra Señora del Antigua, there to adorn her with rich jewels. And here will we raise a town and church in her honor and bearing her holy name. *Oremus*."

He then went upon his knees, signalling us to do likewise: and he began a long prayer in Latin. The *compañeros*, understanding little of the priestly tongue (and fearing a sudden rain of arrows from lurking Indians), could not forbear to raise their eyes to the low hills above us. And as the orison droned on, Francisco Pizarro (who had little faith in the prayers of lawyers) whispered to me: "Behold the truth of the saying, 'No fool can be a great fool unless he knows Latin.' "

The long prayer being ended, we arose and marched in good order along a wide trail toward the inland parts. And when we had gone but half a league, we beheld before us on a low hill a fearsome force of Indians, who by estimation were to the number of five hundred, appareled for battle and in all readiness to receive us.

Enciso, seeing the great number of troops the enemy had and in consideration of our weak condition, was of a mind to send to them a messenger with gifts to lure them to amity. But while he took counsel of us as to what should be done, our enemies began a warlike tumult, blowing on conches and beating their drums. And they uttered great shouts of defiance: and by many dumb signs gave us to understand that we must go back to our ships and leave this land.

Whereupon Enciso commanded us to charge. And it was something worth seeing how such enfeebled men surged forward with the strength of well-nourished soldiers. Our crippled limbs miraculously awoke to life: and our swollen mouths ached with our cries.

Being ignorant in all matters of civilized warfare, the Indians descended from their hill to fight on level ground where the advantage was ours. Thus were they soon confounded: for the noise and fire of our arquebuses and the ferocity of our boar-hounds wrought among them a great fear. And believing that they were not able to make any strong resistance, they sought to secure themselves by flight.

After they fled, we entered their town, which was a fair and pleasant village on the river: and we took the spoil of it. Having not the time to carry and convey away their principal substance, the Indians had left in their *bohios* a good quantity of needful provisions, which we took to assuage our dog-like hunger. Likewise, we found there fine cotton cloth in abundance: some good plumage, apothecary herbs, and other things.

With much diligence we also sought their gold, which we discovered hidden in divers places among the canes and thickets by the river: coronets, anklets, plates, and other ornaments to the value of ten thousand *castellanos*.

Finding the situation pleasant, with good and wholesome air, we resolved to found here the first Christian town on Tierra Firme: and according to our vow, we named it Santa Maria de la Antigua del Darien.

So we possessed ourselves of their dwellings, which were well-made with walls of cane: the roof-thatch smelling of woodsmoke from their fires: and the floors of well-beaten earth, smooth and clean, sloping toward the sides.

Refreshed and eased, we walked among the *bohios* of that town and talked of the good fortune that had chanced to us and of our deliverance from the city of death: that surely it had been by the hand of God.

And I remember the veil of evening slowly covering the face of the day: westward over the rustling *maiz* fields: gathering its folds

67

over the distant sea and among the tall river grasses. How I thought then: this is a strange land, the wind full of dreams and new smells.

And Vasco Núñez, who had brought us hither, counselled that on the day following we send an envoy to find the Indians: for we must persuade them to friendship and familiarity: that they were a poor and natural people, created of God and who might be led to a knowledge of Him, not by the weapons of ravenous strangers, but in peaceful traffic and liberality in all things, as behooves the loyal vassals of a Christian sovereign. For such, said he, was the will of the King our Lord: and we would do well to abide by it.

To all of which Fray Juan Bautista said a hearty amen: but all the others kept silent.

Chapter 5 ~~~~~~~~~~~~~~~~~~~~~~~~~~~~~~~~~~

Now after we had made ourselves secure in the Indian pueblo (which we had dedicated to Our Lady of Antigua), we added thereto many works for our use and comfort.

We cleared a space for the plaza, with the church fronting it. The heavy-timbered *cabildo* was squared on the right hand and the royal house on the left. There was also a market where Indians trucked peacefully with us for Flemish trinkets, cheap scissors, needles, and other trifles.

Yet we were much plagued by the natural character of this land: both by many poisonous creatures that here abound and by the extremity of rain and heat during the wet season.

It was then that the rain came down as a deluge: the sky on the sudden darkened, with a gale of wind and much thunder and lightning flashing out of the clouds. And the waters fell from heaven without ceasing, not with the plash and patter we had known in Spain, but as a marvellous great flood, as it had been the emptying of a vast cauldron from the skies.

After an interval of two glasses, the storm would cease with the same suddenness as when it began. Then the sun would emerge with an extreme force of heat and such brightness as to blind the eyes. Presently, all the lagoons, pools, and marshes of the land began to smoke like the pits of hell: likewise, from the fevered earth there arose hot, pestilent vapors which stifled our breath.

And if some need required us to go forth from our fortified

town into the forest (to course the dogs or for any other purpose) so that we must of necessity put on armor, we roasted as though we were inside an oven: and the sweat streamed down our limbs in such rivulets that it is difficult to believe unless you have witnessed it with your proper eyes.

Yet within the space of another hour, the sun once again was blotted out by scudding black clouds: and once more with lightning and a terrible rush of wind through the palms with a great tearing sound, the downpour began anew.

So it went, day following day. And at night, if we slept inside our houses, we were assaulted by mosquitoes, wasps, winged ants, horseflies, and snakes.

Yet we dared not take our rest in the open air: for there it was certain we would be attacked by ferocious bats, which descended on the town with the coming of darkness. Although they resembled in appearance the bats of Spain, their bite was venomous and deadly. And before the Indians had provided us with a remedy, two of the *vecinos* died of the hurts they thus received: others became very ill.

These evil creatures would suddenly give onset to a sleeping man and, before he could escape, would snip off the ends of his fingers, toes, or the tip of his nose.

And they would suck therefrom such a quantity of blood that all who witnessed it were astonished, and remained in much fear of them. It was also a matter of marvellous wonder that the black fiends would choose the blood of one man over that of his companions and, if they had bitten him, they would return to him night after night, even though he reposed among a great number of other men.

Our sleep being thus much troubled by both winged and crawling things of the night, some (myself among them) arose with the first light to walk in the cool air of morning.

Early on the feast day of Santa Lucia, I being with Vasco Núñez on a fair and pleasant hillside above the river bank, where we were accustomed to give ourselves a little refreshing, we espied approaching us through the canebrakes a small company of *vecinos* from the town.

As they drew toward us we perceived them to be Francisco Pi-

zarro: Pedro de Orduna, with the stoop and lurching stride: Bartolomé Hurtado, always in the lead: Martín Zamudio, the Canta-
brian: Francisco de la Toba, with the fine morion.

Without greeting, without a word, they stood quietly with us,
all listening to the strange cries of the newly awakened birds in the
riparian thickets. A black crow soared above our heads with a
harsh caw and we lifted our eyes to follow its flight. That was a
bad omen: but none spoke of it.

Hurtado, who squatted on his heels, meditatively chewing a
twig stripped from its bark, was the first to speak. Addressing
Vasco Núñez, with a backward look to the town we had left, he
said: "It is an uneasy sleep in that town, *compadre.*"

And knowing well that all the men had fallen into dislike of the
hard rule exercised over them by the Bachelor Enciso, Vasco
Núñez answered him: "The new law, eh Bártolo?"

"One of the hundred new laws, *hombre*: and a thousand more
to come from that Bachelor's evil-breeding pate. 'No *vecino* in
this city of Santa Maria de la Antigua will henceforth traffic with
Indians for gold upon his own behalf: but all goods obtained by
trade, theft, discovery, or seizure are to be submitted to this office
of *alcalde mayor.* Penalty for violation: death.' Death! Who will
abide this scurvy prescript? For my part, not I!"

"Nor I!"

"Nor I!"

"Wait!" Vasco Núñez interrupted them (for he was ready as always to avoid mutiny and rebellion against law). "By what power
does Enciso lay this rule upon us?"

"By the power given him by Ojeda, governor of Urabá," Pizarro
answered.

"Then it is the power of the Crown?"

"Yes." So Pizarro grumbled, admitting it.

"And you would oppose your Sovereign? That is treason."

"The Sovereign, no!" cried Hurtado, jumping to his feet. "But
this monster, this jackass, this howling hinny of a Bachelor, *sí
señor* and amen."

"No, it cannot be," Vasco told them. "We are loyal vassals."

"But we will all lose our goods and our lives as well."

"Let us consider," Vasco Núñez counseled them. "You, Martín, are well practiced in all things concerning royal letters patent. Now, just as a matter of laughter: what part of Tierra Firme was given over to the government of Ojeda?"

"Well, that portion called New Andalucía or Urabá."

"And the remaining portion of the territory?"

"Is Castilla del Oro, the country under the hand of Diego de Nicuesa."

"And the western line of separation between the two *gobernaciones?*"

After weighing the matter, Zamudio smote his knee with his hand. "*Santísima!* What numb-witted pigs we are! The boundary, in God's name, yes the boundary. As Ojeda himself declared it and set his name upon it, the western boundary is the river Darien. We have founded a city in the territory of Diego de Nicuesa!

"And in conquence, Enciso is no more Chief Judge than any of us, nor licensed to prescribe laws. In the absence of Don Diego, the legal governor, we are free to choose whom we will to be *alcalde.*"

Upon hearing this, a great shout went up from the men. And Hurtado placed his hands upon his hips and thundered the question into their faces: "Who, then, is *alcalde mayor* of Santa Maria de la Antigua?"

And we cried as one: "Vasco Núñez de Balboa!"

"And who is that Bachelor Enciso that lives amongst us?"

Pizarro answered him: "The live image of a dead and rotting ass!"

Vasco Núñez held up his hand. "There are men of this colony," he told us, "who hold me in no such good account as you. Therefore, to stay their spirits, let another share the *alcaldía* with me. I counsel Martín Zamudio because he has a following: and for *alguacil mayor,* Hurtado. Let us down to it then, to test what may be the will of the *vecinos.* Though I forewarn you: no violence toward Enciso. I'll spill the first lusty pug who ventures a disorder."

So we marched back to the town, carrying upon our countenances the look of men who were about a serious business.

But as we entered Antigua, Francisco de la Toba (who was much given to compounding doggerel for every occasion) could

72

restrain himself no longer (for he had been silently composing some lame verse during our return) and now burst forth with a roar that awakened the whole town:

> *"Arise betimes, Enciso dear:*
> *Awake and see what now portends.*
> *Thy bum, so firmly wed to bed*
> *May soon be naked to the winds."*

As Vasco Núñez had declared unto us, there were certain malcontents in the colony with whom he was in no great credit. And among those who went about sullenly seeking to stir up the people against Vasco Núñez was a certain Alonso Perez de la Rua, who was a toady to the Bachelor Enciso, ever ready to do what was laid upon him.

In his attempts to cause dissent and tumult, he had some success, because the *compañeros*, having deposed one authority so easily, now believed that they could at any time replace a leader who did not please them or (what is more to the point) one who did not allow them all freedom in their feverish greed for gold, which moved them to maltreat the Indians, both in their persons and in their goods.

Perez fostered this behavior as best he could, throwing out talk of tyranny and encouraging every new grievance against Vasco Núñez: abetting every plot of disobedience to his commands.

The contentions and unrest increased every day. The loyal friends of our Captain (among whom I was one) were always ready to cry down any opposition to him: but the talk of mutiny spread.

"Ay, it's a pretty piece of justice that passes in this town nowadays," cried Perez to a number of men assembled in the plaza one day. "Now that you, *señores*, by your proper 'yes' have set that sow's dug up as alcalde! Our *patrón* protect us! What answer do you carry to his latest ordinance? 'No indigene is from this time forward to be beaten to prostration,' says he, this horned usurper of lawful authority. 'Penalty: blow for blow delivered: lash for lash.' *Santos!* Chew on that. You, gentlemen of Spain, are made equal to the wild and naked people of this region. You, Christians, are to share civility with the squatting heathen. Mercy, he calls it. Perfidy, say I: give it no other name.

"Will you plant the crops, then, on your own knees? Grind the

73

corn with your own pith? Hunt wild pigs on your own bellies? If you give me a 'no,' I ask you then: how will these things be done? You know already what I repeat: for an Indian or a mule, a kick from behind. But I waste words on this—"

"Lies!" shouted Pedro de Orduna, who had a voice like unto a lion's roar. And to the men there assembled he said: "What this slobber-mouth *pisaverde* wishes to say, *compañeros*, is not waste words, but twist words. As for this new law he has gnawed on and disgorged to you, it troubles nobody save the brute and the drunkard, who by their daily slaughter of the Indians bid well to leave the fields vacant and the market-place bare. I marvel you would lose a thought on it. As to the kick from behind, yes and often. But I say lay it on with proper and sufficient reason. Some have made a vicious sport of it, as I have heard it."

"Better a sport of the savages than the cruel oppression of Christians," Perez made answer. "This country swarms with Indians (yes, and each one with an arrow for our guts). But from which of these hills will come Spaniards, men as we are: men like Pascual de los Rios, who but a week past was dispatched outside this very town? Mercy—bah!"

"And bah the other way!" said Orduna. "The proof of our Captain's lenity lives before us (a shameful sight!) in the person of this word-windy goat-skin. A plague seize me if—"

Orduna gave over and cocked an ear: and we were all silent there, for all had heard the distant sound of cannon fire. Ñuflo de Olano, the Negro, who had been sitting upon a cask, slid to his feet and started off in all haste toward a high point that gave a view of the gulf: and he proclaimed as he went: "By the Sacrament, that was the Christian sound of a Lombardy: and I'll hazard to it a pipe of cribble."

From the hilltop we descried smoke signals rising in white puffs from the opposite shore of the gulf: and we heard further cannon fire from time to time.

Whereupon we made fires of reeds and green branches to signal our presence and whereabouts. Vasco Núñez also ordered that the piece which the *Concepción* carried be fired off.

"If those Lombardys betoken an armada from Española," declared Hurtado, licking his lips, "we may well dine this night on figs and the savory cheeses of Castile."

74

To which Vasco Núñez made answer: "Yes, we have gold and half-vacant bellies. And these Christian gentlemen who come with provisions will think strongly on that when the price of their cargo is made known to us."

We had sight of the armada early in the afternoon: a caravel followed by a brigantine. And having seen our signals, they came swiftly across to us, being fully under their courses and bonnets.

The caravel having arrived first and anchored in the road, the Captain and his officers came ashore.

And with watery cheeks we went down to meet them, lifting our hands up to heaven and greeting them with loud cries of rejoicing: embracing them as emissaries sent from heaven.

In command of the enterprise was one Rodrigo de Colmenares, a lieutenant of Diego de Nicuesa. And he said: "We come from Española with supplies for and in search of the Governor Nicuesa. A long time has passed since we had word of him and we are preoccupied for his safety. Have you news of him?"

"Nor a word," Vasco Núñez answered him. "Here, you, Pizarro: you were the last of Ojeda's men to bring notices of Nicuesa. Tell us what chanced to him."

And after repeating his sad relation of finding Nicuesa near death among the mangrove roots (as before told to us) and of their entrada wherein they had discovered the body of Juan de la Cosa, Pizarro said: "Afterward we returned to the ships. Nicuesa then parted from us with his armada. He sailed in demand of Veragua: who knows whether he found those shores? We who remained with Ojeda were put to it for the safety of our own tails."

Colmenares, being as hungry for gold as we were for victuals, ordered provisions brought ashore from his ships. That night we feasted: and being greatly refreshed in mind and body, we began to talk of our situation in Santa Maria.

The *compañeros* were fearful of losing their foothold in the territory of Darien if we did not place ourselves under the banner of some person of rank and quality, who had prepotent influence at court.

Colmenares told us then (with many kind expressions) that Diego de Nicuesa was already our legal Governor by royal *capitulación*: that he was a man who was favored by the King and had good credit with the Council of Indies. Why not gain both his favor and the help in men and supplies that he could enlist in our enterprise, by pledging ourselves to his cause?

Only Enciso and his coterie spoke against the proposal, though I perceived that Vasco Núñez was not happy about it. He nevertheless stood with the *vecinos* in their agreement: but he advertised us thus: "Let us proceed with this business in the manner of one who gathers eggs, lest with undue haste we invite the Governor's greed and he may take all that we have garnered to this day by misery and valor."

So the cause being thoroughly heard, it was concluded by all the company that three proctors should accompany Colmenares on his voyage toward Veragua to seek the Governor: and that if (with God's favor) he should be found, to make known to him our desire to join ourselves to his suite.

The men appointed to the said deputation were Francisco de Agueros, Diego del Corral (a lawyer who had come hither with Colmenares), and Diego Albitez, a regidor of our town of Santa Maria.

Now many things which Vasco Núñez had learned of the Governor Nicuesa while on the island of Española had taken deep impression in his thoughts: wherefore, he did not think it meet to repose trust in a person of his character.

To do the best he could, therefore, to protect the people of Santa Maria, he secretly took Diego de Albitez aside and told him: "Look well to it, by whatever means may be most politic, that we are well-served in the troublous times you will surely find in Nicuesa's camp. And if you find that Nicuesa is the harsh man I believe him to be, who cares not how he grinds and misuses others, seek out the Biscayans among his following (for they will most quickly pact with us) and determine what means may be used to save us from the said Nicuesa's tyranny and greed."

To assure Albitez's hearty compliance with this order, Vasco Núñez delivered into the regidor's hand one hundred *castellanos* in gold. And he further informed him: "If your services prove to be fruitful and well-executed, more gold will be forthcoming, as well as other favors which befit your rank and worth."

Having dispatched all his business in Santa Maria, Colmenares and his men departed and set sail in search of Nicuesa. And from the hilltop (together with Vasco Núñez, Bartolomé Hurtado, and others) I watched the armada sail from the shores of Darien.

And the caravel's tall mainmast having quivered in the noonday distance and disappeared below the hyaline, Vasco Núñez said to Hurtado (who stood beside us, chewing the succulent end of a length of sugar cane): "I fear their early return, Bártolo, with that hungry wolf Nicuesa slobbering to devour the fruits of our enterprise."

Hurtado spat out some ropy strands of masticated cane to answer him: "You think they will find Nicuesa, Captain?"

"Yes, and soon. I have the heaviness of it on my heart. Nicuesa will come punctually to govern in Darien. And what a blessed change that will be! After all the frowns of fortune on sea and our labors on land, we petition new misfortune to come among us. Though, to speak the truth, it is little matter for those fat-witted rogues who have thus sold their parcel for drunken stupors in their afternoon hammocks. *Vaya!* You will shortly hear their roars of indignation, their groans of regret, and finally their howls for a new Governor, more turned to their own advantage."

"Then you will be sent for."

"Well, who knows? For my part, I'm little smoothed to wait for their pleasure, seeing that it changes with the altering moon. Besides, Nicuesa is lawful ruler of this territory and by the King's writ. It's little that opposition will cry down."

Hurtado continued then to munch thoughtfully: and presently he said, speaking slowly around the cud of cane: "I have a plan, *capitán*. When this Nicuesa arrives, let us receive him with a King's grace. Then each day, let one of our feather-footed menials extract a few drops of the juice from the leaves of that tree the Indians call *coyamo* and squeeze the hellish stuff into Nicuesa's bed. That, upon my life, will engage his attention most heartily for days together, without time to spare.

"In the week past I was under such a tree, taking shelter from the rain. Some drops of water fell off the leaves upon my arms and hands. Holy Saints! I am still scratching: and ever sore like a lance wound heated in fire. Look you."

Hurtado held forth his arms for us to see. Large red patches showed on his arm and between his fingers. And viewing them, he dropped the cane and began scratching as it were a dog with fleas.

77

Whereat Vasco Núñez laughed with great humor: but he told Hurtado: "A skittish wile, Bártolo, even to plague Nicuesa. And to no good purpose: we have a rasping, red Governor for three weeks (but still a Governor) and afterward a fiend ready to avenge the outrage with harsh laws. No, I have a gullery worth ten of yours."

"What is your device?"

"This: wherever Nicuesa may be when Colmenares finds him, one thing we can forsee: he will have no prodigal store of provisions. That means, if our own experience has not misled us, that those men under his charge will make against him those impeachments that empty bellies are wont to incite. Even after they are fed, they will still aftertaste the bitterness of their complaints and little desire further exploits under a command that brought them only misery. To shore them up in their discontent, we have our own bellman in their midst. He will keep hot discord among them, or I have misjudged the gentleman."

To which Hurtado made answer: "I draw a short breath today: tell me whom you have sent to the task and how it will be performed."

"Easy. When Colmenares comes to the settlement of Nicuesa, he finds the whole company in sorry plight, lean as blind pigs. Do we not know the story well? Albitez (for he is our *procurador*) goes among them with the good story of our rich gleanings as free men of Darien. At the same time, he draws forth their ugly complaints concerning Nicuesa. He tells them life is but a breath's span and no time to be lost if they are to see Spain ever again, with a fat purse. Think of their companions (may they be in heaven) whom the wild Caribs have devoured, the battles cut down, the sea swallowed. Mother of us all! the hazards are desperate in this country: and a Christian's bones sleep better in Christian soil. Better to search these regions with a good and just man and live than to follow after a cruel and foolish tyrant only to expire in the wilderness."

And Hurtado said: "Lead on: the direction is good."

"When Nicuesa's men are fully tuned to that song, Albitez takes aside that one of their number having the worst grievance, he being in urgent need of succor. Together, they agree what must be said to the *vecinos* here when they arrive. At the same time, Albitez counsels Nicuesa that, the *vecinos* of Santa Maria having

78

petitioned him to be their Captain-General, he ought not to arrive in our midst as a vulgar crow descending upon a carcass, but fully heralded in the manner befitting a nobleman from the royal household.

"To that purpose, Albitez asks leave to return to Santa Maria with Nicuesa's chief officers to announce to us that the Governor has been found, that we may have time to prepare a proper welcome. Faith, and Nicuesa will listen with an open ear to that counsel! As for Albitez, he will bring with him certain members of Nicuesa's company who will bear tidings that will not be of the kind a man may easily sleep on. In plainer terms, my friend, the welcome to be prepared for Don Diego will in no wise be the kind he expects."

"As God's my life!" mumbled Hurtado through a mouthful of cane, "you have the Devil's own craft. But say: what of Nicuesa's lawful writ over this territory? To think of him cubbed up in the mouldy hulks and with His Majesty's seal, as you might say it, like a mare's brand on his rump: the blessed angels guard me! A sudden buffet for an alcalde, yes: a wink at a constable's paper, sí, sí! But to miscarry a royal commission, there Hurtado begins to lose the spirit of the exploit."

But Vasco Núñez belittled his fears and said: "I have never heard of an offense to the Crown that a sufficient quantity of fine gold would not dissolve with the wonderful suddenness of sugar in a cask of Jerez. As for Nicuesa, he is not to see the inside of our jail. The people of Santa Maria will, I think, persuade him not to come ashore at all."

And, having pondered our Captain's words, Hurtado said: "I understand. Nicuesa, if he ever reaches Castile, will plead his cause with nothing more eloquent than a Latin lament. Our cause, on the other hand, will be argued with ready gold and promises of more to come. On the one side, a bereft hidalgo with an empty purse and a lost gobernación: on the other, a company of baquianos led by a man of valor. What decision, indeed? Our course is certified."

"I hope you are right, man: but never praise a bridge until it is safely passed over."

Diego de Albitez carried out all that had been ordained before

79

he embarked with Colmenares to go in search of the Governor Nicuesa. For the condition of Nicuesa and his men, when they were found in Nombre de Dios (a harbor half swallowed up by the jungle), was exactly as Vasco Núñez had forseen it to be.

Within a month after the departure of Colmenares on his quest, a small sea-ravaged caravel appeared in the Darien estuary, and Albitez, together with Corral and two men of Nicuesa's company, came ashore. One of these was so weak and ill-used that he could scarcely endure to walk without the help of his companions. His haggard face, the droop of his shoulders, his sore lips, and knotted hands recalled to all of us our own miseries and accursed privation at San Sebastián.

And when all the people of Santa Maria were assembled, Albitez brought the unfortunate man before them, saying: "*Compañeros*: we who set sail with the Captain Colmenares have found Nicuesa, the gentleman whom you sent us to bring to this town as lawful Governor."

Whereupon someone among the *vecinos* was heard to ask, looking toward the woeful stranger: "Is *that* Nicuesa?"

"The Governor will arrive in good time, *señores*," Albitez continued. "He has sent us before him to proclaim to you his coming that you may receive him in the manner proper to a nobleman of the first rank or (to give it his own words) 'with arches of triumph.'

"We who went over to him from Darien have already told him of you: of your Christian town: of your gold: and of your enterprise in service of the King. We have piled dignity upon dignity. And his answer was that, upon his coming, he will boot from authority those officers we have elected by our vote and punish us, requiring of us that we (as he has said it) 'disgorge all the gold they have illegally taken in my territory.'

"Thus we acquaint you with Don Diego de Nicuesa, whom you have chosen to serve. With your patience, I present to you Fernando Gómez, *regidor* of Nicuesa's government, and who sailed with the Governor out of Española. He will tell you of all that befell them afterward, for he witnessed it with his proper eyes."

Gomez advanced a step or two, but for a moment he did not speak: and beneath his stare, we began to shift uneasily: yet not a word was spoken among us.

80

"Gentlemen of Santa Maria," at length he began (and his voice like an *adios* to hope): "we were seven hundred souls who left with Nicuesa upon that Devil-favored enterprise. Today . . . we are sixty . . . scurvied, feeble, yellow. . . ." He paused and a murmur passed through his listeners. Then he continued: "As for my own plight, my own suffering, it is but a part of the cruel injustice worked upon all of us by a mean-spirited tyrant.

"But to tell you how we came to such extremities: I served with Lope de Olano, who was Nicuesa's lieutenant and a good man. We had scarcely lost the harbor of Cartagena when we encountered a sudden torment: and it was down upon us like a beaten horse in a blind smother. Olano ordered our vessel and those with us to keep good watch and to bear but slack sail, for the *capitana*, which carried Nicuesa, was not in sight. So we found shelter from the storm under the lee side of an island. When daylight was come, we coasted all shores in demand of Nicuesa. He had stood out to sea (as we supposed): and we believed he had perished.

"We proceeded therefore and came to the river called Belén. There we landed all our goods, for our ships were greatly ravaged by the cursed *broma* and would soon sink beneath us. . . ." Gomez drew a long breath: and after a brief silence, he continued. "From the wreckage of our ships we built meagre cabins upon those shores. But new storms arose. The waters rushed upon us, and our shelters were washed away, while we were severely tried to save our lives. Some drowned: some were swallowed by the sands. Holy Mother! It was a heavy affliction. Hunger gnawed at our guts: fevers came, and more storms. In great tribulation, many died.

"I tell you the Devil has domain over that country. The bodies of our dead that were buried in the sand were consumed in eight days as if they had rested in a grave for fifty years. And we who saw it all returned to our encampment crazed and speechless. We remembered then the great comet, shaped like a naked sword, that had blazed across the sky over Española before we had sailed. And we took it for an evil sign.

"So, out of wreckage, we built a brigantine to bear us from those shores of death. We had but finished the vessel when a ship's boat put in to us with four Castilians. They told us that Nicuesa still lived, though in misery, on a distant island which they had named Isle of the Deer. So we crossed over to him with all haste.

"But when we had come to the island, Nicuesa clouded over with ire: and, charging Olano with treason for having lost the company of the *capitana*, he sentenced him to death. Such was to be his recompense for fealty and good services. But all of us as one man opposed that harsh judgment and made loud appeals for mercy. So Olano was saved from death. Yet all of us who had been with him in his ship were chained and beaten. As for Olano, he was bound in harness like an ox and made to grind a few husks of grain. So does he still, though from sickness and famine he can no longer walk, but must crawl upon his knees to pull the heavy dragstone. Ah!" The man's voice deserted him and he shook with sobs.

Whereat a certain Biscayan of Santa Maria, unable longer to withhold his wrath, shouted: "A blade to the sagging belly of that swine Nicuesa, say I!"

And other Biscayans, as Vasco Núñez had foretold it, roared with anger.

And Gómez continued: "Take warning, men of Darien, by all that has passed with us. We too sent relief to Nicuesa and rescued him from death: and he repaid us with misery and chains. And when those who were about to perish of sickness and famine implored his help, his answer was: 'Get out! Get along to the dying ground!' Such is the recompense you may expect from his hands. Already he has said it (as your own emissary has truly told you) that he intends to take possession of all your gold. Finally you will know hunger as I have seen it. Ay, *señores*, what I have seen! Spaniards, men of good cape, scrabbling for unclean and rotten carrion.

"Yes! The carcass of a starved and scrawny dog for the pot sold for twenty *castellanos* in gold: the water in which he was simmered went for a peso a bowl. And one day Gonzalo de Badajoz brought in two ugly toads and they were like viands from the King's table: and we bid for them. They went to Diego Ribero for six ducats: but he, out of compassion, had them prepared for one of our men who was sick unto death and because he begged for them with such piteous cries."

Gómez began to pant, being short of breath because of the

82

exertion of his speech. His last words ended in a long, trembling sigh. But after a moment of silence, he resumed: "What evil demon has magicked you, *señores*, that being your own masters, and free, you have sent for this monster to devour your gains and rule over you? You have invited suffering and death. You are like sheep that have asked the wolf to be their shepherd. May God . . . have mercy . . . upon . . . you!"

Having spoken thus, the wretched, sick man staggered and would have fallen had not Albitez held him up. Then, leaning heavily upon Albitez, he walked away toward the house of Martín Zamudio. The people started to surge after him, but Hurtado held out his arms and stayed them.

He told them sternly: "Let the *pobre* have rest! And meanwhile let us consider the extremity of our own estate. It is plain that we have erred: but thanks be to God, there is yet a cure for the evil. That devil Nicuesa still has not set foot upon these shores. I ask you, *compañeros*, will he ever beach his boat on the free strand of Darien?"

And they answered him with a great shout: "Never!"

Hurtado pressed the advantage. "Well said! Now, as you all know me to be a plain and blunt man, I do not hesitate to tell you this: we are traitors to an honorable man. We have sadly recompensed him who saved us from death: who brought us over to a land of good portions: who put down tyranny: who retained to us our parcels when they would have been taken away from us by unjust laws. Judases! You set him up once and you prospered. You followed him in battle and you tasted victory. Need I name the man?"

Whereupon I cried as loudly as I could: "Vasco Núñez! Viva Vasco Núñez!"

And all the others joined together in a mighty shout: "Viva! Viva Vasco Núñez!"

Thus in accord again, they began to look about for the man who might once more lead us out of our present affliction. And Pizarro, pointing across the plaza, said: "There he is."

And turning to look in the direction he thus gestured, we perceived the Captain seated alone upon a bench, his head inclined as though weighed down by heavy thoughts or at his prayers.

83

Thereupon all of us repaired amain to that side of the plaza to learn of him what counsel he might give to us.

Our captain called together all the company and told them: "Do not despair. If we all act in concert to thwart the evil which threatens us, we can afterward (if the need be) plead that we, for the very safety of our lives, were constrained to put down a great injustice which would be contrary to the will of His Majesty our King as well as to the royal laws of his realm."

To give good color to what otherwise might appear a treasonable act, we resolved to draw up a document setting forth Nicuesa's crimes and excesses and asserting that, as men pledged to Ojeda, we were not bound in allegiance to the Governor of Veragua.

Furthermore, to present a show of unity and to discourage any man from changing sides after the arrival of Nicuesa, a written vow was laid down by the notary to which every *vecino* was to swear and sign with his name or mark.

And to bind every man more fully to his vow, we executed it in the church before the Holy Sacrament, in manner thus:

On a fair cloth spread before the altar was placed a copy of the Holy Gospels and upon that a crucifix, as in the observance of Holy Thursday and Good Friday. Then, one by one, every resident and sojourner of Santa Maria approached the altar to take his oath, beginning with Vasco Núñez (who was highest in rank) and so proceeding with his co-alcalde Zamudio: the treasurer, the chief constable, the *regidores*, the *veedor*, the *escribanos*, and finally the *compañeros*.

Placing his right hand upon the cross, each of us swore in the name of God and of the Holy Mother not to receive Don Rodrigo de Nicuesa as our Governor.

We understood thereby that in all that was brought to pass, we would act not as separate men, but as members of one body. And every soul in Santa Maria (even unto the Bachelor Enciso and his suite) set their names to the paper and took their oaths.

It would be well not to tell how Nicuesa behaved after the departure of Albitez and the others to return to Santa Maria.

As I have heard it credibly reported (and hold to be true) he made prodigal use of the stores brought in the ships of Rodrigo de Colmenares: and each night there was feasting and a celebration with much wine and music. And the principal diseur at these lavish repasts was the Governor himself (for, as it is well known, he is the most accomplished guitarist in all of Spain).

At one of these banquets he also exhibited his great skill with a carving blade (he having been chief carver of the royal household). And he sliced and sundered a whole chicken while holding it suspended in the air, a feat for which he had been greatly lauded in the court of the Catholic King.

The brigantine *Trinidad*, bearing Nicuesa and all who had been with him at Nombre de Dios, came to anchor in the estuary of Darien shortly before sunset on the last day of February in the year 1511.

And perceiving from the ship a multitude of people on the shore, the Governor supposed them to be gathered there to receive him with high honors and to entertain him well.

And to Colmenares, who stood beside him, he spoke his thoughts: that he felt then as without any doubt he would on the morning of the final judgement day when he would be called forth from the tomb. His eyes grew moist as he remembered the hell which they had called Nombre de Dios only because they had come to that harbor in such a state of wretchedness that he had cried out, "In the name of God, let us stop here." He shuddered a little, recalling that even the stones in that country were long and white, like unfleshed bones.

"There was another peculiarity about that purgatory, Rodrigo (which all have seen many times and attested to), and it is this: that no man dies there except when the tide is ebbing. Is that not strange?"

Not since the easy and languorous days of his youth in Spain had Nicuesa known a more mellow dignity. His flesh being now appeased, his mind was tranquil: and he was in all ways ready for the glory that was soon to clothe him.

As they were lowering the boat, Nicuesa continued to stare with a smile of pleasure on his countenance. He drew forth from beneath his lace cuff an immaculate napkin and delicately wiped his face and tucked it away once more. Whereupon one of the mariners whispered to another: "Behold how, less than a week past the shores of death, he begins to eat with the greed of the Devil's private hog, and so sweats like a bag of suet in the sun. *Fo!* It is little

85

else than chicken bones they will get from his rule, and those picked clean."

But Diego de Nicuesa did not hear this. As the sailors rowed toward shore, he sat regally in the stern, humming and singing a somewhat indelicate song he had learned during his student days at Salamanca. It was called "Juego de Amor."

> "Who wishes to play the game of love,
> Heed these directions, I implore:
> First, close the shutters and sneck the door.
> Then drawing her nearer. . . ."

"Alto ahí!"

This rude command to halt came at the precise moment Nicuesa's boat touched the strand. Now, he saw clearly the hostile faces of the people. In front of them stood the Chief Constable, his arm upheld in a gesture of prohibition. Beside him was another official with a document in his hand.

"What passes here?" the Governor mumbled in confusion. "Is there a plague in the colony? A mutiny? Impossible. What then?"

The mariners who accompanied Nicuesa were also bewildered at this kind of reception. They sat motionless, their oars in the air, unable to speak or move.

"By order of the people of Darien, the men of Ojeda," Zamudio now read from the document he held, speaking with authority: "—to Don Diego de Nicuesa: Item: you have declared your intention of seizing all lawful gains heretofore falling to the Christians of Darien by traffic and conquest: That, Item: you have shown no mercy, but rather barbarity, ill-usage, torture, outrage, and brutality to those who served you well and were loyal vassals of our King: and cruelty to those who brought you succor, especially to a certain Christian free man—"

"Villainous pig-snout!" Francisco Benitez, the Biscayan, interrupted, crying it out in a rage.

"That, Item: because of your crimes and excesses, committed in these Indies, you are a traitor, answerable to God and to the Crown. Wherefore, you are forbidden to land upon these shores and to enter into this territory: but you are ordered and commanded to return with all haste to your rightful province, to Veragua. Signed by my hand and by the hands of those whose names

86

follow, by petition and testimony of the people of Santa Maria de la Antigua, on the twenty-seventh of February in the year of Christ, fifteen hundred and eleven."

Now fully understanding the situation, Nicuesa stood erect in the boat, steadying himself upon the shoulders of the mariners.

"Cavaliers and men of quality," he addressed the people in a calm voice. "I have come hither at your own request and by entreaty of your emissaries who came to me saying that you desired my *gobernación* as that one duly appointed by royal decree. I perceive, however, that in the while I came over to you, complainers (offended at my justice) have already got them among you, corrupting the public ear with falsehoods and—"

"Bah! Go back and crow on your own dunghill, Nicuesa!" Benitez shouted.

There was now much stirring and talking among the Antiguans. And in a loud voice, Vasco Núñez commanded them: "Let Nicuesa speak!"

The noisy bustle ceased: and Nicuesa inclined slightly to Vasco Núñez: then he resumed: "If you do not wish to receive me, *señores* (knowing, however, that I am lawful Governor of this territory and generous to your cause—)"

"Ah! Ah!" [It was Benitez again.] "Generous, he says, *compañeros*. Well, the carrion beetle wouldn't lose the drippings of his nose. Generous he—"

"Shut up, Benitez!" Vasco Núñez again admonished him.

Nicuesa continued his appeal. "As I was saying, if you do not wish to receive me as your Governor, at the least remember that you are gentlemen of Spain and men of honor. Allow me to land, therefore, and, by my life, after a day's proper reason, I will abide by your commands. You have heard against me: will you then not hear my cause? Shame, Castilians! that you are so easily moved to treason."

"Return, Nicuesa!" It was Zamudio who spoke, more calmly than the others, but as one empowered to impose justice. "We are loyal men: but loyal to our Sovereign, as our lives shall answer to it. To allow you to come among us is to invite tyranny. And tyranny, Don Diego, like disease, comes on horseback and goes away on foot. Tarry no more. If you have a peso's worth of good coun-

87

sel, you will go back to your ship and withdraw from these shores."

But Nicuesa would not heed Zamudio's words. And he said: "Gentlemen of Santa Maria, for the sake of Christian brotherhood do not, because of ancient oversights, consign me to the wretched death that awaits all who beach ship on those heaven-despised shores. Already, *señores*, hundreds of Christians lie in the unknown sands and none to tell if they be husbands or brothers or sire. And I from my own kin, who wait—"

"*Basta!* Shut off the spigot and let it out the bung!"

Benitez once more. And I perceived that our Captain was much annoyed at his conduct and ready to rebuke him when Nicuesa, with a look of resignation, sat down once more in the boat and ordered the men to return to the brigantine.

Early on the day following, as I watched with Vasco Núñez for the brigantine to sail (believing as we did that Nicuesa had accepted his fate), we saw a boat put off from her side and row toward shore. We easily descried the figure of Nicuesa, in a resplendent cape with its gold crosschain flashing in the morning light.

"The fool!" said Vasco Núñez. "He will persist in his folly until he pays for it with his life."

And he started in great haste toward the strand, I following. And at the landing we found a number of Biscayans gathered, awaiting the arrival of Nicuesa's bark. The Governor, smiling cordially, stepped from his boat with confidence, as though he expected to be received with an embrace of brotherhood. It was then clear to us that the Biscayans had plotted to deceive him. And as soon as he was ashore, the men, led and conducted by Zamudio and Benitez, ran forward to seize him.

"*Que hay?*" shouted Vasco Núñez.

The Captain's unexpected appearance and his words stayed them for a brief instant. And it was in that breath of time that Nicuesa, perceiving how he had been tricked with promises of good will (by a messenger who had been sent aboard his ship) took to his heels with astonishing fleetness. He was at once pursued by the Biscayans. Vasco Núñez followed both: and it was plain to see that his anger was rising.

Nicuesa's legs had in them a swiftness that was surprising for one of his noble birth. He easily left his pursuers behind him, taking refuge in the dense thickets a short distance up the river. Vasco Núñez once again shouted at the men, and now with such rage that they halted.

"Rogues! Sly gypsies! Have you forgotten the strong jail and executioner's block in this town? By the Mass, not one of you will live his natural age if violence is done to the person of Nicuesa. Now, Zamudio, speak for your men."

And looking about guiltily at his men, Zamudio answered: "We wished him to stand trial for his crimes."

"The proper place for a trial is in a tribunal: though little good in it I warrant. You have already given your oaths in the presence of the Blessed Sacrament that you will never receive him as Governor."

Vasco Núñez then left them and went forward toward the place of Nicuesa's concealment. Seeing that our Captain came alone and recognizing him as the man who had spoken in his behalf, Nicuesa came readily from his hiding place.

"I am Vasco Núñez," our Captain told him. "I have persuaded them to hold a peaceful inquiry. I offer you protection, with my life in gage for it."

Nicuesa bowed gracefully. "Diego de Nicuesa, at your command. As for my letters patent, you see, *señor*, that they are addressed to lawful subjects of the Spanish Crown. Evidently I have fallen among pirates, who are without any allegiance."

"What you say has truth to it, and I counsel you to hide your tongue in this affair or you will stir them too strongly and we will both be undone. Come with me: I will meet their threats with my sword. That is something they have seen and understand."

Nicuesa bowed again. "I have heard it related, Vasco Núñez, that you are an hidalgo. Permit me to add that you are a cavalier of Our Lord Christ as well."

Thereupon Vasco Núñez turned aside as if in shame. He said: "*Vámos.*"

The inquiry was poorly heard and done without good order, being much marred by the tumults and outcries of the Biscayans. Vasco Núñez spoke persuasively for the safety of Nicuesa: he reasoned, he advertised them, saying that he would not permit any man to there commit any such thing as would redound to his dishonor and to the dishonor of our Sovereign.

Yet were the men not moved by it, they believing his words to be a windy show of justice for the King's chronicle.

Observing to what little effect Vasco Núñez heated their ears, Nicuesa put aside caution once again and acted as his own advocate. But his words were received with taunts and loud ridicule. The Governor then wrung his hands, saying: "Admit me only as a *compañero, señores:* as one of the meanest, the poorest in your company."

To which the men made answer: "Never! After the collar cometh the halter. A sweet wile, Nicuesa!"

"As a prisoner, then, in the wives even: but do not command my return to Nombre de Dios, *señores!* For the sake of God's love and holy mercy, not to those coasts of famine, poisoned arrows, death: not to the misery of—"

But they cried him down: and uppermost in the noise of derision was once again the voice of Francisco Benitez. Now as Nicuesa, bowed by adversity and fear, began to weep before them, Benitez bellowed: "Let him weep: he will piss the less!"

Vasco Núñez beat upon the floor with a pike staff to restore good order. Then he said to them: "Let Nicuesa find at our hands some mercy, which will redound as much to our profit as to his own. Let us victual a ship withal, and send him to Española and thence to Spain to answer for—"

But Benitez again overcame all other speech, bawling in a loud voice: "No, no, no! Not a smallest morsel for this dribbling fribble!"

Thus he brought an end to our Captain's patience: whereupon he threw down the pike he held and walked across to Benitez: and without word or warning, he struck the Biscayan full in the mouth with his fist.

An instant quiet fell upon the assembly. And Benitez was so arrested by the unexpected blow that he stood blinking stupidly, one hand held before his mouth.

Then Vasco Núñez spoke his will: "I, Vasco Núñez de Balboa, as lawful alcalde of the Christian city of Santa Maria de la Antigua, hereby order one hundred lashes to Francisco Benitez, delivered upon the back. Roldan, execute the sentence."

And as all looked on in marvellous astonishment, Benitez was led out, protesting loudly, to the whipping post. And the sound of his punishment thereafter greatly chastened the remaining arguments at Nicuesa's inquiry.

But Vasco Núñez made his plea to small purpose: and perceiving at last that they would, contrary to all his entreaty, go about to withstand any charity to Nicuesa, he remained contented that they should give the Governor a ship and deliver to him victuals (at our Captain's charge) necessary for a voyage of seven days. It was also agreed that they would allow his serving men and familiars (and such others as were willing to go) to accompany him.

Thus did Nicuesa and seventeen of his company embark that same day. And the ship given them for their voyage was a worm-ravaged vessel which (God knows) was weak and ill-appointed: her seams had been caulked with a blunt tool and her ribs were soft as suet.

Vasco Núñez watched them set sail with great sadness of countenance. And to me he said: "Mother of God! This day savors of cruelty unto death."

At that same instant, Diego de Nicuesa gave himself up to prayer. And his voice was carried back to us like an ominous rising wind: "Show thy face, O Lord!" he cried. "And we shall be saved!"

But in our hearts we perceived that to which the future would bear witness: neither Nicuesa, his ship, nor any member of his company would ever be heard of again.

Chapter 6 〰〰〰〰〰〰〰〰〰〰〰〰〰〰〰〰〰〰

After the events I have described, Vasco Núñez had all things at commandment in Santa Maria de la Antigua. But had his early years in Spain been those of a courtier rather than of a soldier, he would have known that one cabal must lead to another: that the banishment of one adversary would be followed soon afterward by the disposal of a second: and the departure of the second by the rising threat of a third.

For if he would keep his place (as all who climb to honors and high offices well know it) a man must not allow his foes and rivals the time and the alliances wherewith to work him ill. Ambition, whether it be a lust for gold or a thirst for honor, is (as the blessed San Bernardo has well said) the mother of hypocrisy, skulking in corners and dark places, but ever with an eye to advancement.

But Vasco Núñez did not know this. Nor did he ever learn it: and therein at the end lay his ruin. For his was a guileless craft, loath to offend and ready to forgive. So his purposes were cleverly devised and quickly carried out.

Thus the departure of the unfortunate Nicuesa having removed the most instant opposition to his authority, he now bethought him of some remedy against the troublesome discontents by which he was yet plagued at the hands of the Bachelor Enciso and those who resorted to him.

The said Bachelor continued to stir contentions among the *vecinos* and to draw up legal writs wherein he made divers demands, not the least of which was that all gold in the treasury was to be handed over to him without question or delay.

Pricked on by these and other acts of effrontery in a similar sort, Vasco Núñez and his officers arrested and stayed Enciso: and they charged him with violating the pact made with those who enrolled in his enterprise when he sailed from Santo Domingo: with attempting an unlawful seizure of the King's property: and with assuming authority by illegal means.

After diligently examining all the particulars of the cause as near as might be in the course of our royal laws, the Chief Justice ordered that Enciso be set at liberty upon his promise to quit Santa Maria de la Antigua and to convey himself to Española or to Spain, there to answer for his unjust acts in Darien.

As for the Bachelor, this judgement gave him the greatest pleasure. His most devout prayer (so he said it then) was to appear before a fully qualified tribunal of gentlemen who knew and respected the laws of our realm. There he would surely vindicate himself and at the same time have these villainous outlaws of Darien (the mangy pirates!) thrown into the dungeons as well.

Our Captain, fearing that the Bachelor made no idle boast, but that he would do us great harm by writing memorials and making suit unto the King, persuaded the people to give their consent that Enciso remain in Santa Maria: and (to smooth his vanity) that he be appointed Chief Constable of the town.

But Enciso scorned this grace, declaring: "When I return to Darien, it will not be as an obedient servitor to that pork-barrel admiral, and my life to it. You will all receive punishment according to the quality of the offense."

So saying, he bought passage for himself and two serving men aboard the nao of Rodrigo de Colmenares, which was in readiness to depart for Española.

It was resolved that in the same ship with Enciso would go Martín de Zamudio as our *procurador*: for, as Vasco Núñez told Zamudio's following and familiars, he was the better qualified to plead our cause at the Court in Castile.

"I am but a poor *escudero*," he said to them, "with a good right arm for the marches and the battles that lie before us. It is Don Martín who has the polite words that will win favor in high places. Let each of us, therefore, serve as God wills it."

The Biscayan's suite being thus assured and of the opinion that this was very good counsel (as indeed it was), Zamudio was given carefully written reports for the King, together with a certain amount of gold as a gift. The letter asked for royal favor and help to bring to pass the enterprise we had begun in Darien with so many great mischiefs, dangers, and losses. We likewise petitioned His Majesty to confirm by his assent and seal appointment of a new Governor of Darien, preferably our freely elected alcalde, Vasco Núñez de Balboa.

Juan de Valdivia, one of our *regidores* (and a man strong in Vasco Núñez's cause) also embarked with Enciso to serve as our proctor in Española, there enlisting the help of Admiral Diego Colon and of the King's special emissary to the Indies, the royal Treasurer, Miguel de Pasamonte.

On the night before their departure from Darien, Vasco Núñez drew Valdivia aside and delivered into his charge a heavy leather bag, carefully secured and sealed.

"Take this darkly to Pasamonte in Santo Domingo," he ordered the *regidor:* "and look to it that his ears are dilated with a good report of our cause. He is a cavalier whose word reaches the King like an arrow from Ponce's crossbow: for they have between them a secret sort of writing which no other may intercept. Tell him that for our part here in Darien, we need men of good pecker. Likewise we need good weapons and such supplies as he can provide. Tell him we are toward new discoveries, as we have set forth and declared in the reports you carry: and make clear to him that such undertakings will redound greatly to his profit, and to the profit of the King."

Vasco Núñez, of whom it had been said that he could not remain quiet even while his bread was baking, now turned his thoughts to how he might best carry out an *entrada* into the lands beyond our stronghold, and what direction it should take.

Being a careful and prudent man in all matters that concerned the Indians, it was his desire to learn as many secrets of the country as possible before leading a march into unknown territory.

But in the meantime the men who had come hither moved by a desire for profit and conquest began to grunt and chafe like boars in a frank.

And our Captain heard them talking together in the plaza and about their doorways in the dusk: that they were soldiers, not planters: they had come to these Indies for conquest, not for a few pesos' worth of inferior gold that the naked natives cared to exchange for civilized trifles. Inland were surely rich chiefdoms to take and nuggets to be gathered from the streams of those hills. What did they there in the empty clay streets of a fool's town? And had they desired a long life in a peaceful country, they had remained in the known streets of Spain. Well! Had they seen their last battle then? No! It was time to take up arms and march. What was this Vasco Núñez waiting upon? Had his gall turned rotten with easy living?

Yet Vasco Núñez was not ready to risk our scant supply of men and weapons against an enemy of whose strength and numbers he had no certain knowledge. It had been made known to him by certain Indians who had come to traffic in Santa Maria that to the northwest, twenty leagues by estimation, lay a chiefdom called Careta that was rich in gold.

He therefore ordered a force of six well-practiced and valiant *baquianos* under the leading and conduct of Francisco Pizarro to make a careful discernment of the region. They had gone but a few leagues before they were attacked by the Cacique Cémaco (whose principal town we had taken and dedicated as our city), accompanied by four hundred of his fighting men.

It fortuned that these Indians did not employ bows and arrows: and being so great in number, they thought it best to fight at handystrokes with the six Spaniards. In a short time, however, a great number of them were killed by the superior weapons and skill of the white men: and those remaining took flight.

Fearing a new charge by an army which so greatly outnumbered his small company, Pizarro withdrew in all haste to the town, leaving in the forest one of his men who had been gravely wounded in the skirmish.

Upon learning that one of the men had been thus deserted by his retreating comrades, Vasco Núñez was greatly angered: and he sternly told Pizarro: "Go instantly and bring me Francisco Hernan: and as you value your life, never again leave one of my soldiers alive upon a field of battle!"

96

And with another force to the number of twenty, he returned with all speed and brought back to Santa Maria the said Francisco Hernan, who in the course of time recovered from his hurt.

While Vasco Núñez was pondering how best to adventure an *entrada*, the two brigantines he had dispatched to bring over to us from Nombre de Dios the men of Nicuesa who yet remained there, arrived in Darien. And with them came new tidings and knowledge which put us in good circumstance for our march. For the pilot of one of the ships brought with him two Spaniards who had lived more than a year with the Cacique of Careta and, being his trusted lieutenants, had full knowledge of his ways, as well as the tongue of the region.

"Being in want of fresh water, we had been inforced to seek the shore to fill our butts [the pilot said]: and as we were thus employed, Johan Garcia, who was one of my oarsmen, gave a word of warning. We unbent with good haste to see two Indians coming at us from the forest. Crespo took aim with his arquebus to accord them a loud welcome, when one of them cried out in clear Castilian: 'Hold your fire, man! As I'm a Christian!' We remained astonished that these men, naked and with their skins marked from the dyes of the heathen, could so turn Spanish words on their tongue.

"Then seeing still our unbelief (for they were stained with root juices all over their bodies and carried plumes in their hair), one of them said, 'God, who knows it, can witness this is true, *señores*. We are men of Spain. We came to these coasts with Diego de Nicuesa. But we were lost from him and have dwelt this while with the Indians of this region, which is called Coiba. I am Juan Alonso: my companion is Sebastián Henriquez, the Biscayan.' And he spoke true! They were Spaniards, men as we are: but you must see them with your own eyes. They bring news of a rich kingdom."

"Tell them to come in."

The pilot thereupon conveyed the two men (who were waiting outside the door) into our presence. And when the two strangers entered the room, we held them in marvellous wonder. Though they had once again put on the clothes of their native country, their faces were the faces of Indians: brown, bony, and marked between the eyes. Even their hair had lost the fullness of Spanish hair and lay flat and sleek against their heads.

Juan Alonso spoke for both of them. He was quick as a monkey with his hands, though he walked slowly, being as plump as the capons which housewives fatten in their cellars.

His comrade, the Biscayan, spoke but little, but stood apart, taking view of us with a heavy face and doleful eyes. From time to time, Juan Alonso called to him to verify his words, whereat he would emit only a deep grunt of affirmation.

"You have passed more than a year with this cacique?" Vasco Núñez asked him at length.

"Over a year: *sí, señor*. We abode with the ruler of that realm, who is an Indian of wealth, called Chima. We had been lost from the company of Don Diego, and we carried so great a hunger that when we saw an Indian village, we hastened into it without fear, preferring to perish within reach of food than to die of slow famine in the forest.

"But our saints favored us. The cacique addressed us with gentle words and gave us food and drink. We did not understand his greeting, not at that time having the tongue of the Indians. But he made signs and his meaning was: 'Strangers, who are you and what is your desire in food and women?' Faith, and we were not slow in acquainting him with our preferences in both.

"So this Cacique Chima [Alonso continued] entertained us well: and we were in such credit with him that he made us officers of his army, which in number is about two thousand. We have passed the time well, with never a vacant belly nor an empty hammock. In short, what we wish to say is this: we know well the times and ways of this Chima and have spied out his land. We likewise have the tongue of the country. We can well serve you in an *entrada*."

"You say the lord of Careta treated you with a generous hand?"

"*Sí, señor*, even unto a choice of his own women."

"And you desire to recompense this good man by loosing upon him and his people an army of ravenous strangers and their dogs, who will plunder his land and peradventure slay the cacique himself?"

Alonso turned aside, but answered him: "They are unbelievers, *señor*. They worship idols and salute the stars as souls of the dead. They burn copal and *maiz* in the secret places of their filth. They grow drunk on the wine of plantains and twist in the lascivious

98

dances. They mock the holy sacrament of confession by dropping to their knees in short shrift to any menace, even to wild beasts in the forest. By the Blood it is true, eh Sebastián?"

The Biscayan grunted.

"Yes! I have seen them, when beset by a wild animal, to go upon their knees in our manner of prayer, making holy signs and confessing to the beast all their past wrongs, crying, 'Have mercy upon me: do not cause me to perish. I have committed this or that sin, for which I truly repent.' Are such men of darkness to be spared and their hoarded gold left to dress their heathen gods, while Christians want for food and goods?"

Vasco Núñez thought well upon what Alonso had told him and then answered: "There is, I ween, reason enough in what you say, though little enough of charity. Still . . . charity for the Indians never filled an empty stomach nor fattened a poor soldier's purse. In truth, your coming hither is in good season, seeing that we are already preparing for an *entrada*. We will go well-favored with you who have knowledge of that country and the tongue of its people. Perhaps we may even have what we desire without giving battle."

"One thing more, Señor Alcalde."

"Command me."

"A friar will go with us on this march?"

"Such is our custom and desire: yes. Would you have it otherwise?"

"Ah, no. I—that is to say—it is a good thing for the Indians to receive the True Faith."

"You had no other reason?"

"I have a bastard. I thought . . . perhaps a baptism, lest I foredoom Castilian blood. . . ."

To which Vasco Núñez answered him: "It appears that your conscience is not all ashes. When you blow hard enough, you get a little smoke from underneath."

Our Captain called all of us together and said: "Gentlemen, we are soon to march."

Whereupon there arose great shouts of rejoicing from the men.

"We go to Careta: that is a country well-peopled and the defenders not feckless as I hear it. Accordingly, we must go properly

99

armed. Therefore, look to your weapons, Castilians. Inquire diligently of your own estate: whether you need purging or anything else that will keep you from sickness and other discomforts. Pack away your velvets for the moths, give your testaments to the scribe, and bid your mistresses a worthy patience."

For the business at hand, Vasco Núñez mustered a force of his best soldiers to the number of one hundred and ten: and all things being in readiness and brave order, we left Santa Maria de la Antigua on the feast day of the Holy Cross, in the year 1511.

We journeyed for seven days without perceiving any similitude of habitation, although certain of the *compañeros* one night said they heard Indian drums: but both Juan Alonso and Sebastián Henriquez (who had full knowledge of the country) said no.

Juan Alonso, who went ahead of us as guide, entered a wide natural aisle in the forest (that being a dried-up river bed), where we found firm ground under our feet and thus made our way with greater speed.

When we had sight of the Indian town (which was the seat of the lord of that province), Vasco Núñez halted the company and ordered Alonso and Henriquez to continue into the settlement alone. These two, already familiar to the inhabitants, excited no alarm: and they greeted the two Spaniards with friendliness and respect.

The white men entered a large *bohio* near the center of the town, which we took to be the house of the cacique by reason of its size and stateliness of structure (as in reality it was). Very soon they came out, followed by the cacique and a small retinue of servants and important personages. Four of his servitors or slaves carried above his head a fringed canopy of bright blue to protect him from the hot sun. The Indian lord walked with great dignity and royal bearing, such as would be worthy of the best people of rank and quality in Castile. Over his shoulders he wore a mantle of indigo, in one corner of which was a blazing gold sun and in the opposite corner a silver crescent moon. His head was adorned with a kind of crown formed by brilliant plumes, which were affixed to a band of gold.

As they drew near to us, Alonso came forward in haste and said softly to Vasco Núñez: "It is better to parley now and make no attack. At the first cry, they will hide all their gold and provisions."

The cacique Chima commanded his retainers to halt: then he walked forward alone. He instantly knew Vasco Núñez to be Captain: and he saluted him in the manner of those people. Alonso translated his words: "I raise my eyes to you, stranger. My house is your refuge from the fiery-eyed tiger: it is likewise your place of rest. Will you ask more?"

And in answer, the Captain made a bow of courtesy. "Tell him that we come as friends and in the name of our Sovereign, the great King of whom we are all vassals and unto whom belong all the Indies and other dominions that lie beyond the sea."

And this having been said, the Captain ordered that Chima be given certain fine articles of clothing, lace-points, and other things, with which he was greatly pleased. Then Vasco Núñez turned to Alonso and said: "Tell him that we have great need of provision from his stores for our soldiers and for the people who reside in our town: that he will be well-recompensed for these."

Unto which the cacique answered: "To every traveler whose shadow has fallen upon this land, I have given shelter, food, and drink. Gladly would I grant your request, but alas, we are war-returned and you are many. We have little in the shelters and we will ourselves weep for *maiz* before the time of harvest. All night the *eebee* cries in the forest. We shall know grief. Gold we hold in small account and possess little."

Alonso added then his own words: "He throws out great lies, *señor*. In the graves is a great quantity of gold: and the corn-bins are full. Still, it is best to give the face of belief and to retire until nightfall, for he has many warriors ready."

After carefully weighing and digesting Alonso's words, Vasco Núñez said: "Tell him we wish to remain in the forest for a day that we may hunt wild boar. Tell him that we will depart when we have taken provision for our hungry men."

In answer, Chima offered to send certain of his best huntsmen to help and to guide us.

"In God's name," the Captain told Alonso, "persuade him from that noble grace. Faith, and it would be small surprise we would carry with his spies in our midst."

Alonso once again spoke rapidly to Chima. The cacique inclined himself to Vasco Núñez and returned to his canopy. At his word of command, the retinue then returned to the town.

101

When they had thus departed, Vasco Núñez asked of Alonso: "What did you say to him?"

"I told him that Sebastián and I have knowledge of these forests and could guide you well. I gave it out also that the Indians, being in no wise familiar with our weapons, might be hurt by no intent of ours."

"And he received your reason?"

"Completely, *señor*. I swore by my tooth (which to them is the same as a Christian oath upon the Holy Cross) that we would return for a visit to his town before departing this land. Ha! A visit this very night, eh Captain?"

"Yes: though I have less taste for it than you who chew treachery like a ripe fig."

We then entered once more into the forest: and, believing that Chima would surely put his spies to watch us secretly, we counterfeited a boar hunt until it was dark.

We found a clearing and prepared camp as though we would resume our hunt on the morrow. We built fires at each end of our encampment, as it was customary to fend off beasts during the night: and the Captain ordered our sentinels to keep good watch.

When all signs of movement by the Indians had ceased and we believed them to be asleep, the Captain ordered Alonso and Henriquez to scout about the village in order to determine the situation of Chima's army and what guards may have been posted, who might alert them to our attack.

We waited in the night's stillness, listening to the divers sounds of all the creatures that inhabit those forests and were aprowl in the darkness. We heard also the cries of a nightbird which we took to be the *eebee* of which the cacique had spoken to us.

Alonso and Henriquez returned saying that Chima had taken few precautions, having placed only two sentries to watch the whole town: and that these simpletons were already lulled half asleep by the cicadas.

Vasco Núñez thereupon divided the company into three parts, so that we might assault the town from three sides. And it was his will that the mounted troops charge first, they being the swiftest and because the Indians held our horses in marvellous fear.

Accordingly, we arranged ourselves as quietly as we could

102

among the trees around the town. And the Captain's order was that only warlike Indians were to be slain: and that those who made us no resistance or who fled were to be spared.

Our trumpet sounded and we charged, bursting the silence of night with our loud cries of "Santiago!"

The cavalry swept through the village as it had been a sudden scourge of God (or an evil whirlwind, released by the Devil): and infantry followed, swarming among the *bohios*. The town's inhabitants, awaking thus to terror descending upon them, had little heart for combat, but fled shrieking into the surrounding hills. A few of the more valiant sort quickly closed ranks and surrounded the cacique's house in final defense of their lord.

They released a marvellous number of arrows for so few bowmen: and their shafts clanged loudly against our bucklers and breastplates. It was an honorable though foolish thing to do: for most of them were soon slain and the remainder were quickly put to flight by their fear of the dogs which were set upon them.

Vasco Núñez and certain of his men (I among them) entered the cacique's house. And being come inside, we halted because of the dimness of the place, which was lighted only by the banked embers of *maiz* cobs, heaped in a shallow pit in the center of the room.

The cacique Chima at once perceived our difficulty and ordered a servant to light a torch. When this was done, we looked about to find ourselves in a large chamber that measured (by the estimation of it) nine paces in length and five in breadth. Chima was seated upon a split-log taboret, attended by two of his wives. Although the house was clean-swept and well appointed (after the Indian custom), it held little of value. Yet, if Alonso spoke the truth, the cacique here before us possessed sufficient gold to buy a better house than many princes of royal blood in civilized countries. Yet his life (for us) held such privations as would make the most fervent monk bewail his vow of poverty.

Chima spoke rapidly to Alonso in his tongue: and the Captain waited calmly to know his words. Alonso interpreted them thus:

"He says: 'What ill have I done you, Powerful Stranger, that you set upon my village by night? When your white brothers came to me, they were sheltered and fed. And when you came to this land of Careta, did I meet you with a javelin in my hand? Did I

103

not offer meat and drink and other refreshing? Leave me in freedom, therefore, with my family and people, and we will serve you with the yield of our earth. You seek gold: you will have what we possess and more, for we can guide you to greater abundance in the lands beyond Coiba. The *tequina*, who understands the omens of birds and of clouds, has told of it: that Chima will be the friend of a great Tiba, who will send a powerful army against my enemy, Ponca.' "

And Vasco Núñez asked of Alonso: "Who is this Ponca?"

"He is overlord of a province to the westward: and against him Chima has made war these years without victory. This same Ponca has much gold."

"Tell him that we will march with him against his foe when the time is proper for it: that we welcome his friendship and loyalty. And to give that God's truth, he is to return with us to the Christian city of Santa Maria, where we will make a feast and celebration of our amity."

When Chima had heard this, he saluted the Captain with his hand to his head: and, through Alonso, declared: "I and my people incline to your command. But I beg return to Careta before the first night of *tula toreba*."

To make his meaning plain, Alonso said: "*Tula toreba* is one of their heathen festivals which they have at the time of planting certain crops. It is a season of great wickedness, drinking, and lewd dances. My counsel is—"

"Tell him that we will not stay him: that he may return."

Whereat the cacique was well-pleased and, henceforth from that day, not a single thing did the Captain ask of him that he did not do it to the uttermost of his power.

It was at the fiesta of Chima that our Captain went soft about a girl: a young *espave* (which in their tongue means a maid of noble rank): and she was the daughter of the cacique himself. She was a slender creature of great loveliness and fine spirit, and was ardently desired by many. But she cared only for Vasco Núñez: and, indeed, in all patience and virtue has continued in that love unto this day.

After the many hardships and dangers we had passed through, the music, wine, and dances of our carouse made us act as children

104

at some carnival of make-believe: and when we had sung each oth-er's songs and had feasted and drunk together, we embraced the Indians as though they were brothers or *compadres*.

Then to exhibit before the cacique a good show of our strength and skill as men at arms (that he might advertise his neighboring lords of the same), Vasco Núñez ordered a joust and other warlike games within the lists.

The lord Chima, as well as all the other naturals of the Indies, had our horses in marvellous fear and at first could not be per-suaded to go near them, believing them to be ferocious in propor-tion to their size. His eyes flashed with wonder and admiration when he beheld the Spaniards mount the beasts and ride them in the mock combats.

Being a man of uncommon valor, he was persuaded at last (with many smooth words and counselings) to mount and ride one of the steeds himself. And in boyish mischief, they gave him Valder-rábano's mare, La Torbellina, who would suffer none but her owner to ride her. Almost instantly, upon being left alone in the saddle, Chima found himself flying through the air. He came to earth upon his thinly appareled rump, unhurt, but with a look of great amazement on his countenance. Though we near burst with laughter, we froze our faces and assisted him to rise, saying our kind souls ached for him.

Then the Captain said graciously to Chima: "Let your musi-cians advance that we may hear the sweet harmony of these forests and join with you in treading the measures of your people."

So it was done: and in a great circle, with arms across each oth-er's shoulders, we stamped and shuffled to the heavy beat of their drums, accompanied by the bleating conch, the chattering gourd rattles, and the wailing of the pipes and flutes.

And when fatigue had paralyzed our limbs at last, we threw our-selves down in the shade of the walls and porticoes. Whereupon, the lord Chima led forth his daughter, dressed in much beauty, with bracelets of gold and necklaces of pearls and blue stones, that she might dance and sing for us.

At her father's command, the drums began anew, and that flute they call the *camó*, whose sound is plaintive and mysterious like the music of the Moors.

We were much moved and pleased by the beauty of her dance,

wherein she imaged the slow opening of a flower. For she seemed, in truth, to become the swaying stem of some strange blossom of her native forest. Her head trembled as a newly awakened bud that would burst into bloom: and her arms slowly entwined like curling tendrils. The heavy drum rumbled the thunder of an approaching storm and her body quivered with the sound. The *camó* whistled a chill, strong wind from the hills and she swayed with it. Finally, with the tempest past, the tender flower once again opened the heart of its being to the sunlight of renewed life.

There were three other dances I can give no account of, save the last, which our Captain found so much to his liking that he entreated that it be done twice. And when he asked how it was called, Alonso turned it to the Castilian tongue as *Dance of the Moonlight Gloom*.

The girl's movements were entirely of flesh and muscle, for her feet never left the ground except in a hesitant step forward, followed by a quick withdrawal as in fear of the unknown. Her supple body, full of sadness and melancholy, trembled beneath a robe as thin and iridescent as an insect's wings.

At one side, the *tequina* chanted her lament to the mournful treble of the flute, and I remember certain words, repeated like a wafted sigh:

> *"The sky-man seizes my throat for his* camó,
> *And the night for his despair. . . ."*

At the end of it she swooned (as it were) in her dream: and after a moment's death, sprang up and came before Vasco Núñez. She unclasped her arms and spread them wide as if to receive and fondle him: and her small, bare breasts rose and swelled. The musky odor of her glistening body tingled in his nostrils like a witch-brewed love philtre.

With his left hand he wiped his moist brow: and with the right, he lifted his wine cup and in a hoarse voice: "I drink your beauty, daughter of sorrows."

And all who witnessed it knew then that she held his soul like a small bird in her fist.

But Andrés de Garabito, who could not moderate himself, and who was now blear-eyed, lurched forward and greedily reached his

106

hands toward the girl. Whereat the Captain frowned severely as his anger flared: and he ordered Garabito to leave her alone or get ready to take care of himself.

Hearing which, Garabito withdrew, for he knew the terrible swiftness of our Captain's blade.

As evening came on, the friars began to speak to the lord Chima of our Holy Faith, urging him to accept baptism. With Alonso to interpret their words, they said: "You have this day marvelled at many fine things. And we have given you certain presents for the sake of friendship. But the best gift is not ours to bestow, though we have borne it hither from our distant country. It is the love of God which, though you cannot see it with your eyes, can save you from the darkness of death. For that holy purpose, He sent his Son into the world, whom our ancient progenitors saw and heard and who lives with us yet, we who partake of the sacrament of His body and blood.

"You may also receive this divine and profitable gift and with it our love and charity. You have but to bow down as you are wont to do in the temple of your false gods, acknowledging that One who created us and is the Father of all. Then will you be baptized with water, not for our pleasure or in fear of us, but because you desire it in your heart. Afterward you will study and deliberate upon this mystery and will listen to our words, we the religious fathers who have come hither with us and who will expound it to you. Would you, then, receive this spiritual seal, and become a Christian?"

After the cacique had pondered the matter well, he answered them.

"I receive your words with joy, but I do not know how to answer them. I am silent. As we say it, the great *waree* sits upon my tongue. For these are things of the sky. They come like dreams in the middle of the day.

"We know it is true that there is one Father of us all, the great sky-man whom we call Chipirapa, the giver-of-life who shines in the sun and moon and all the stars. Of his son our priests have not spoken. Still (as you say it) he lives with you and you have brought him in your great canoes across the water. By his terrible sorcery he has made you lord of these lands against our bravest warriors. So I lift my eyes to you. I say: let me and my people receive water from that god and become his vassals. For even as you, white strangers, I would serve that god who serves me best."

At these words, Father Perez gave a deep groan: but Fray Antonio, speaking in a kindly sort: "You cannot understand and penetrate this mystery in a single day. The knowledge of God ripens slowly like a rare fruit, reverently husbanded. But come now and by our sacrament of water, we will wash away the sins that are the cause of your present blindness, that thereby you may be admitted into eternal life."

Vasco Núñez embraced the cacique with joyful tears in his eyes: and, taking him by the hand, he led him to the church, his people and the Castilians following.

There they were baptized, beginning with the cacique and continuing to the servant of lowest rank. Chima was given the Christian name of Fernando in honor of our Sovereign: and his daughter was christened Maria after the Holy Virgin, while all the officers and people who filled the church witnessed it and thought well of it.

Afterward the cacique, now called Don Fernando Chima, made a pact with Vasco Núñez, binding them both to certain undertakings and enterprises. For his part, Don Fernando promised additional supplies for the *vecinos* at Santa Maria: a number of his vassals skilled in planting to clear and harvest the land surrounding the town: and guides for future *entradas*. Most of the gold from his province had already been taken by the Spaniards in one way or another, but he agreed to seek more.

In return, Vasco Nunez vouchsafed an early assault on the Indian lord's enemy and neighbor, the cacique Ponca.

To seal their compact, Don Fernando sent his daughter (with her full consent and liking) to live with the Captain in his house. That same night she silently crossed his threshold: and with the mysterious contentment of her kind she merged her life with his. They had no need of words: they squandered none of time's sands in the civilized game of conquest and surrender. Mutely and without shame, she yielded herself, as the great plantain leaves beside the walls that enclosed them suddenly threshed about in the wind and the rains came down, whispering into the thatch roof above their heads.

For her it was the supreme ritual of a woman's life. The priests of her people supplicated heaven for rain that it might impregnate the earth. They sacrificed to the *maiz* goddess that she might conceive in her golden womb a greater abundance. They sang to their God: "Thou art the dew of heaven: thou art the dew of the clouds."

Thus she became in that hour the earth longing for sunlight and rain. She became the earth in darkness, awaiting the bridegroom of light.

Infuse me with the vital seed and I shall be renewed of life. Join your breath with mine and I shall bear forth in summer: I shall be immortal.

Chapter 7 ~~~~~~~~~~~~~~~~~~~~~~~~~~~~~~~~~~~~~

Having brought all pending affairs to such an estate as seemed good to him, Vasco Núñez kept the promise he had made to Don Fernando Chima to take up arms and to march against his enemy, the cacique Ponca.

The seat of the said lord Ponca lay several leagues westward of Careta and was difficult of access, being reached by a twisting and scraggy pass.

So we followed our Indian guides with much labor and travail: and, in truth, we did not march, but clambered upon that stony trail, grinding our teeth and clawing blindly at rocks and hanging vines. We were eighty companions (with two hundred of Careta's fighting men behind us): and it was our Captain's will that we hold ourselves in readiness to repel any attack from ambush, our enemy being accounted very cunning.

On the third day, we came to Ponca's principal town, which was by the river called Moretí: and we took our careful view of it from afar off through a red and purple haze of twilight. Perceiving no signs of life, Vasco Núñez sent two Indians of our company to scout around the *bohios*. They returned to report that Ponca and all his people had fled into the forest, leaving their town empty of all save silence, and the smoke of their fires, and peace.

Careta's soldiers were of a mind to pursue the people of Ponca that they might be discovered and slain: but Vasco Núñez said: "Leave them to their covert. They will receive punishment

111

enough by all they have lost when our greedy soldiers have done with their homes and all they have left therein. Never again will they war against Careta, knowing they will invite thereby the wrath of the powerful strangers who pact with you."

The *compañeros*, expecting booty, marched down in all haste and ravaged the town. We found gold, pearls, cloth of fine cotton, and an abundant store of food, which the Indians in their great scramble to get away, had left behind them. And when we had taken the spoil of it, we committed the whole village to the flames.

Don Fernando Chima rejoiced that his hitherto undefeated foe had been thus vanquished. He then told the Captain of a fair and very spacious kingdom called Comogra, whose people numbered ten thousand or more and whose cacique could muster an army of three thousand notable and valorous soldiers.

The said cacique (so Don Fernando declared it), being his friend, might easily be brought to league and amity with us, thereby giving us possession of such rich wares and commodities as the country yields, not by bloody battle, but by profitable traffic and tribute.

Vasco Núñez received these tidings gladly: and he readily consented to a peaceful meeting with the powerful lord of Comogra.

Accordingly, in aid and furtherance of the plan, Don Fernando sent as emissary to Comogra a certain *jura* (which in their tongue means a noble of princely blood) named Zebaco. This young man had been a friend of Alonso and Henriquez, when the two Spaniards had sojourned in Careta: and he had been also a counselor to the aforesaid cacique of Comogra.

Now Zebaco laid open the case to Comogre, saying that the Castilians sought nothing else than his amity and to traffick with the people, whereby he doubted not but that great profit would grow to them from so honest and reasonable a request.

But the cacique answered that the friendship the bearded barbarians from the sea had shown Chima's people, and more recently, the domain of Ponca, was not the kind he found to be of his liking.

Thereupon, Zebaco pressed to a closer engagement, saying: "It is only against their enemies that they thus conduct themselves, Sire. It is better therefore to be their friend. For in their warfare, they come with the swiftness of a wizard-wind. Fiery serpents leap from their breasts: and they attack seated upon great plunging beasts that do their bidding, trampling all beneath their pounding feet. Raging brutes of a smaller kind, but twice as savage, are also loosed from long cords. These mad creatures leap upon three or four men at the same time, ripping them open with terrible fangs. This I have seen with my own eyes, Sire. It is better to walk with these white devils than to run against them. See how Chima has won much in becoming a brother to them. He has put down his strong enemy, Ponca."

After Zebaco had delivered this or some such like speech (as it was related to me), the lord Comogre, contemptuous in his strength, said: "But what was Ponca? He had an army half as large as mine, and they with a chicken's courage. The white *quebi* has fewer than a hundred men, and you ask Comogre the lord of three thousand to turn him a good face. The battle of Careta's town has wilted your arm."

Zebaco was patient. "Sire, it is not a hundred men you would fight," continued he, "but all the lightning, all the demon-beasts, all the deadly sorcery that the evil gods of these white strangers have given them. And their friendship may be had for little. What they desire more than any kingdom, more than life itself even, is a fool's bauble. They desire gold. Only gold, Sire. For them one grain of it has greater worth than a handful to us."

To this, Comogre: "You say they are cunning men, yet they hone thus after the sun-metal. Why is this so, Zebaco? Do they desire it because it shines? There are river stones of better color. Do they desire it for craft tools? The black palm wood is stronger and more easily fashioned. Are their dead so many that they require it for them, or their gods so greedy that they ask always more?"

And in great perplexity, Zebaco answered: "Of that I know little, Sire. Two of the white strangers who lived among us spoke of nothing else, even during the harvest songs and dances. When I asked them why they so greatly desired the sun-metal, their answer was that in their own land they could exchange the thinnest dust of it for whatever they desired: houses, servants, women, food. For which reason they gather all of it they are able to do and send it upon their great canoes to their own realm."

113

Comogre was further confused by this answer. "Why do the people of the distant lands so greatly reverence it that they are willing to give their houses and women and food in order to possess it?"

Zebaco was much grieved that he had no reasonable answer to lord Comogre's query. And he said in a disquieted sort: "This I also asked the white strangers and they replied that people will give their possessions for gold because they in turn may exchange it for whatever they most desire."

Whereupon Comogre grew to some silence and, after weighing the matter, declared: "The question is not answered. They are madmen. Still, since their favor is so easily won, we will send messengers to them to come to us in peace, before they set upon us with the demons you say they have at their commandment. To engage their fancy, I will make them a gift of some of the sun-metal they dote upon. Let my will be proclaimed to my sons and have them come hither to behold the foolish white strangers."

The lord Comogre sent messengers to our Captain, inviting him and his company to make a visit to his domain: and he sent also guides to conduct us thither.

When we came out of a pass and first took our view of the cacique's principal city (after a long and tortuous journey through some high mountains and along hazardous rivers), we halted a bow-shot off and stared in speechless wonder.

For, all the towns and dwellings we had seen in these Indies were much surpassed and excelled by the great beauty and elegance of the city we now beheld.

It stood before us on a green and spacious tableland over against tall mountain peaks. Row upon row of well-built houses with strong walls and high-pitched roofs spread outward from the cacique's palace, which rested upon great and solid pillars of wood.

Surrounding the *alcázar* aforesaid was a stone wall of formidable appearance, the first of its kind we had found in these regions.

"Blood of saints!" Hurtado exclaimed after some silence. "Not even the Gaul has written of a sight like this! And all the work of skilled hands, with good masonry and excellent woods used with marvellous art."

Vasco Núñez also stood gazing silently at the view before us. And after carefully contemplating the palace and all about it, said he: "As I measure it from here, the castle is no less than 150 paces in length and perhaps 80 in breadth: and 80 in height. The white space on the left is a large court: on the opposite side, an orchard. Faith, and Comogre is lord of some good fortune. Let us look to it that we do our homage with great solemnity: and we may obtain very fruitful results in this city."

And knowing full well the knaveries our soldiers were wont to commit on such occasions, our Captain spoke to all of us in serious sort, of how we ought to behave and conduct ourselves toward the people of Comogra, who had invited us to their great city. That we were not to molest their women (there would be enough shameless rollicks with those who were appointed to us for our pleasure): that gambling with our Indian friends was forbidden and punishable by fifty stripes (for we were cheating gypsies and they but children to be cogged by our wiles): that, above all else, we ought to avoid the brawls and tumults that come of too much drink: and that, whatever secrets we might learn, not to lodge them with the town crier: for some of us were accustomed to go about drunkenly braying like a lame ass.

As he was speaking, we descried a fair-sized cortege coming out to us upon the trail from the city. In the distance we beheld the brilliant plumes of their feathered diadems: and we blinked in amazement at the burnished gold of their great round breast-plates, which glimmered in the sunlight.

Upon their near approach, we perceived Comogre the King in their midst, borne upon a richly adorned litter covered with embossed gold and carried by long poles upon the shoulders of his *naborí* or slaves. Certain other manservants walked beside him, waving blue and yellow fans.

In good array behind the cacique marched his seven sons, all apparelled in red and white robes of fine cotton, down to the ground, and fringed at the bottom. And their heads were attired in coronets of woven cane and bright plumage. (And it was Comogre's boast that each son had a different mother.)

There came likewise in the monarch's train six grave and ancient personages, wearing robes of red and blue, with mantles secured to the left shoulder by means of a golden brooch. And these we took to be priests of their pagan cults, for they had the eyes of sorcerers: and we had seen their likenesses graven upon stones beside the trail.

So they came with great pomp and magnificence, followed by nobles, henchmen, and people of meaner station, to the number of about three-score. And when the cacique had commanded that his litter be put down, he stepped forth to salute us with much formality and gracious flourish.

He was a well-favored man, tall and of regal bearing: apparelled in a white tunic of finely woven cloth, fringed at the bottom. And he wore divers ornaments of gold and emeralds, with necklaces of jaguar teeth in serrate pattern upon his chest. Entwined in his golden crown were fine plumes of green and yellow and ruby-red. And in his right hand he held a shining scepter, thin as a reed, and of pure gold.

He stood there before us in the sun's blazing rays: and he turned and waved his scepter like a wand toward that rich land of *maiz* fields and meadows about his city: and he said: "Strangers whom the birds foretold: this land awaits your footprints upon the pathways. Come, for you will have good lodging: you will have good fare. You may sleep all night without a sentry, for danger is distant from here."

Thus did he welcome us and conduct us in great honor to his town. And there we were quartered in clean and spacious houses whose walls were of fragrant woods, which he had ordered prepared against our coming and wherein we found many comforts and good means of refreshing.

He appointed to us also many servitors, both men and women, all ready to do what we would require.

In order to be certain that we should not want for anything the place could yield us, Comogre likewise laid upon his eldest son, Panquiaco, the duty of preparing feasts, dances, and boisterous masquerades in our honor: and of acquainting us with the ways in which his people went to hunt and fish: how the goldsmiths and artisans plied their skills: and with many secrets of the land, which we rejoiced to learn.

The Prince was a proud youth who (having been told of us before our arrival) thought us to be powerful barbarians: but he desired to know more of us and to examine our possessions and dress.

Our principal and urgent desire was to visit forthwith Comogre's palace, wherein he kept his court that we might see with our own eyes what wonders so large and rich a house might hold. When this request was made known to him, Panquiaco was pleased to conduct us there, being himself impatient to show us the excellency of his father's estate.

To maintain good order, Vasco Núñez commanded that we make our visit to the palace aforesaid in five different companies, beginning with the Captain and his officers and so proceeding to men of lesser rank and quality.

And being thus conducted into the King's house, what we there beheld did very well amaze the *compañeros* and dashed them out of countenance (though our Captain was not much moved therewithal, but bore himself with impassive mien).

We found the edifice to be constructed of heavy timber and masonry, the upper portion walled with wood cut from sweet-scented trees like cedar: and the beams artfully carved and intertwined to form a great loft, which was divided into many apartments and corridors.

Upon passing from chamber to chamber, we observed that none of the rooms had windows, their only openings being tall narrow doorways without any kind of door, but set on either side with beautifully chiseled slabs of stone. And these were marvellously carved with the images of men and of animals, all of them engaged in some kind of movement. The floors were of polished wood, artistically decorated.

All the rooms received their light from doorways which opened upon outside courts and balconies which the building had on four sides.

And when we were come to a certain apartment (before we entered therein) the prince Panquiaco made us to understand that by custom it was a place of deep veneration and honor.

"In this place are preserved our brave and well-remembered fathers. Here also they are prepared for their long sleep, being dried above the sacred fires the *tequinas* keep."

Inside we stared as haunted men: as those who wake to night-

117

born visions that arise from wine and torpid sleep. Before us, from the beams of that great room hung the husks of long-dead men: life-drained and shrivelled dry as the insect shell caught in a spider's web. Swathed in cloths of painted cotton interwoven with threads of gold: curiously embroidered with pearls and gems: and their cindered faces covered with gleaming masks of gold: they turned slowly in the gentle breath of wind at our passing.

When a cacique of these people died, there were long days of mourning during which time (as Panquiaco described it to us) the corpse of the deceased King was suspended from a crossbeam over a large clay pan of hot coals, kept glowing by the squatting priests, who fanned them with palm leaves.

And when all the humors and fluid substance had thus dripped slowly from the body and it was light as pith, the priests wrapped it in its final shroud of fine weaving and hung it there in the company of the other ancestors.

Panquiaco led us from that hall of death (with our liking and relief) and thence to large storerooms where the royal provisions were preserved. There we beheld such an abundance as we had not believed to exist in all these Indies.

Remembering then our past hungers and the hard days, we stood speechless before roof-high bins of white and yellow *maiz*: we passed our calloused hands over smooth, ripe melons musky fresh from the harvest: and with humble reverence we broke the honeycomb like holy bread, tasting its soothing sweetness in our heat-scorched mouths. And we snuffled up the full-fragrant smells of pineapples, coconuts, custard apples, and other fruits, merged with the peppery sweet odors of red and green chilies that hung in long strings around the walls.

We had in great admiration the huge mounds of little orange potatoes which this country yields (and which are as well-tasted as any in the whole world). There was in like sort a wonderful profusion of baskets heaped high with divers seeds for the planting: herbs and all kinds of pulse and roots.

We walked between big stacks of flat round cassaba bread, higher than our heads: and we felt the ghosts of famine swoop through our dazed minds as we contemplated a vast store of smoked fish, pork, and venison.

So we shuffled like crazed gluttons through that mouth-watering

118

paradise, reaching our greedy hands to touch the red and purple ears of corn that hung by their shucks from the ceiling, like rows of dead birds by their yellow wings.

In the cool cellars the prince showed us long rows of glistening big earthen jars wherein were kept the monarch's wines, both white and red. And smoothing back our beards, with our cupped hands we dipped and gulped down each draught with gurgling sounds and murmurs of delight. The tawny liquor made of dates and different sylvan fruits we found to be as sweet as boiled honey: others were tartish on the tongue, being brewed from fermented *maiz*.

Thus were we given good entertainment: and afterward we repaired to our appointed lodgings to make ourselves ready for the feast which the lord Comogre had decreed for that same night to do us honor.

We sat beside our doorways in the tranquil air of evening and through the thickening light gazed on the movement of life in that rich and curious town. In the streets and byways young girls appeared, carrying big jars balanced upon their hips: and walked with mincing steps toward the river to fetch water, swinging their buttocks and proudly lifting their shapely breasts as they passed by. And seeing that we were attended by women (the most beautiful of them) they giggled shyly and made much talk of it among themselves.

We heard bats squeaking in the dusk of the trees' branches, as they awakened and readied themselves for their night's evil hunting: and distant voices and cries and an infant's wail. Old men shouldering baskets of ripe fruits, or carrying dangling fowl in their scrawny hands, moved with unsteady gait on their stork-thin legs toward the cacique's kitchens.

We watched the slow drift and swirl of azure smoke from the grills and ovens where they were preparing the feast: and we breathed deep the scent of many savory and nourishing foods borne on the wind and mingled with the smell of rank vines growing against the shadowed walls.

The sound of drums and conches burst forth from the hillside temple where their priests made obeisance to the departing sun which (lacking the light of our Holy Faith) they falsely worship, believing that great fiery orb to be the father and creator of all.

119

"He inseminates the whole world [they say]: and brings forth life under all the heaven." Knowing only this their native land that is lush with natural growth and increases, they perceive not the sun to be an insufficient lover of the earth, whose golden fertility is not enough to fecundate the countless wombs of the world. Wherefore the land dries into deserts, freezes into rimy crags, ossifies, rots, decays. Ah friends, cannot you see: his vivifying kiss with all its ardor cannot warm up again the cheek which has known the cool, dispassionate caress of death?

When the messengers came to call us to the banquet, Vasco Núñez ordered us to march in array and to observe good order. And being thus conducted into a great courtyard beside the King's house, we found Comogre seated upon a high and stately taboret, apparelled with a white robe of fine quality, bordered with a curious design: and upon his head was a diadem of bright plumes. Around him were the headmen and courtiers seated in order of rank, all of them attired in fair, colored cloth and adorned with many gold ornaments and gems.

Ordinary vassals to the number of several hundred occupied a large clearing on the lord's right hand.

Our men were seated before him at long tables: and in front of each of us (on the diner's right hand) were a small lump of salt; a bowl made of polished gourd, embellished with gold and filled with water: and a drinking cup of withes so finely woven that, when filled with wine, not a single drop passed between the strands.

The cacique removed his gleaming gold nose-ring and placed it upon the table, which was a sign for the feast to begin. Thereupon scores of servitors arrayed in yellow livery began to place upon our tables such a great bounty of victuals that in brief time they were so laden that there was no room for more.

I cannot remember all: but I may not forget five kinds of fish sodden, boiled, and roasted: meats in great measure and of every kind: fowl, both large and small, for every taste, together with peanuts and pot herbs of good savor: divers fruits and bread and wines.

And these people took their food after the manner following:

120

they ate without the aid of spoons or other utensils, using instead the two forefingers of the right hand, which they curved into a kind of hook, which they dipped into the dishes of hot food. The quantity so obtained they conveyed hastily to the side of their mouths, moving the hand from left to right in a stroking motion that cooled the food sufficiently to be taken into the mouth. The fingers were then instantly plunged into the calabash of water at every man's place, as I have said.

After they had taken three or four mouthfuls in this manner, each diner took up the lump of salt and brushed it gently over his tongue with a great show of pleasure.

The *compañeros* being nothing dismayed withal, followed their example: and after divers attempts (which accorded the Indians much pleasure and laughter), we learned the art as well as they.

At the end of the feast, the dancing and songs began at once, before the men had risen from their seats. And certain of them, who felt cramped from sitting so long in one place, now stood up to ease themselves. They stretched shamelessly, belched, and prodded one another with their elbows in ill-bred horseplay. And Francisco de Lentin, the Sicilian, said in a loud voice to Hernando Hidalgo (whose eyes had never left the large gold ear-rings worn by the Prince Panquiaco): "It will take many a night to sleep out the pleasant vision of those golden pendants, eh Hernan?"

And Hidalgo, giving no heed to our Captain's frown, answered him: "Blessed Jesus, yes. The sight haunts me like a Devil-sent revenant. A hundred pesos in Christian gold, hung in the rotten lobes of that heathen dapper, like braid on a donkey's rump. And I miss my share of the melt when the time is at hand, let me pocket up my paltry gewgaws and return to Castile."

"A noble vow!" cried another companion across the music, "and one you may well keep, seeing that I have some cheap scissors and Parisian tops that are excellent merchandise of good request with these people. And being of a womanish heart, I will let them bubble me out of my last trinket for their heathen frumpery."

Then perceiving the look of ten demons in the Captain's eyes, the men grew to silence and sat down.

The dancers now put on colored masks, becoming hideous

121

monsters in the torches' flare. They also wore heavy necklaces of jaguar teeth and belts and ankle bands loaded with thin shells that clattered as they leaped about.

Drums and flutes made up the principal musical accompaniment, while old crones with sharp faces and leathery skin shook gourd rattles. The *tequina* droned out a monotonous chant that never rose above the sound of the drums and crackle of the maracas.

Comogre himself soon tired of it. He presently motioned for Panquiaco to come to his side, and whispered into the youth's ear. The young Prince saluted his father after their manner and went inside the cacique's house.

In a short time he reappeared, followed by several slaves. Each of them carried a wicker container which was set down in front of the cacique.

Comogre then dismissed the musicians with a regal gesture and beckoned to Alonso, who was seated near the Captain. At the same time, Panquiaco busied himself with the baskets, directing the slaves to remove the lids, which had been secured by strong pieces of sinew. The cacique then arose and began to address the Spaniards. Alonso interpreted his words.

" 'Strangers from the distant forests: it has been told us that you have found great pleasure in the sun-metal of these lands. It is said that you have fought battles for it and were glad in its keeping as a new bride in her blue vestment. See, then, how we have here brought forth gifts made thereof and fashioned into the shapes of birds and of fishes and of drinking cups. Some stand in the wild hare's likeness: others—' "

The *compañeros* (being joyful and warmed by the liquors they had drunk) waited to hear no more. They scrambled to their feet and pressed about Panquiaco, who knelt before the baskets, taking out the gold figures and ornaments.

Vasco Núñez commanded them to be seated, but they either did not hear him or they pretended not to hear, all shouting and talking at the same time.

"—*pesos de oro*, or my opinion is corrupt as a hogsty. Witness this—"

"—say I, and not one piece to hide from boast. After the *quinto*, we will each fortune a generation—"

122

"—as you might appraise it. Have I said appraisal? Where are the balances? *Patrón!* We are not without the balances?"

Whereupon the Captain stood up and, walking over to an Indian drum, struck it with two or three hard blows. And the companions, perceiving the wrath of Vasco Núñez, hastily returned to their proper places and sat down. Our Captain then turned to Alonso.

"Tell Comogre that we deeply regret this interruption. Ask him to continue: that we will follow his words like a holy service."

When Alonso had translated the message, Comogre saluted Balboa after their manner: but he hastily concluded his oration.

"This, which is the bird-of-a-hundred-songs and a good talisman for the *maiz* harvests, we send to your monarch beyond the water."

Comogre then placed the image in our Captain's hands, who received it with a courtly bow. The cacique then took up a breast-plate of gleaming gold.

"This breastplate, marked with the good signs of the sun-god, the moon, and the stars, is my gift of friendship to you, lord of the white strangers. Wear it in battle and you will be preserved. But remove it always from your person at nightfall."

Vasco Núñez accepted with high courtesy, after which Comogre made a gesture toward the remaining articles and (through Alonso) said: "These are for the warriors. You, Tibá, will allot them as you desire."

Our Captain then spoke to all of us: "Get to your feet and make a bow of Christian gratitude."

Mutely we obeyed, inclining in the fine unison of trained soldiers. Then he said: "Montejo, bring forward the balances and weigh these pieces. You, Gutierrez, keep the count. Do you carry paper and seal?"

"*Sí*, Capitán. Ready to hand."

As the weight of each piece was called, a murmur of joyous surprise broke forth from the men, who watched every move of the procedure with lickerish eyes. Comogre and Panquiaco (as well as all their court) also observed the weighing with much interest: but they thought it would not stand with their dignity to ask the Spaniards what they were doing.

123

"Is the bird to be reckoned as a portion of the *quinto* or apart?" asked the *veedor*.

To which Vasco Núñez answered: "It is a separate gift to the King. As for my own favor, the breastplate, reckon it with the common lot."

After the King's fifth was put aside, Bartolomé Hurtado began to distribute the remaining treasure, beginning with Vasco Núñez and continuing down the ranks. Under our royal laws, the Captain was allowed nine days in which to apportion the gold: but it was resolved by him (with the consent of the companions) to make an instant sharing out, both to cool their greed and in order that the cacique might witness their pleasure in receiving it.

But our men, upon seeing so much gold, could in no wise forbear: and they began talking excitedly among themselves and disputing with Hurtado about the count. Some swore that their weight had been shorted and cursed him for a stinking filcher, a scurvy falsifier of measures, a cheat, a *bribón*, and a rotten guilt before God.

And growing hot upon it, they began to bicker and to fight among themselves. Gerónimo Olea brought about an outright broil by giving one of the Biscayans a rude shove backward. To be short, they were soon an angry, scuffling rabble, swinging their arms like madmen.

The Captain was readying to restore order by a few decisive blows upon the more violent heads, when the skirmish was on a sudden halted by another and unlooked-for means.

Panquiaco, moved with anger and disgust at the disgraceful behavior of the Castilians, threw himself among them. With his fist he knocked the balances from Montejo's hands. The weights rolled in all directions beneath the men's feet.

The companions stopped fighting and stood staring at Panquiaco in amazement. His daring assault so took them by surprise that they did not know what to do about it. The young prince addressed the whole company in rapid sort which (it was clear) was meant to chastise them for their bad manners.

And Alonso gave us his words thus: "He says: 'What means this, white strangers: that for metal you contend with snarls and blows? And why do you scrabble like stupid fowl with a bug over what my father has given you? Is it for so small a thing that you loot the peaceful lands, banish yourselves from your own firesides, sicken your bellies with hunger, and spill blood in battles? If such be the desires that bring you and your miseries to these peaceful forests, your gods are false to you. In this land is but little of the sun-metal. But I can show you a region where there is more of it than would be needed to satisfy even your mad cravings.' "

Upon hearing this, the companions once more broke into a wild confusion of speech. But our Captain made a sign for silence and then told Alonso: "Ask Panquiaco to describe the way to this rich land of which he tells."

In answer, Panquiaco pointed to a range of mountains south-ward of us and several times traced an arc in the air with his right arm, moving it from east to west as though indicating the sun's passage.

"He says: 'Southward from Pocorosa, south from Tubanamá: east of the mountain passes: the journey is not done in six suns. There you will find an ocean sea like this near which we dwell: and ships like yours (though not so large) with sails and oars: and there the people eat out of vessels of gold, which is more common than the metal of which you have fashioned your many weapons.' "

The *baquianos* began one to look upon another and to swallow down their spittle. They rejoiced with themselves and conceived a hope that they would all live to behold that kingdom whereof the Prince spoke, and to share its great riches. They imagined then that they heard the cry of battle: and they saw the Indian armies advancing row on row, with their lances of solid gold glimmering in the sunlight. A rain of golden arrows whirred through the air and clanged against their bucklers with a welcome sound. They could not fight for gathering up the arrows. And they begged the foe for more!

"Ask this Prince [Balboa commanded Alonso] how it is that he, living so far away, knows of that country and that sea."

"He says: 'I have heard many times of it. And here [pointing to one of the nobles seated near Comogre] is one who was once taken captive to those lands and has himself been upon that sea. But do not think that you will come to that country with ease. Great mountains lie between. There the rivers rise and are deep and swift. There the lords are violent men and their warriors many. You must march by the sword and by the long spears and by the fire-weapons: and with an army of a thousand men. Our fathers and those of Querequá and of Tamame thought once to take that land. They joined their arms and marched: and their lances outnumbered the *maho* leaves in season. Yet were they driven as the smallest dust before the wind. Could we but bring low our ancient enemy Tubanamá, no sacrifice would be too great. Therefore, prepare your army. I myself will accompany you with the best warriors of our hosts. Guard me well: and if my words prove false, hang me on the nearest tree.' "

We marvelled greatly at these words of the cacique's son: and our Captain pondered in his mind and earnestly considered his sayings.

So we continued in drinking, talking, and making good cheer three days following, with good fare and all things correspondent.

And after hearing the doctrine of the Holy Gospels expounded to him by Fray Andrés, the cacique Comogre yielded himself and the greater part of his people to receive the waters of baptism: whereof the Castilians rejoiced, seeing how, by their mediation, so many Gentiles were thus converted from paganism to Christianity. And thenceforth the lord of that realm was known as Don Carlos Comogre, the Christian name by which he was christened in honor of our Prince and heir apparent.

So with great contentment we took leave of them to return to Santa Maria, where Vasco Núñez determined to make ready everything necessary for our venture in search of the other sea.

126

Chapter 8

We returned to Santa Maria with the words of Panquiaco still ringing in our minds like an anvil struck with force. And when the *vecinos* who had remained in our town (as well as those who had come thither with Valdivia during our absence) heard the tidings they were moved with fierce hope and a great hunger for gold. There was a day of public rejoicing: and we began to speak of the other sea as though we had already seen it with our own eyes.

Our *regidor* Juan de Valdivia had gone to Española (as I have related) to petition the Governor for supplies and soldiers: and to enlist the help of the Royal Treasurer Pasamonte. And while Vasco Núñez was in Comogra, together with the eighty men who had accompanied him, the aforesaid Valdivia came again to Santa Maria aboard a caravel laden with provisions and bearing a certain number of men who desired to enroll in our enterprise.

And upon our coming to Santa Maria, Valdivia warmly embraced the Captain, saying: "I bring excellent news. First, from the Governor Don Diego, a *cédula:* you are by official writ made Captain-General of Tierra Firme. Now, let the groaners cry that down!"

He handed Balboa the sealed document with a bow. "By my saints, I would not have believed that the amount of gold you sent would buy so much at Don Diego's sweet court."

"Gold and promises, Juan. Don't forget the promises. What other information do you bring?"

"A pledge from the Royal Treasurer. His word was: 'Tell Vasco Núñez that my letters to the King our lord will be his good envoys. Tell him that the ugliest butt-end of a fine ingot is more beautiful than a thousand compacts wrapped in visions and tied with the red string of hope.' "

"And the Governor sent provisions?"

"Not all that was asked: but enough to assuage our present hunger at least. We brought meat, drink, and apparel: also seeds for planting, cheeses, edible oil, ten *hanegas* of lentils: thirty *arrobas* of sugar: three hundred strings of garlic."

"You bring also powder and furniture for the soldiers?"

"Everything you ordered, but not of the quantity you desired: though we have Don Diego's affirmation for more to follow. And his bidding was: 'Inform Balboa and the Christians of Darien to be of good cheer and they shall lack nothing in the days to come. Tell them that I have at my commandment no larger ship to send them a greater plenty of supplies at present. But I will dispatch such provisions as soon as a vessel arrives at these shores, as must soon befall.'

"As for weapons [Valdivia continued] he shipped over thirty new suits of armor: twenty-five Bilbao sabres: five thousand arrows: two score pikes: and ten pipes of powder."

With grave countenance, Vasco Núñez answered: "That is not the beginning of what we will need for our intended exploit. But when the Governor is certified of all we have learned, he will without a doubt send what is required. In the meantime, I hope that the purveyance you have brought will provide for us until that day. We have been too often worn out of apparel and hungry as the grave."

But our Captain's hope became, instead, a dire prophecy. For in the space of five weeks a violent storm came down upon us from the mountains round about us: and it ravaged our town almost to extinction.

With horrible thunder and lightning, the tempest rushed through Santa Maria like the furies of hell, carrying therewith a great overflowing of waters which drowned our sets and fruits.

And when it was past we went forth to take careful view of the damage. We perceived then that all the benefits of nature we had

128

so carefully husbanded were washed away: the flourishing millet, lentils, and chickpeas lay submerged: the *maiz* fields were muddy tracts of spectral, twisted stalks.

Being thus sorely vexed and so frustrate of the increase of our seeds, we were very heavy and sorrowful. After taking counsel with his officers, Vasco Núñez determined to send Valdivia once again to Española, there to deliver to the Governor an epistle signifying to him our great extremity and also relating to him what we had learned from Comogre concerning the new sea and the regions toward the south. And the Captain asked for five hundred or a thousand well-practiced soldiers (together with all necessary munitions) with which he might forcefully make his way across the high mountains and unknown territories to discover the said ocean sea.

Balboa also sent with Valdivia the King's fifth of the treasure we had brought back from the Careta *entrada:* and the same *quinto* was in amount, 15,000 pesos in good gold.

"Enough to tempt St. Anthony [as Hurtado said it]: and I know of no saints in Castile."

But though Balboa could have no knowledge of it then (for those things lay unborn in the dark womb of future time) neither that gold nor our loyal and courageous *regidor* was ever to reach Española, he and all his company being (as we believe) cast away at sea.

After the departure of Valdivia, we who remained in Santa Maria conferred about the hard difficulty we were in by reason of our lack of victuals, and by what means we might stay alive until we received the succor promised us by the Admiral.

Almost all of the provisions Valdivia had brought from Española were already consumed or had been lost in the recent floods. And being thus pricked forward by exceeding privation, we resolved to search the inner parts of the gulf in hitherto unknown places.

With a force of *baquianos* to the number of one hundred and sixty, we embarked in a brigantine and a fleet of small native boats which the Urabaes call *uru.*

Coasting the shores of that wide gulf, we found them to be a drowned morass of salt marshes and mangrove swamps: and per-

129

ceiving the flotsam adrift upon all the waters, we feared that our ship would strike a log or go aground upon the reefs that lay beneath them in that region.

Proceeding thus, we made our first landfall on the eastern side, where we beheld firm earth. And before us the forest went up like a wall, strange in the bronze light of afternoon: and we were caught in the suffocating airs of rotting frith. Great alligators descended the muddy banks and beat the dark waters with their scaly tails, like fierce dragons.

We saw also many butterflies of rainbow colors weaving through the last sunlight of the day. And the shouting voices of the men at their tasks startled the bright-plumaged birds from the thickets, sending them up like a scattering of live embers blown on the wind.

From there we passed to a chiefdom called Cercana, journeying for a distance of nine leagues. We gave upon the principal town, which we found deserted, the cacique (one Abraibe) having fled with all his people: for he had been advertised by our old enemy the lord Cemaco that we had entered his territory.

The *compañeros* made careful search through the forsaken houses, diligently seeking both gold and victuals. The Indians, who had taken their departure in haste, had left most of their possessions behind them. There was a great store of bows and arrows: household goods such as baskets, looms, and dye pots: and calabash utensils of divers kinds. They discovered also a great abundance of fishing nets, for the Indians of that region could not cultivate their land by reason of the many marshes and fenny places, but subsisted upon what they could gather from the river and the trees.

The nets were of fine and artful workmanship: and they had been laid out in such great numbers that our Captain named the wide stream there the River of Nets.

A good quantity of gold had also been left in the *bohios* by the Indians, the count coming to more than seven thousand pesos when the final discovery was entered.

But of foodstuffs (for which we would gladly have exchanged all the gold) they found very little. So we took our leave of that town with much grumbling and discontent, the companions saying among themselves: "We have garnered gold, but we eat the air.

130

Our bellies retch for bread and our mouths are famished for the taste of roasted *maiz* and savory fish from the coals. Mary, Mary, succor us or we fain will perish all."

The Captain now divided his company into two forces of equal number. And one of them he placed under the leading of Rodrigo de Colmenares, while the other followed him.

As for Colmenares and his men (among whom I was counted one), we took our direction eastward toward the mountains. And after we had journeyed twelve leagues more or less, we descried along the river bank the cane-made shelters of an Indian village.

And even as we pondered whether we would send scouts to know if the people were armed and hostile, some of the Indians came out to us and greeted us with signs of friendship.

By diligent inquiry, Colmenares learned that their *chebí* (or overlord) was called Turvi. They spoke freely and without guile, saying that they had little gold in their village, but that they possessed a store of victuals with which the strangers might refresh themselves if we desired to take our rest in that place.

As Vasco Núñez had previously ordered us to do, we sent the *chebí* some gifts of mirrors, green beads, and other Spanish things that we might entreat him to trust and friendship.

In consequence we were received with smiles and rejoicing. Finding a plenty of food in the town, Colmenares called his men together and addressed them in a solemn manner: "Gentlemen: we are much bound to Providence in this affair, for here we have good food to assuage our outrageous hunger, which has hollowed our bodies these many days. We may here sleep safely (with one eye, that is to say!) among these shelters. The situation is pleasant, with wholesome air. And already I perceive that the women take it for a decent thing to serve us in all our needs. Here, therefore, we will await the return of Vasco Núñez."

While we were thus refreshed and eased and entertained with many singings, maskings, dancings, and wrestlings (after their manner), our Captain and his company took their voyage back to Darien. His purpose in returning to Santa Maria was to learn whether men and supplies had come over from Española and to deliver our treasure to the safe keeping of the town.

But as Balboa and his men entered the wide gulf once again, on a sudden the wind began to grow very great: and the canoes in which they had embarked plunged like chargers in the confusion of the waters. And they all thought to have perished, being then helpless as logs among the roiling waves.

But as it fell out, their clumsy barks survived the violence of the storm, all save two which they had taken from the people of Cercana. And in these (as surely the Devil willed it) were the gold and other treasure taken during the *entrada*.

When the storm had passed, Vasco Núñez did not tarry to mourn our losses, but ordered the surviving boats to direct their course again toward Darien.

And arriving in Santa Maria, they found the town as we had left it, there being no tidings of the reinforcements and provisions promised us by Don Diego. The Captain embarked again, therefore, to return to the business of our present exploit. Sailing up the same river we had explored, he and his company came to Turvi, where the Indians cheerfully ministered to their relief and comfort.

All our company manifested great contentment at seeing the good reception that was given us: but it was our Captain's will that (in order not to lose time or to use up food without advantage) a start should be made at once on what was to be done.

Therefore, on the second day following the arrival of Balboa and his soldiery from Santa Maria, after having heard the Mass with great devotion, we set out, marching in the good order of a military parade. And thus pursuing our incursion into unknown regions, we passed among the many rifts and breaches of those coasts.

Our advance was greatly hindered by mangrove swamps and by the venomous hosts that inhabited them: giant stingrays, scaly monsters, sharks, and divers kinds of fanged fish that tore at our flesh.

In the drier uplands, some of the companions began to sing a ballad of Castile: and a multitude of monkeys answered them with screaming clamor from the trees.

So we marched: and Colmenares, laughing: "Look, *compañeros*, how we have increased our ranks with yet another army." And, looking down, we saw beside the Spanish column (as if in unison with us) an endless moving file of leaf ants. They went forward as troops toward a battlefield: and each creature carried, as it were, an oval green banner, freshly cut from a leaf.

On the morning of June 24th we came to a vast, languid river, which the Indians called Ata-dó, that was to say, the Grandfather of Waters. But Balboa named it the river San Juan, that being the saint's day on which we discovered it. And we stood a long time watching that mighty flood: and the spread of it: more than a league across: with whorls and eddies, slow as waters flow in a dream.

We entered a vast green strath that spread before us hot and moist like a valley of the Last Judgement. We lifted our eyes to the towering blue *cordillera* which walled us in, and beheld along the lofty ridges a bank of clouds resting motionless and dark against the sky. And some of the companions imagined their shapes to counterfeit certain castles in Spain.

But the land beneath our feet little resembled the kind Castilian earth of the past: for there were perils and hardships in that country. Every step was menaced by coiling snakes that carried a powerful venom. We had in marvellous fear also the sudden thrust of the scorpion's poisoned lance: the burning pain of the centipede: the feverish sickness of spider bite: and all the unknown plants that blossomed death along the way.

And Vasco Núñez told of it (afterward) in a report to the King: "Do not think, Your Royal Highness [said he], that the swamps of this country are so easy to penetrate that we dallied pleasantly through them: for it often happened that we went a league or two or three through the marshes and water naked, our clothes bundled together on bucklers on top of our heads. And having emerged from one morass, we entered into others and marched this way two or three or as many as ten days."

Albeit, our Captain determined to extend our discoveries as far as possible in spite of the great difficulties and risks encountered. So we followed a toilsome trail through the wet lowlands. And torrential rains fell upon us days together, quenching our cooking fires: and we ate our meagre food cold and raw, the taste of it nauseous in our mouths. Some of the *compañeros* were sick and some lame, their limbs swollen with poison from bites and stings.

The Captain went among them with words of good cheer: and he dressed their wounds with his own hands.

133

When we had come thirty leagues from the guld, we had sight of a second large river, its black waters slow and deep where it flowed into the wide San Juan.

We made our night's camp upon an island between the two streams: and finding there some trees laden with a beautiful ripe fruit, the *compañeros* fell to devouring it. But in this they prepared their own miseries: for the fruit was a purgative more violent than anything known before that time.

And all that night they who had eaten of it rolled upon the wet earth with loud groans, believing that their guts were dissolving away within their bodies: and expecting death at any moment. But none died: and some were even the better for that terrible purge.

Having thus escaped the dire fate they had expected, they sang the praises of God, the Holy Virgin, and all the saints. Thereafter we marched upon an Indian district called Abanumaque, which lay eastward on the bank of the river opposite the island whereon we had encamped.

The Indians of that region used no bows and arrows, but they fought valorously with lances and clubs. But when Vasco Núñez ordered the arquebuses to be fired off, they took to heel, shrieking like demons with fright.

Pillaging the five hundred houses of that chiefdom, we found only scant stores of food and no gold. And our Captain stationed half of his men in the town with orders to keep good watch and ward and to search the forest around them for food and treasure.

With the others (among whom I, Juan de Toledo, was one), he then proceeded up the river to the domain of the cacique Abibaibe. There we found that the inhabitants had built their dwellings in gigantic trees. The companions fell to disputing the size of the leafy towers. Joining their hands, therefore, they encircled some of the larger trunks to measure their girth. And they found that these were of such size that it required seven or eight men with their arms stretched to full length, to reach around them.

Among the high branches, the Indians had erected *bohios* of considerable size, some of them having several rooms. And the householders reached these strange dwellings and left them by means of ladders, one for going up and another for descent.

And it was a sight worth seeing how the women of that town

could, at the bidding, climb these vine ladders with the swiftness of monkeys, carrying their infants upon their backs.

The Castilians hastily surrounded the big tree in which the cacique had his lodging. There we found that the liana ladders had been drawn up to prevent our ascending. Our interpreter Juan Alonso shouted for the cacique to come down to us, assuring him that the white strangers came in peace, which they would prove to him with wonderful gifts if he would descend.

The lord Abibaibe, however (peering down at us from his secure height), refused to stir. And he said: "Go away, strangers: I know you not as friends or foes. Here I abide in my own house after our custom. Here I survey the land in all directions. I will not come down to see whether you speak the truth. Go now, go back to the sliding river. Follow the spirits of the rain. Go, go!"

Perceiving that words of persuasion were to no purpose, Vasco Núñez fell from fair promises to threats and menacing gestures.

"Tell him that except he come down to us with all his family and familiars, we will cut down his tree and thereby overthrow his house and all who are in it. These we will slay and we will make faggots of their bones."

But the cacique's only answer was a hail of heavy stones which rattled off our armor. The Captain then ordered a force of men to begin to hew down the tree with axes. And Abibaibe (who had never before seen a tool of steel) was greatly struck with fear at the sight of chips flying from the big tree on every side. Whereupon, lowering a ladder, he straightway came down to us, followed by two of his sons.

The cacique told us then that neither he nor any of his people had any use for gold: that they had it in no more esteem than the river stones and therefore possessed none of the bright metal. But when we were instant upon him, with great swearing and ado, he promised to seek for some of it in certain places among the mountains whereof he had knowledge. And promising to bring us a large amount of gold on an appointed day, he departed with his men. But he did not return on the day agreed, nor indeed on any day thereafter.

Our Captain's faith in the word of Indians (whom he dealt with fairly and expected them to act in like manner) thus proved almost calamitous to us, as the sequel was to show. For the lord Abibaibe did not gather gold while we awaited his return, but he was even then joining with other Indian rulers in a conspiracy to attack us. By secretly gathering together both men and supplies, they intended to make a surprise assault upon the vastly outnumbered Castilians and to kill us all.

Upon our return to Abanumaque we had grave tidings from the men Vasco Núñez had left there under the charge of Colmenares. In the absence of our Captain the *compañeros* (finding themselves under loose rein) had formed small companies and had gone off in all directions to make raids upon certain Indian settlements. One of these foraging parties, a force of ten men led by a slapdash cavalier named Antonio Raya, met and joined battle with a well-armed Indian horde to the number (by judgement) of seven hundred. And in that skirmish, Raya was slain, together with two of his followers. The others saved themselves by a swift retreat back to the garrison at Abanumaque.

Greatly emboldened by this triumph over enemies whom before that time he had believed to be invincible, the cacique Abibaibe called together the Indian lords Abanumaque and Abraibe: and with them he secretly conspired to pounce upon the company of Castilians who were at Abanumaque before Balboa and we who accompanied him should return.

And so they did: before the breaking of the day, they came: naked: leaping like cats from the darkness, with their wild animal cries: and the mighty blasts of conches: and the beating of drums.

But the Spaniards had posted sentries at each of the four quarters, keeping good watch: and they had slept with their swords and bucklers at their sides. Being thus in all respects ready for attack (and having been that same night reinforced by thirty men that Vasco Núñez had sent ahead of us), they put the enemy to rout in brief time, with many of them slain and taken captive and without the loss of a single Christian.

The Captain, utterly misliking this report when he arrived, ordered a force of thirty men and a priest under the commandment of Bartolomé Hurtado to remain in Abanumaque to keep the Indians in view and to discover all the secrets of the country that it was possible to do.

But shortly after we returned to Darien (without any recompense for our tedious travails) two score soldiers of those who stayed at Abanumaque fell sick and could not be cured. Hurtado therefore allowed them to embark in a large canoe (together with certain Indians taken captive) to make their way back to Santa Maria.

But they went only a scant three leagues down the river before a hundred warriors of the cacique Cémaco set upon them from ambush, sallying forth from beneath heavy boughs that overhung the water. And our men (who were not prepared to defend themselves by reason of their weak condition and because they were not accustomed to fight in canoes) were all drowned, save two. These two escaped by concealing themselves under driftwood which was floating down the river, by which means they reached shore. And when they returned to Abanumaque and told Hurtado what had happened, he and the other Christians remaining with him abandoned that place and came back with all speed to Darien.

Chapter 9 ～～～～～～～～～～～～～～～～～～～

Heaven favored our great enterprise in Darien: have no doubt of that, my friends. And had it been otherwise, we should have perished all, either from the great hunger and privations we there endured, or from the spears and arrows of the Indians who were (by judgement) fifteen thousand men, all lusty and in good state of body: while we were only three hundred and with some of the companions in ill case by reason of fevers and other sicknesses and hurts.

Howbeit, the Indians feared most our valor, not alone our arms: we who had pledged our lives to one sword, one monarch, and one Holy Faith. As for our Captain, Vasco Núñez de Balboa, many of them believed him to be some kind of god, wherefore they called him Warrior of the Sun and Emissary from Heaven.

Even so, they took counsel among themselves as to what craft and cunning they might best use to kill this same white god and all who resorted unto him.

And thus did they fall into the snares they had laid for us: thus were they put to the edge of our blades and scattered in confusion like dust before the wind.

The things of which I now speak all happened after the manner following:

The cacique Cémaco whom our Captain had not been able to bring to amity either by gentleness or by rigor, now sent fifty of his vassals to us in Santa Maria: and the message they brought was that their lord had ordered them hither to make his humble suit and to establish peace between him and the great Tibá: for they were men well-practiced in the tending of crops: that they would labor in the *maiz* fields to bring forth a bountiful harvest.

And Vasco Núñez (whose single fault was that he could not for long believe evil of any man, be he Christian or pagan) welcomed them with many good words, using them with all kindness and favor.

But the recompense by which they villainously planned to requite his gentleness was death: and their orders were to allure him into the fields alone and there to fall upon him from every side and to kill him.

Yet, even as they lay in wait (having enticed him to a certain place among the *maiz*) their hearts failed them. For, as they beheld him riding forth mounted upon his mare, and seeing how he loomed above them in great majesty, with his crimson plumes and regal look, their hands began to quake: and they stared as men bewitched, awestruck and mute.

And later some of them confessed it: but he would not suffer any of us to mete out to them a just reward for their treachery. For (said he) the story they would have to tell the cacique Cémaco who sent them, would be greatly in our service.

After this, if there yet remained any doubt that our Captain had an advocate in heaven, surely it vanished when it was miraculously revealed to us that our lives were yet in great peril: for by means of that disclosure we were saved: and our enemies were brought into our power.

It befell that on a certain day Vasco Núñez was awakened by one of his mistresses (an exceeding well-favored *espave* called Fulvia, who was much in his eye: for her comeliness was a matter whereof there was great talk among the *compañeros:* and her breasts were so beautiful they raised the passion of every one of us, old and young alike, who looked upon them).

When the Captain opened his eyes, the girl was beside him, holding one of his hands: and she wore an air of grave concern.

"Tibá, my lord [she said to him, laboring over the Castilian words] during the night past came my brother to me secretly: and he has said that the caciques of Darien have reared such forces as they might and wait for the night of no moon. Then they will come over this town and kill all the Christians in it, to the last man. They are many, my lord: you must give them the fire weapons at once."

The aforesaid brother of Fulvia was a noble in the service of the cacique Cémaco: and it was his love for his sister that brought him thither at night to warn her of what was to befall. But Fulvia's love for Balboa was even greater: and being thus made privy to the Indians' evil designs, she straightway gave notice of them to Vasco Núñez.

Our Captain received these tidings with a very grave countenance, for the caciques concerning whom Fulvia had spoken were Cémaco, Abibaibe, Abraibe, and Abanumaque: and it was known to us that together they could muster an army (by judgement) of five thousand war-hardened fighters.

Balboa was instant upon his beautiful consort to reveal to him the place where the Indian troops were hiding that we might make a surprise attack upon them. But the girl's brother had not opened that information to her.

Howbeit, she told the Captain that the Indian youth had promised to return that same night to take her away before the town was attacked and burned.

When he heard this, Balboa ordered the Constable's guard to conceal themselves near his house and there to keep good watch and ward and to seize the brother of Fulvia when he would come.

So it was done: and during the second watch of the night, he was taken and brought before Vasco Núñez and the principal officers of the town. He stood there with a calm and resolute countenance: and it was plain to see that we would find it difficult to force from him the knowledge we had to have.

To Alonso, who acted as interpreter, the Captain said: "Ask him where the warriors of Cémaco and the other caciques are hiding. Say that, if he give us this knowledge, his life will be spared and his sister Fulvia rewarded. But if he withhold, he must surely be given to the dogs to devour."

But the young *jura* would not thus easily betray his people. Alonso gave us his answer: "He says: 'You speak as the crazy bird, *xkan-xoc*, that cries, Who comes? Who comes? For such there is no answer.'"

"Tell him to think well and twice again. We are patient men, desiring him no wrong. But if he refuses us, he will be put to black-faced torture, for our lives lie in forfeit."

The brother of Fulvia made no reply, but stood staring into the candle flame.

"Give him the bow-string," Vasco Núñez said sadly. "It's more than tender sop that's needed here to have the word from him, and all to be lost for the want of it."

The Constable then brought a length of strong bow-string and a piece of wood from inside the *cabildo*. Two guards secured the youth's arms behind his back and forced him to drop to his knees. Tying the two ends of the bow-string they placed the loop loosely about the Indian's head and into this they slipped the stick which, when it was twisted, tightened the thong.

God knows it, he had great courage. And there was no shame upon him that he spoke at last revealing to us where the Indian armies were gathered. For, as Mendana continued to tighten the bow-string, the thong bit deep into his forehead: and drops of sweat glistened upon the bloodless skin. His eyes bulged from their sockets. He screamed in agony then, and Mendana loosened the cord, perceiving that he was now of a mind to speak.

And in a faint whisper, he said: "Tichiri."

Having thus discovered the hiding place of our enemies, Balboa made his will known to us: that we should arm ourselves and depart at once. A force of sixty men under the charge of Rodrigo de Colmenares set forth for Tichiri in four large canoes, guided by the brother of Fulvia.

Vasco Núñez commanded another company of seventy (among whom I, Juan of Toledo, was one): comprising twenty horsemen and fifty foot: and we proceeded in haste to the village of the cacique Cémaco: for it was he who had united the others against us.

But when we reached that settlement, we found only a few Indians remaining there, their fires banked and their eyes heavy with sleep. These we seized, and continued on to Tichiri: a long file of shadow-men that climbed the dark, wooded slopes and passed across windy, fair uplands, spectral as a burial ground in the moonlight.

Just before the breaking of day, we espied the Indian encampment in a deep hidden valley. And Cémaco, being certain in his own mind concerning the complete secrecy of their warlike designs, had appointed no sentinel to keep watch through the night.

Our Captain drew rein and sat quietly looking upon the sleeping Indians spread out below us like men already fallen in battle. He dismounted and bade the other members of cavalry do likewise, which we did. And we threw ourselves upon the ground to await the arrival of the infantry.

The night's chill was still in the air: and a sticky dampness clung to the earth and to the thick foliage around us. We huddled beneath our cloaks, conversing in low voices.

Cristobal de León, the silversmith, had had another of his long, prophetic dreams: and he told it all to us, grunting and groaning and drawing it out like some tale of Amadis.

Presently, through the misty half-light we descried the tips of pikes moving along the trail behind the low hills: and we knew that the foot soldiers were arriving.

Having arrayed our forces in their best strength, our Captain ordered the horsemen to remount. Then he gave a signal to Barrantes the bugler, whose gleaming horn seemed to waver through the morning mists as he held it to his lips. The clear, rippling tucket echoed down the valley: and distantly we heard the rearguard answer.

Vasco Núñez spurred his horse, and we charged down the incline, crying to our patron: "Santiago!"

Taken by surprise, the Indians were slow to rise: and we rode over the bodies of many. Despite their great number, they were assaulted so suddenly that they had no time even to seize their weapons. So they turned us their backs and fled in confusion and fright.

Only a few valiant fighters were bold enough to make a stand: but because of their bad order and our superior weapons, these brave defenders soon lay dead upon the ground.

And that was the end of Indian revolt in Darien: and such leaders as fell to us were put to the sword, for they had well-deserved their death, by reason of their treachery.

So we returned again to Santa Maria, carrying with us the abundance of stores which the caciques had brought together for their war against us. Yet well did we know that the supplies that by good Providence had thus come into our hands would not suffice to keep us alive for many months.

We were therefore much troubled that the Admiral had not kept his word to send us victuals and furnishings from Española. Some months had passed since our emissary Valdivia had departed for Santo Domingo, carrying our petition and our gold. Yet, as we all knew, the voyage was one requiring no more than one or two weeks, even when the winds were contrary. Some of the men, therefore, began to complain that our *procurador* had betrayed us all to the crows and (as they said it) "in some peaceful country jigs a merry passion with our gold."

Vasco Núñez rejected these suspicions out of hand. Valdivia, he said, was a loyal and honest man in whom we could repose full trust, even though he carried thirty thousand *castellanos* in gold. That it was more reasonable to believe his lieutenant had perished in some tragedy at sea or (God forbid it!) served up at some devilish Carib feast.

After the matter of our situation had been well pondered by all, the *vecinos* resolved that another deputation would have to be sent to Española and thence to Spain to seek help from the King for our intended enterprise.

Balboa gave out that he was of a mind to go himself, for he knew all the secrets of these lands and could therefore make a very good representation at the court in Spain.

But the people (even those who had been his enemies), when they heard this, did not cease to protest until it was agreed that the mission would be entrusted to another. For such was the respect they had for his good qualities that they feared the settlement at Santa Maria might well perish in his absence.

Some of the men who had been of Nicuesa's suite put forward Alonso Núñez de Madrid as emissary. But the *baquianos*, recalling that he had a wife in Spain, feared he might find the comforts of home beguiling and never return.

After much deliberation, Juan de Caicedo, the elderly *veedor*, was chosen. He was a Crown official, already known personally to the King: he had passed many years in the Indies and could make a worthy report of our needs. To insure his return, he would leave his wife, Doña Inés de Escobar in Santa Maria.

Howbeit, having in mind Caicedo's advanced age and the rigors of the long voyage back to Castile, we resolved that a second *procurador* should accompany him. And for this mission, we appointed Rodrigo de Colmenares, in whom Balboa placed great confidence. (But, as the sequel has shown, he was a devious man who even at that time was conspiring with the Captain's foes in Darien.)

There being no ships left capable of making the voyage to Española, Vasco Núñez ordered a vessel built, using timber and materials from two brigantines which, by reason of the *broma*, were no longer seaworthy.

When the craft was ready, Caicedo and Colmenares were given our petition, properly drawn up and signed by all the *vecinos*. They also carried with them five hundred pesos of gold for the King, and certain private gifts which the *compañeros* sent to families and friends.

With a crew of eleven Castilians and two Indians, they sailed from these shores on the 4th day of the calends of November, 1512.

For us whose hopes and fortunes went with them in that ship, it was a sad departure. For the brigantine's tackle had been made from tree-bark: the masts were dressed in faded banners: and only a large stone rested upon the bow as anchor.

There is no case for a man in waiting: and for those who tarried in the streets and dooryards of that steaming town, it was not enough merely to look to our safety and honor until such time as reinforcements came. Our breasts throbbed with impatience: great greed and craving beclouded our vision.

There was much talk then of that rich cacique Dabaibe, whose golden city (it was said) had many palaces and treasures: and in a temple of their mother-goddess were gems and pearls of great worth adorning her altar.

As for the said Dabaibe, he had a large gold smelter in his house, whereat more than a hundred men labored continually. In his strongrooms were certain large baskets of gold, of such great weight that only a strong man could lift them.

Thus, time wearing away, our stores of grain and food supplies diminished. We were put on short rations: and hunger began to nibble at our bellies like a ship-rat at a morsel of cheese.

A shortage of candles left most of the houses in darkness after sunset. Some of the men, urged on by their Indian women, tried to use torches made of a resinous wood: but these smutty flares

145

soon filled their dwellings with a heavy pall of smoke and fumes: and few could abide it.

Being thus impatient of idleness, and being pricked on by fear of famine, the companions went about bickering among themselves and giving voice to loud complaints. When they were together, whether two or twenty, they filled each other's ears with dire prophecies and talk of their Christian bones lying unwept in that cursed, wet, and shallow glebe.

Leading the loudest faction of faultfinders and grumblers was Diego de Corral, a bachelor of laws whose laziness and ceaseless effort to stir up rebellion only proved the reasonableness of Balboa's hatred for lawyers.

Aided by the great unrest in the settlement, the aforesaid Corral, together with certain other malcontents, brewed a conspiracy against Vasco Núñez and the officers who had all matters at their command in Darien.

To that end they employed a secret, counterfeit investigation of Balboa's official acts, setting down therein many false accusations against him: and all of them done over the seal of a corrupt notary who impugned his own sacred oath.

Believing that by this sham legal document they had given good color to their villainous cabal, they first attempted to take the chief constable, Bartolomé Hurtado.

But it pleased God that tidings of the foul plot should reach our Captain by privy report from the women of his household (who had learned of it from a certain *espave* whom Corral had taken as mistress).

And when he heard that Alonso Perez meant to lead a band which would seize Hurtado, Balboa ordered the same Alonso Perez to be taken and stayed.

That arrest provoked a great tumult among the Corralistas: and they appeared in the center plaza of the town, fully armed and ready to do battle with Vasco Núñez and those *baquianos* who supported him (among whom I, Juan of Toledo, was counted as one).

We were prepared to charge, when the priest, Padre Andrés, stood between us in the role of peacemaker, declaring that the only victors in such a fight as we were about to undertake would

146

be the Indians, who would divide our possessions, and the crows who would pick our bones.

Being persuaded, as well by the great fear they had of Balboa's terrible skill with the sword, as with the good words of Padre Andrés, the rebels put down their weapons. On his side, Vasco Núñez agreed to release Alonso Perez with a warning not to risk his high indignation by provoking future disturbances.

But men of ill will are never peaceable. Barely a day had passed after this reconciliation before that spite-weaver Corral was at work again in the public eye.

Addressing the *vecinos* in the principal plaza, the lawyer told them they had all been robbed and ruined by Balboa and the ravenous wolves he had placed in authority: that they were ill-paid for all their labor and fatigue in that conquest of the new lands.

As for the gold we had garnered with our travails: "Whose gold is it, compañeros?" asked he in a loud voice. "Your gold, say you? Bah! I call that mine which I may use when and how it pleases me. This gold of yours is locked in the keep until that sweet noble, Balboa, feels of a spirit to apportion it. Even then belike the bastard gypsy to cog you of your just shares, and who's to say him 'Cho!' My counsel is, if you would pull down your proper meed, as I mine, that we get us to the casting house tomorrow and make our own parcels as free men. Alonso Perez has a sturdy sledge for the lock and I a keen blade for the *veedor*.

"What say now, *señores*; are you men to possess your own grist by the soldier's good arms, or sucklings to lick the pestilential gall of that tricky tyrant, Vasco Núñez? For my part, I will claim my share tomorrow with a quick blade. You who are of a humor to follow, come forward."

The first to respond to this call of mutiny was Francisco Benitez, whom Balboa had caused to receive one hundred stripes at the trial of Nicuesa. Others followed, crying "Forward!"

Thus impelled by their consuming greed, which was at all times greater than their loyalty to God or man, the people arrayed themselves beside the traitors.

Andrés de Valderrábano (who had witnessed it from the edge of the crowd) was amazed at the speed with which the *vecinos* could change their allegiance, turning against that man who had saved

147

them from peril and used them better than any Captain who had come out to the Indies.

He left hurriedly for the house of Vasco Núñez to inform the Captain of what was afoot. And he found him swinging meditatively in a hammock outside the doorway to his house.

Gasping for breath, Valderrábano said: "The dogs are . . . going to . . . seize the gold!"

Vasco Núñez ceased moving and regarded his lieutenant with a tranquil look. "Which gold?"

"The gold in the strong-room. They plan to take it by force of arms."

"Well, calm yourself, man. This is not the first or the last piece of treachery to pass in the Indies."

"It will be the last for us, unless you send the guard for those stinking instigators Corral, Benitez, and Perez."

Balboa began once more to swing back and forth in his hammock. He stared quietly at the sky. And after waiting a long interval, Valderrábano asked: "What will you do?"

"You mean about the Corralistas?"

"Yes, and all their adherents."

"I will hunt the boar, Andrés. We will leave tonight. Have Hurtado come here: also Pizarro, Muñoz, and Gutiérrez. Tell Muñoz to bring food for a day's journey. *Purísima!* I do like to hunt the *pecarí.*"

Valderrábano was much perplexed at this answer. He said: "If you leave the town, those devils will surely take all the gold. Corral has said that he has a blade for the *veedor* and Benitez has a sledge for the locks."

Upon hearing this, Balboa ordered that the door to the treasury be left unlocked: and that the sentinel should yield without resistance to the demands of the rebels.

"I do not understand your reasons," said Valderrábano, "but it will be done as you have commanded it."

"What a simpleton you are, Andrés. Have you never watched the dogs besporting the one with the other in a way that proclaims them better friends than we to our *compadres?* But throw a joint of meat among them. Then you will see. You will see."

And so it fell out as the Captain had said. On the day following,

148

shortly before midday, three of the *vecinos* came seeking us where we had made our camp to hunt the *pecarí*.

We heard their horses crashing through the thickets, but at Balboa's bidding we put ourselves to be examining the muddy bank of a stream for *pecarí* tracks. As we were so engaged, the emissaries from the town came upon us. Benito Buran led them and spoke for the *vecinos* who had sent them.

"Captain [said he], there has been an act of disorder in Santa Maria. But people of reason gave only their tongues' and not their hearts' consent to it, as was seen in the civic tumult later."

Vasco Núñez feigned surprise. "A rebellion, say you? What has passed in the town, Buran?"

"This, Captain: in the night past, the chief *vecinos* of Darien, with the bristling words of that Bachelor Corral to prick them on, vowed them to seize the gold. Afterward, they were to cry you down and seat that meddling ass, Corral, as alcalde. So they looted the gold, but in the division of it, Corral was seen to favor his own familiars, and thus begot a loud discord and a shout of 'Cheating gypsy!' And that Balboa—so they said it then—was never the scurvy crimp as was Corral. Some of the men, then, and I among them, began the cry of '*Viva* Balboa!' So we pledged our loyal faith, and all of them with their names for it, save Benitez and Corral, who were not consulted. I was sent to ask your return at once to Santa Maria, for a strong hand is needed. Here I bring the pledge taken down by the *escribano* and signed by us all."

Vasco took the document with an air of seriousness.

And slowly shaking his head: "They cry '*Viva!*' today and '*Muera!*' tomorrow." Then he turned again to Buran. "What of Corral and Benitez?"

"They have been lodged, like two giddy parrots, in Santa Maria's cage. There their loud squawking is heard, but not regarded."

Being once more in full authority in Darien, Vasco Núñez ordered an investigation made of the insurrection, with a report of the findings to be sent to Spain.

At the same time he did not impose any severe punishment upon the leaders of the treason (as he ought to have done), but released them into the charge of the Franciscan friars. Thus did he preserve his worst enemies that they might do him even greater evil in the future.

149

The true cause of the outbreak (he said) was the artifice and cunning of Corral who, being a lawyer, was skilled in the devilish art of misleading and confusing men.

And being hot upon it, a short time afterward he wrote to our King a letter wherein he begged His Highness to forbid that any lawyer be allowed passage hither:

Most powerful Lord:

I desire to ask a favor of Your Highness, for I have done much in your service: and it is that Your Highness will command that no Bachelor of Laws, nor of anything else, lest it be of medicine, shall pass over to this part of Tierra Firme, upon pain of heavy punishment which Your Highness shall order to be imposed. For no Bachelor comes here who is not a devil and who does not lead the life of devils. And not only are they themselves evil, but they stir up a thousand lawsuits and quarrels. This mandate will be greatly to the advantage of Your Highness's service, for the country is new. . . .

With the passing of time, our situation became ever more perilous, as one misery after another began to fall upon our necks. We endured great want of victuals: and sickness was so common a thing among us that hardly a man escaped one form of infirmity or another.

The companions searched the sky and hills for fell portents: a plunging meteor over the town, a bird cry in the night, strange sounds in the dark forest: "Silence! Listen! Who calls out like a wounded comrade? Ahhh, *compañeros*, he falls back groaning. So shall we all, God forgive us our sins!"

And a company of them, seeking game in certain inner parts of the country, came upon a mysterious tree, each of whose leaves bore a curious design drawn in black, as though some ghostly hand had etched it there. These drawings were in divers states of completion, some being just begun and others seemingly done.

And the Indians who went with them were awe-struck by these leaves. "This is the Tree of Life [said they]: when the medicine picture is finished, the leaf falls, and the man falls and his heart is turned to the great source of waters: and it is soon over: and he feels no more pain. You who come from beyond the foggy mountains: you too will die when your leaf falls."

150

The Indians reverently gathered up the leaves which had al-
,ready fallen to the ground, to carry them to their *tequina* to be
used in magic rituals.

Watching them, the Spaniards signed themselves with the Holy
Cross and murmured a prayer to our sweet advocate, the Holy
Mother, to deliver us from these things of the Devil, and from the
death that passes over that country.

Succor came to us only when our extremity was such that, had it
been delayed yet a week longer, we would have perished all. For
the famine had grown to be so great that we held our very souls
between our teeth to prevent them from departing our bodies.

Such was the case when two vessels—a caravel and a brigantine
—arrived, laden with bacon, wine, oil, biscuit, cheeses, and other
provisions sorely needed in Darien.

We who were almost consumed with hunger welcomed these re-
freshments with as much gratitude as the Israelites who received
that marvellous bread which the Lord gave them in the wilderness.
And many fell upon their knees along the shore, loudly giving
thanks, weeping, and making such other signs of rejoicing as the
occasion seemed to require.

In command of the vessels (which had come over to us from Española) was Sebastián de Ocampo, a gentleman of quality whom
Balboa received with great pleasure, for they had been friends
from the time of our Captain's sojourn on that island.

And Ocampo brought word that Colmenares and Caicedo
(whom we had sent as our envoys to the Court of Spain) had
turned traitors to our cause: and they conspired with the enemies
of Vasco Núñez to misrepresent him to the King.

Having received this intelligence, Balboa resolved to counter
these lies and false accusations (concerning what had happened
with Enciso and the unfortunate Nicuesa) with a full and true account of his life in these Indies and of the very great and loyal
services he had rendered the Sovereign.

He sat down in his house and began to compose a long letter to
the King: it would be dispatched to Spain with Ocampo, accompanied by a quantity of gold and an Indian slave who knew their
secrets of treating metals and could explain these to His Highness.

And he wrote late at night (as he told me) by the unsteady

flame of a smoky candle. Its wavering light raised a large crucifix from the darkness of the opposite wall and played across the body of the agonized Christ our Savior, whereon he looked as he pondered his thoughts and his words.

As for the governors Ojeda and Nicuesa, he gave the King to understand that they were the cause of their own perdition, being selfish and cruel in all their dealings both with their own men and with the Indians of these lands.

"After coming to these regions, they were so presumptuous and high-handed that they imagined themselves to be lords of the land: and that they could rule the country and fulfill the needs of government from their beds. And so they did: for, from the moment they arrived here, they felt they need do nothing but give themselves over to dissolute living.

"But the nature of this country is such that, if he who has charge of the government sleep, he will be caught asleep when he should be awake: for this is a land that requires that the man who governs it pass over and around it many times."

The worst fault of these governors, he informed the Sovereign, was their mistreatment of the men who served under them, whom, from the first, they used as one would slaves. When loot was taken in raids, they refused to distribute so much as a *real's* worth among the soldiers, with the result that the men were so dejected that, even if they saw gold lying alongside of them, they would not care to pick it up, knowing they would receive precious little of it themselves.

He cleaned the point of his quill with a small piece of cloth, as he considered the weight of his words: black, squirming creatures of thought which must speak for him before the throne. And he was much perplexed to give clear and agreeable account of his own services.

He combs his callous fingers through his hair: feels the sword-scar behind his ear, as he stares deep into memory's well. There in the confusion of shadows are the hunger-ravaged faces of the companions. And so many are the faces of dead men, it causes grief to think of it.

"Since coming here, I have thought of nothing night and day save how I may protect and support the handful of men God has placed in my charge, and to sustain their lives until such a time as Your Highness sends reinforcements.

"Very often I have wondered how it has been possible for us to survive, seeing that we have been as badly succored from the Island of Española as if we had not been Christians.

"I have taken great care that none of my people shall go hence unless I myself shall go in front of them, whether it be by night or by day, marching across the rivers, through swamps and forests, and over difficult mountains.

"I, my lord, have always looked to it that everything that has been obtained up to this time should be fairly divided (after the portion belonging to your V. R. H. has been set aside): the gold and pearls, as well as the clothing and edibles. But up to now we have esteemed the victuals more than gold, for we have had more gold than health. And often I have cast about in all directions with a greater desire to find a basket of corn than one full of gold."

Mindful of our Sovereign's express command that his Indian vassals in the new lands be treated with kindness and Christian charity, the Captain wrote: "I have tried wherever I have gone in this land to look to it that the Indians are treated well, allowing no man to injure them unjustly, and giving them many things from Castile, whereby they will be persuaded to friendship with us.

"By thus treating them fairly, I have learned from them many secrets as to where great riches in gold may be found, by which your very R. H. will be well served."

Balboa put down his quill and flexed his fingers. He threshed the air irritably to fend off the insects buzzing about his ears, as he sought for words wherewith to persuade the King that our pretended enterprises would be greatly to his royal liking and profit.

"I desire to give an account to your very R. H. of the great secrets and marvellous riches of this land of which God has made your R. H. the lord and me the discoverer before any other, for which I give many thanks and much praise every day of the world, and count myself the most fortunate man ever born on earth.

"In this province of Darien have been found many rich mines, and gold in great quantity. Twenty rivers have been discovered:

153

and there are altogether thirty of them that flow from the mountains only two leagues distant from this town, all of them carrying gold.

"Thirty leagues up this great river [San Juan], on the left side, a very large and beautiful stream flows into it, and two days' journey up this stream there is a cacique who is called Dabaibe: he is a great lord over a large and populous territory.

"All the gold that goes forth from this gulf region comes from the seat of this cacique Dabaibe, as well as all that belonging to the other caciques of these regions. And it is reported that they have many pieces of gold, curiously wrought, and very large. Many Indians who have seen them tell me that this cacique Dabaibe has certain baskets of gold, and that it requires the full strength of a man to lift one of them upon his back.

"This cacique does not gather the gold himself, because he is far removed from the source; but the way in which he obtains it is that, two days' journey from here there is a beautiful land in which dwells a very evil and cannibalistic people; they eat as many men as they can get. These people, who are godless and obey no one, are very warlike. Each one is a law unto himself. It is they who are owners of the mines which, according to my information, are the richest in the world. . . .

"There are two methods for collecting the gold without any labor. One is to wait until the river rises in the ravines; when the freshets drain off, the stream beds remain dry and the gold, which has been robbed from the hills and brought down in very large lumps, is laid bare. The Indians describe them as being of the size of oranges, or of a fist; others say they are in the form of flat slabs.

"The other manner of gathering gold is to wait until the grass on the hillsides is dry and then set it afire. When it is burned off, the Indians go to search in the most likely places and collect large quantities of very beautiful grains. The Indians who gather the gold, bring it in grains to be smelted; and they trade it to the cacique Dabaibe in exchange for youths and young boys to eat, and for women to serve them as consorts, whom they do not eat. They barter with him also pigs, of which there are many in this land; a great deal of fish; cotton cloth; and salt: and such pieces of wrought gold as they desire."

Having thus spoken of the great abundance of gold (which he

154

knew to be the monarch's heavy concern), our Captain did not fail to mention the reinforcements we needed to obtain it and (above all else) to make our way to that other sea whereof the cacique Comogre had informed us.

"Your very R. H. should order that two hundred crossbows be brought, made to exact specification with very strong stocks and fittings . . . and with long ranges. They should not be of more than two pounds in weight. From these, much money would be made, because every man here is glad to have one or two crossbows, as they are very good arms against the Indians and they keep those who own them provided with an abundance of fowl and game.

"Two dozen very good espingards of light metal are also required, made of bronze, because the iron ones are soon damaged by the constant rains and are eaten away with rust; it is enough that they be twenty-five to thirty pounds in weight; and not too long, so that a man may be able to carry one of them wherever it may be needed. Very good powder is also required.

"What I recommend, most powerful Lord, is that more people should come so that, if it please God, from these two stations, the one at Dabaibe and the other at Comogre, we may explore the land and learn its secrets, and more concerning the Other Sea which is on the other side, to the south; and everything else that is needful.

"It is also necessary that Your Highness command that skilled artisans come to keep the crossbows in repair, because every day they get out of order, owing to the heavy rains.

"In everything that I have suggested, money will be made, and it need cost your very R. H. nothing, except providing the necessary reinforcements; for I dare, through the help of Our Lord, to undertake everything in these lands that is necessary in the service of your very R. H."

As he thoughtfully wiped the nib of his quill once more, Balboa bethought him of similar promises made by those captains who came out to the Indies before—men like Ojeda, Nicuesa, Enciso. And had not these men returned with only a dreadful loss of life and failure to their credit? He therefore wished to assure his King that he was of different mettle.

"I do not desire to build air castles as did the governors whom

155

Y. H. sent out before me. Your Highness must consider all I have done and discovered and endured with these people, without any help save that I received from God, and by my own labor.

"I can certify that I know how to minister better than all those who have come here hitherto: and that Your Highness may fully understand what this means, consider how little those Governors have discovered up to now: how they all have failed and have departed, leaving these shores full of graves. And although many Christians have been buried in the earth, it is also true that many of those who have died have been devoured by dogs and crows.

"I do not wish to enlarge upon this, except to indicate to Your Highness what each man has been able to do and has in truth done up to now."

Before concluding his long letter, Balboa arose and went across to a Spanish cupboard, from which he took a *botija* of Jerez and a heavy glass. He poured himself a liberal portion of the golden wine and held it up toward the candlelight: he admired its clarity and elegant color. Seating himself once more, he set the glass down before him, alongside the unfinished missive. For a long time he sat looking at a spot of radiance in its depths: a reflected point of light from the candle flame. Then he soberly lifted the glass as though making a toast: and, after a moment of reflection, he drank.

"Most powerful Lord [he resumed] I am sending Sebastián de Ocampo that Your Highness be informed of all that is happening here: and I entreat Y. H. to give him full credence, for he has been apprised by me of the whole truth concerning all that should be done in the service of Your Highness and of what is required in this land.

"May Our Lord prosper the life and royal estate of Your Highness by the addition of many more kingdoms and dominions to your sacred rule: and may all that is discovered in these regions come directly under your charge, as your most R. H. may desire: for there are greater riches here than in any other part of the world.

"From the town of Santa Maria de la Antigua, of the province of Darien, in the gulf of Urabá: today Thursday the 20th of January in the year 1513. The creature and servant of Your Highness, who kisses your most royal hands and feet.

Vasco Núñez de Balboa

The *vecinos* had also procured that a letter to the King be written for them by the notary. And in the said letter they greatly praised and extolled Balboa as a just and worthy Captain who knew best how to conduct men-at-arms during the serious business of conquest and discovery: and they respectfully entreated His Highness to confirm his authority in Darien by appointing him Governor of that province.

They also begged the Sovereign that he reduce the Crown's share of the plunder taken during our *entradas*, from one-fourth to one-fifth: and that certain spoils of lesser value (such as gossapine cotton cloth, canoes, dyestuffs, and household goods) be left to us free of all royal impost.

The two vessels of Sebastián de Ocampo put up sail in God's name on the 28th day of January in the afternoon: and with a fresh wind, they departed Darien, bearing our petitions and gold.

We stood a long time on that strand watching them go: and none spoke a word. After a space, the sun went down and the shapes of the two distant barques seemed to shiver and to fall to pieces in the water. We knew this to be a counterfeit begotten of the evening mists: yet did we pray in our hearts that God might suffer those ships to come safely into their appointed haven.

On the ides of June, two Crown caravels, well-furnished and provisioned, arrived in Darien under the conduct of one Cristobal Serrano. And those ships brought us not only victuals and weapons (whereof we were in great want) but also a writ from the King which was the cause of great rejoicing by our Captain and by all of us who were his loyal followers.

The said document was a royal *cédula* appointing Balboa Governor and Captain-General of Darien.

And upon finding himself thus ennobled and made secure in his command by order of the King himself, as an act of grace, Balboa forthwith set at liberty his worst enemies, who were being stayed for notorious acts of mutiny. Thus did he show again his tragic fault: for (I say) he was merciful to the point of weakness.

Even as these treacherous rogues came forth once more to devise his ruin, those whom he had before shown lenity and warmth of heart were at work in Spain befouling his honor in the court of the Catholic king.

Martín Zamudio, whom we had sent as *procurador* in Castile, told it all in a letter which came in the same ship which brought his brevet from the Sovereign.

The King (he wrote) was weary of the many failures, complaints, and cross-complaints reaching him from Tierra Firme. Therefore he had resolved to create a new *gobernación* in Darien. To that end he had already chosen a Governor to send from Castile, empowered to take full command of all civil and military affairs in these lands.

"Beware of this man, Vasco Núñez, when he is come over to you. He is by name Don Pedro Arias de Ávila, called (with good reason) Furor Domini. He has a certain evil spirit in him, for he was once dead, having lived up a full life: and for an entire night a death watch was kept over him by the nuns of Torrejon. And so, too, a mass for the dead was said. But as his body was being lowered into the grave, one of the mourners who threw his arms about the coffin heard some sound within. Forthwith they raised the lid. *Dios y santos!* He had returned to life. Surely he has a devil in him.

"And (they tell) this Pedrarias each year, on that day which marked his death, has a requiem mass said in full for him, to which he listens with great devotion, standing in the open grave that had been prepared for him. Also, when he goes forth from his city, he carries with him that coffin wherein he lay. It is placed in his bedchamber as one would place a familiar chair or a holy relic.

"Not only is he exercised by Satan, who raised him from the dead for the carrying out of the tempter's evil deeds on earth: but he is also the grandson of a *converso*.

"Take heed, therefore, for it is little else than the toe of his boot he will treat you to."

The Captain-General was greatly troubled by these tidings: and he was left in hand the election of two evils: either to set forth in our present poor estate to find the other sea, or to abide the coming of a new Governor who would surely himself become the discoverer of that great sea and of those rich lands whereof Comogre's son had given us knowledge.

Intending not to be barred of his glorious enterprise, therefore, Balboa at once set on foot certain plans for passing forward while his fortune held so much promise: to pursue with vigor the obligation laid upon him by Providence and by the just desires of his men who had served with such constancy and good faith in the time past.

And though the cacique Comogre had delivered it as his opinion that we would require a thousand brave and lusty men to cross those high mountains in order to find that other sea (greatly amplifying the dangers we might fall into), he did not know as did Balboa the desperate boldness of our company.

So, ordering us to assemble in the town square, the General gave us a clear understanding of his pretension: that if we were of a mind to follow, he would no longer fob off the prosecution of that great discovery, lest others come and take away from us the profit and glory that were justly ours. That nothing could be so odious and dishonorable as for men of valor (such as we were) to shun great attempts because our numbers were small or because difficulties and hazards barred our way.

Were we then steadfast (as he was) in our first resolution: that we would bring to pass that great enterprise or else die the death?

And all of us who were present answered him with great shouts, signifying to him that we were ready to undertake at once that high and notable exploit.

Accordingly, Vasco Núñez hastened to put all things in order as best befitted our pretended campaign and the welfare of the companions.

Chapter 10 ~~~~~~~~~~~~~~~~~~~~~~~~~~~~~~~~~~~~~~

Of that journey (now lost among the shadows of yesterday) how can I speak except with voices of the dead: or how look back without seeing it through a mist of tears? For it was the acme of our lives: the moment (as it were) when our souls were lifted up as the consecrated host is elevated above the holy chalice: and the sacring bell sounds, proclaiming a miracle.

Our memory encompasses a whole world: we who followed the leading of that valiant Captain by day, and by darkness the twinkling fireflies which he ordered attached to the back of each companion, that none might lose his way along those perilous footpaths of their forests. We who listened for words on the wind: and looked for omens in the shape of things hidden behind the flapping leaves of that sylvan wilderness. We who marched through the high passes and pacified the warlike people and brought them into friendship: and I see them come forward to meet us a bowshot off, all elegantly appareled in brilliant feathers and blue stones which they wear for comeliness: and a great noise of drums, rattles, and trumpets. And the red and yellow birds that flew up from the river marshes beneath an ochre sky.

The sun appeared: and it set that green world ablaze: and afternoon tongues of fire fell upon our steel armor. Then night came: and the moon descended, scattering stars across the sky like sparks from our windblown campfires.

All these things and others most serious befell us who marched

161

through those lands, to the south and westward with the sun: our banners before us: until (staring mute as wakened sleepers) we beheld the other sea: that blue profound, which mirrors the depth of the sky.

Now having foretold in part the strange and wonderful events that attended our passage thither, I will relate in full the circumstances of that great exploit.

Upon Thursday, which was the first day of September in the year of our Redeemer 1513, after hearing early mass (with great devotion), we embarked in a brigantine and ten large canoes, in squadron formation. And in our company were one hundred and ninety companions, all of them men of good pecker and ready with one accord to undertake whatsoever charges might be laid upon them.

We directed our course to Careta, the seat of the cacique Don Fernando Chima (whose daughter Balboa had taken for a wife): and the ten canoes arrived at that port on the fourth day, while we aboard the brigantine came to anchor on the day following.

There we were well received and entertained: and we might have tarried happily in that place while we were refreshed and eased: but the General, being impatient to begin the *entrada*, was instant upon us to put all things in readiness to march.

Accordingly, on the following day he mustered a force of ninety-two of the most valorous and experienced *baquianos* among our people: and we departed from Careta and marched forward toward the territory of the cacique Ponca.

Also in our train were certain Indian guides and many servants, women, and laborers that the lord Fernando Chima had given us to bear our furnishings and commodities, whereof there was considerable store: armor, crossbows, gunpowder, baskets of victuals, merchandise for trafficking, small cannon, and arquebuses.

Yet withal (and I speak as truly as at confession) never a gallant company great or small undertook an *entrada* into unknown places so weakly provided and with so small means to help themselves. But as heaven guided our course and high courage our behavior, we had some good hope of attaining to a happy conclusion of that enterprise.

Our men went forward on our journey at the beginning with

lightness of heart and good great passing of the time: some sang along the trail and laughter rang out. But the farther we went on (our strength decreasing and the hot moist air breeding great faintness) the more the companions began to trudge along in silence, their heads down and their faces pocked and swollen from the fierce bites of midges and gnats, which swarmed out of every thicket we passed, thirsting for our blood.

Each time our General ordered a halt to rest, many fell to the ground as though struck with an arrow and would fain have lingered a greater time than was allowed.

Toward the evening, we made camp beside a clear stream which passed through a fair and pleasant vale in an excellent prospect. On the banks of this river we found divers sorts of trees of excessive height. There were also herbs and flowers of sweet scent, of such great variety that (as our friar said) there was the substance of six good herbals if he but possessed the strength to gather all we beheld.

Being fully spent, as soon as we had satisfied our hunger, we threw ourselves into the hammocks the Indians had prepared for us. Yet did we have but scant repose that night: for a storm began to rage with terrible thunder and lightnings and strong gusts. Heavy rains came down in great torrents and we were put to much labor to protect our gunpowder, slow matches, victuals, and sundry possessions.

On the morning following, the weather waxed reasonable and we went forward once again, already fatigued before the march began. And before the sun had dried our apparel, our shirts and breeches clung wet to our bodies from the steamy heat. Andrés de Vera, the *clérigo*, lifted the skirt of his cassock and secured it in the girdle about his waist, saying that necessity was the superior of modesty.

Early in the afternoon, Balboa sent forward a patrol to scout the country, for we were in the region ruled by the cacique Ponca. They returned shortly before nightfall and informed the General that the principal village and seat of the aforesaid overlord Ponca was only two or three leagues ahead: that the cacique and his vassals, being advertised of our coming, had deserted the town and sought shelter in the forest.

We proceeded therefore to the village and encamped therein:

163

and Balboa ordering a sufficient guard upon every quarter, we slept with the angels, every man giving thanks for shelter and good rest.

Meanwhile, our General (who always entreated the Indians with great patience) sent certain of Chima's men to seek for Ponca, to reassure him that we came in peace: that he had nothing to fear, but ought to return to his town. And to further entice him to amity, he sent him gifts of copper chains, bracelets, and other fine stuff from Castile.

After the space of five days, the cacique appeared with a large retinue. He was of high stature and noble bearing: his long black hair disposed behind the ears. While his henchmen whispered among themselves at our (to their view) strange appearance and manner, Balboa warmly embraced the Indian lord and through the interpreter spoke many fair words, persuading him to friendship and promising him our defence against his enemies.

Ponca (to knit up this knot of concord) gave our General a number of pieces of wrought gold to the weight of one hundred and ten pesos.

Then Balboa (to recompense our gain with another) delivered to Ponca several of our axes to fell trees. And this gift was greatly to the cacique's liking, for those people lacked all metals save gold, and had our instruments of iron in much account.

The aforesaid Ponca also spoke of the Other Sea and privily related to our General many secrets of the land, which he was rejoiced to hear.

We continued in that town yet another week in order that by laying down a good foundation beforehand, all things would go forward in due course: for the most perilous and difficult part of the *entrada* was yet before us.

Twelve of the companions had been seized with fever and continual agues: and the General commanded that these sick men be taken back to Careta, there we had left ninety-six of our company to build a fort. And so they were, being borne thither upon litters carried by the laborers the lord Chima had sent with us.

Then, leaving all things in amity and safety at Ponca's seat, we marched off toward the hazy blue mountains, following the conduct of guides provided us by the overlord of that region. And these scouts made their way forward by secret signs and marks on rocks beside the rivers and trails, which the army of Ponca had used in times past to invade the neighboring dominion of Querequá: for there dwelt warlike and evil Caribs: a people who roasted and ate their enemies. And also they had many times carried away the women and children of Ponca.

As for us that plodded behind those guides, we fared less well than they: for we were strangers to their regions and our passage was much hindered by the thick bushes and prickles of the windings and turnings which they took.

Only Vasco Núñez bore himself in very manly sort: and where even the indigenes were brought to despair, with the meanest of the laborers he laid axe to the matted forest lying in our way.

And one day seeing him thus engaged, Pizarro said to Fabian Perez: "That man is exercised with a demon. And we come to a mountain, he will move it; count with it. If a forest bars our way, he will hew it down. He is no longer a man, Perez. For my part, I will forge no more against his will. His arm has God's strength in it . . . or the Devil's. Look: he has cleared the way."

Thus did we painfully drag ourselves forward. Our clothing mildewed: our wounds festered: and we were blind with nausea, begotten of the noxious vapors that rise from those putrid marshes.

We were likewise plagued by many vipers, which in those parts have six fangs and are very poisonous. Spiders as large as a man's hand, also venomous, came forth from the craggy rocks: and they threatened us constantly with their bites.

Nor found we any secure place of refuge: for if we sought repose in a vale, sudden storms raged in the hills, bringing down upon us a great flood of waters: if we halted on a mountainside at a safe height, many of the companions were stricken with a mysterious sickness, turning pallid and bleeding from the nose and mouth.

"We are cursed by the Devil!" cried Juan Gallego, as we swung perilously, one by one, across a great river by means of big vines that grew at some height on one bank. Then he went weak in the arms and fell into the water and he was in great peril of drowning among the wonderful eddies and strong currents. Yet with God's help, we pulled him upon the shore.

When night season came and we encamped, the sounds of the wilderness were about us like a murmuring sea: and prowling beasts came near: so our fires were kindled: and they shone back

165

like glowing rubies in their eyes. Even our pack of war dogs whimpered: all save battle-scarred Leoncico (the mastiff of Balboa): he growled defiance and pulled at his leash.

I remember the fireflies, infinite to be numbered, like tiny stars twinkling in the black depths of the forest: and the great moths with their moon-white wings, descending like large snowflakes from the darkness to perish in the flames.

Our men rolled restlessly in their hammocks: and some could not sleep, but sat dumbly staring into the campfire.

And even when our bodies rested, our souls did not: for (as Tertullian has delivered) receiving no help from our weary and weakened limbs, they set forth upon their own.

So we slept among our miseries: and our sleep was a perilous journey, wherein the phantoms of our minds walked forth unfranked. And they trembled ahead of us on the shaded footpaths of that dangerous forest. There we do not know what is real and what is a counterfeit. I think I see an Indian kneeling with his bow to release an arrow into my throat: and I run him through with a pike: and afterward they tell me it was our General.

I seem to go back to the home of my childhood: and I see the walls of our garden and doves in the olive orchard, so far, so strangely known. My father is there. And my memory, as always, dresses him in black. His face is stern: and his tiger's eyebrows move upward. He says: "My son, what do you here?" And I do not know what to answer him. Softly the wind stirs in his fine hair and I feel a great melancholy (for I know he is dead).

Then I awake to the other dream, which is our march across this the undiscovered country: to yet another dream beyond the dark sierra: the dream of a swelling sea whose roaring waters foam against those shores of the world's end.

We resumed our march with the breaking of day: and Balboa conferred with the guides respecting what distance we might yet have to traverse: for we had been five days upon the trail: and we were enforced to draw ourselves to harder allowances, wherefore our stomachs had begun to gnaw apace. Also, some of the Indian porters had deserted, taking with them as much of our scant provisions as they could carry away.

Now scorched, suffering from calentures and fluxes: fatigued to

166

a very sweat of death withal, the companions began to despair. Then Vasco Núñez passed among us, with much jollity, heartily cheering us to show courage: and pointing upward from the foothills we had entered, "The final mountains, gentlemen! [says he]. And beyond, the time of our triumph, thanks be to the Blessed Virgin and to your strength."

But they were too weak to answer him and could but murmur faintly among themselves.

As night drew on, our guides halted of a sudden and began to converse excitedly in their Indian tongue. Our Captain-General commanded that the interpreter be sent forward. And, upon questioning the guides, he made known their words and counsel.

"They say that enemies are hiding in the *arroyo* ahead. This is the realm of the cacique Torecha, who is the foe of Ponca."

Upon hearing this, Balboa gave it as his opinion that in our encounter with those man-eating Caribs, we had no shift but to make battle. Therefore, he ordered the firearms put in readiness.

And with slow matches lighted and our targets upon our shoulders, we went forward.

Even as we thus arranged ourselves in good order and prepared ourselves for conflict, the army of Torecha rushed forth with one accord from their hiding place. And with a great noise of shouts, rattles, drums, and the winding of conch horns, they came toward us.

While they were yet a bowshot off, the General ordered our men to discharge the arquebuses. The thunderburst of the guns, accompanied by the sight of their front forces laid low, bloody, and writhing from no visible means, caused the Indians to stay their assault.

And as they hesitated in terror and fear of us (who appeared to have at our command the very powers of heaven) the battle dogs were released. Behind them the Castilians, who but a brief while before were weary unto death, now surged forward, miraculously renewed of spirit and limb, crying: *"Santiago y a ellos!"*

A furious and bloody skirmish ensued, in which great slaughter was made.

We fought like demons amidst the dust kicked up by scuffling feet and through the sulphurous smoke of the guns. And some of the Spaniards of the more nimble sort (being enflamed with battle lust) pursued the fleeing Caribs and with their two-handed swords hewed them to pieces after the manner of butchers at work in the slaughtering pens: from this one his head, from another an arm, from him both legs, from that one a buttock. And some, trailing bloody entrails, yet dragged themselves like writhing serpents into the underbrush. And thus perished in that cruel carnage a great number of those naked Caribs who had come out so proudly against us, their mouths twisted in mockery: they could not prevail against the flesh-tearing quarrels from our crossbows, or the flashing steel of our swords: but their weapons were darts, slings, and lances made of fire-hardened palm wood.

And their lord Torecha had the high honor of being dispatched by Balboa's dog Leoncico, who tore the cacique's head from his body and (as it were) playfully tossed it into the air.

And when we had done in this place all that we had to do, we departed in haste toward the Indian town: for darkness had come and the night stank with the odor of death and the bitter smell of new-spilt blood.

When we arrived in their settlement, our men lighted torches and searched all their *bohios* for loot: and there were great confusion among the people and loud cries of grief for those who had been slain.

Pizarro appeared in front of the cacique's house, driving before him about two score Indians whom we at first took to be women: for they were appareled in bright *enaguas* and adorned with bracelets and pearls after the manner of girls in those parts. But when they drew near, we perceived that they were young men, effeminately decked and of a smooth sort, who had clothed themselves as women.

"Well, General!" cried Pizarro, giving one of the captives a shove toward Vasco Núñez, "look you what strange fish have been caught in our net. Name the creature if you have the proper syllables, and I will announce him to the gentry."

And when our General inquired into the matter, it fell out that those wretches (who were *sabras*, which is to say, nobles of the cacique's own household) were a filthy kind of men, guilty of unnatural lechery. And all of them were of the suit of the cacique's brother, who all his life had worn women's apparel and had applied perfumed ointments to his skin and hair.

168

By report of the other people who dwelt round about, it was disclosed to Balboa that the said brother of Torecha had abused many with outrageous venus. And his crimes were most grave, notorious, and conclusive: all of which and more was confirmed when in his house were found certain statuary ornaments of men coupled in sodomy.

Being thus condemned of committing the abominable sin, and of other vile deeds, those lewd get of the Devil (who in the Indian tongue are called *camayoas*) could only await the just recompense for their great wickedness.

Balboa took counsel with his Captains as to what punishment should be meted out to them. Pizarro said that heaven was too just to allow them any mercy: that they should be put to the slow and torturous death as required by our laws of Castile.

But after earnestly pondering the question, the General shook his head. "Time will not suffer us [said he]: let the dogs judge them."

And so it was accomplished with all care and punctuality. The provost, being a man who rejoiced to rid the world of such pestilence, and desiring to affirm before all, the unhappy end of such evildoers, released them to the ravening dogs one by one, beginning with the cacique's brother.

Their execution being hard by, our ears were greatly assaulted by their screams which (I protest before God) were in the voices of women.

In the cacique's garnering rooms we had good store of smoked fish, hens, bread, and divers sorts of excellent fruits: and greatly refreshed therewith, rested the night.

On the next day following, our General took a force of sixty-six and departed into the final mountains which separated us from the Other Sea. And before setting hence, he ordered the residue of the troops (who were in sore need of repose by reason of great fatigue and sickness) to remain there in the town of Torecha until he would send for them.

We who had the strength and the resolve to march forward, followed the guides whom we had taken in Querequá: and so travelled up between the distant, drawn knees of that mountain until we reached the seat of the cacique Porque. There we found the

169

town empty of habitude, the lord and his vassals having fled at our coming.

We did not tarry in Porque, except to eat of their stores and drink of their artificial wines: but passed on, pursuing our journey with much vigor. Thus did we climb the steep slopes, enduring the labor and evils of many hindrances and chances. The underbrush thinned out, but sharp stones began to appear beneath our feet and these were a grievous affliction to the many who marched barefoot or wearing hempen sandals.

As we went upward, the air freshened and was prickly on our skin.

When night came, we took shelter against the high craggy hills. There we huddled about small fires, marvelling greatly at the brilliance and nearness of the stars, as we stamped our feet to keep warm.

During one encampment, in the dead time of the night, a bird came near and shrilled a half-human cry: and Malpartida (the superstitious fool) discovered in the sound a portent of ill fortune.

"Listen, compañeros: you hear it? [he said, and his countenance disfigured in the firelight]. As I'm a Christian, there is an evil omen in that bird's throat. Does it not say, '*Ya acabó! Ya acabó!*'?"

And opening our ears, we who sat sleepless on a high rock in that dazed air, heard in very truth the words (as of a lost soul calling), "*Ya acabó!*— It is finished!"

But our General (who had the craft of the Devil in him) turned even the cry of that unseen feathered oracle to his own service. With slow, firm strides he came among us: and he spat three times into the fire to dispel the ill luck that Malpartida had pronounced upon us. Then he addressed us: "How is it, *baquianos*, that you who have fought in these lands for the profit of our country and the honor of our holy faith, thus take fright like tame boys at the mere croaking of a nightbird in the forest? What mean these words, then (if indeed they be a message from the darkness)? *What* is finished? What, indeed, but our travails and hungers and the sicknesses of the long journey? Is not the meaning clear: that we have overpassed all that barred us from our ultimate triumph: that this day your eyes will leap with your hearts at the greatest glory ever beheld in these Indies?"

At the first show of clear light among the stars, Balboa ordered us to assemble. We knelt about Padre Vera at his rock altar and received the Holy Sacrament, our hands numb with the cold. Then we ate a scant and hurried portion of roast fowl and cassaba bread.

We set forth upon the trail: and the wet leaves were cold as they brushed our faces: forward, choosing our way with great care, our heads down, the steel of our armor frosted to the touch.

And Francisco Pizarro, squinting his eyes upward, the wind in his goat's beard, mocked: "Your sea is just behind the sun, General!"

We came upon the rocky bed of a stream, now firm and dry: and this we followed upward through the narrow cleft of the hills, and so by main strength and the help of the Virgin, attained to a mesa on the heights. There we tarried to catch our breath: and our eyes turned toward the first aureole of sunlight behind a rounded tor on the left hand. That peak was the shape and likeness of a great shining monstrance: and now the golden rays shone forth upon the sky behind it, as it had been a holy vessel upon the altar of God. And all of us with one consent willingly and joyously gave thanks: for this sight seemed to portend a good success to our enterprise.

And so it did: for about midmorning of that day (which was the 25th of September of that year one thousand five hundred and thirteen) we came to the base of a pyramid-shaped hill, which rose in stately height above those surrounding it. The guides we had from Querequá there affirmed that from the top was visible the great main sea which would be the reward of our long labors and travails.

And immediately upon hearing this, Vasco Núñez commanded all our company to stay: and he went himself alone to the summit. He climbed with all haste (as though the vista there awaiting his gaze might vanish): clawing at the big vines by which he drew himself up that steep hillside, and tripping over the nets of loose creepers which plaited the rocky earth. So he reached the peak and stood still in the wind.

There we who watched below beheld a wonderful thing. Our Captain-General knelt down on both knees upon the ground, then lifted up his arms, looking to heaven in the manner of a saint who sees a vision: and turned and beckoned us to come up: and cried out: and his voice echoed down like a battle cry.

"The sea! The sea!"

Pizarro started forward in great haste saying, "He has indeed discovered the Sea of the South!"

Trotting after him was our friar, Andrés de Vera, who intoned as he ran: "Blessed be God!"

And the soldiers, following upon his heels, answered with a great shout: "Blessed be the Mother of God!"

And when we had ascended to where he was, we beheld in the far distance a large gulf or bay entering into the land: and beyond, the austral sea that reached into the distant sky and shimmered on into its depths. Faint and far, we perceived the foamline on the remote shore: and felt the beating of the surf, that ancient heartbeat of the world. And the companions in great joy embraced each other: and their eyes ran wild and brimmed with tears, which tumbled down their cheeks and glistened in their shaggy beards.

"Look you, *compañeros* [said our Captain-General, stretching forth his arm toward the far-off water], the long-desired sea!"

And he ordered us to kneel there with him and to give thanks and to pray devoutly that we whom Providence had thus allowed to do so great a service to God and to the Most Serene Kings of Castile by discovering a new sea, should also be permitted to learn its great secrets and to possess the riches which lay in that sea and along its coasts.

And when we had done so, he exhorted us to lift up our hearts: and he spoke to us in these words: "You see before you, gentlemen and children mine, how all that we have so earnestly desired is being accomplished. Of that we ought to be certain: we have proven to be true all that King Comogre's son told us of that sea, we who never thought to see it. So I hold it to be certain that what he also told us of there being great treasures in and about it, will likewise be fulfilled.

"As for you, my companions, I say: be loyal to me as you have done in the time past and you will be richer than Kings. All that we have this day looked upon will be to your advantage: and yours will be the highest deeds ever done in the service of the King our lord."

He then in a loud voice proclaimed: "In the name of my Sov-

172

ereigns, I take and seize real and corporeal and actual possession of that Sea of the South and of its islands and firm lands."

When he had uttered these words, he ordered us to raise a certain heap of stones as a token of possession: and he caused a fine, straight tree nearby to be felled, which we fashioned into a True Cross. This we implanted at the same place where that austral sea was first seen. And with a ship's knife, Juan Garcia (a sailor from Guadarmes) carved upon it the names of our Catholic Kings and the date of the discovery: September 25, 1513.

Afterward, he—our General—commanded Andrés de Valderrábano (the royal notary) to write down a true relation of that glorious exploit and to list therein all the names of the sixty-seven caballeros, hidalgos, and worthy men there present.

And he also willed that the gulf whereof we had first had sight from that mountain be called the Gulf of San Miguel, there being only four days remaining before the feast of that archangel.

Padre Vera, whose voice was beautiful as music full of memories, called upon us to conclude those ritual acts with the hymn of the holy doctors of the Church, Ambrose and Augustine. Thus, spreading his big hands, he led the liturgy: and all of us joined with him: "*Te Deum laudamus: Te Deum confitemur. . . .*"

Having done everything in such manner and form as the occasion seemed to require, Vasco Núñez turned and said: "Now, my gallants, let us down to wet our very loins in that sea, before it disappears like the false-followed chimeras of the desert."

Continuing our march, we descended from that bare, high hill, toward the distant shores: and (lest any who came after us might pretend to some claim upon these lands) our Captain-General caused to be inscribed in the bark of trees both upon the right hand and upon the left, the name of our King.

Upon reaching the seat of the cacique called Chiapes, we were threatened by that ruler; for seeing the small number and wretched condition of the invading Christians, he took courage and set upon us with all speed.

Perceiving that words would avail us nought, Vasco Núñez set the companions in battle array, ordering the arquebusiers and war dogs to the forefront, with infantry following.

The ensuing skirmish was brief: for those Indians had never before known gunpowder. And when they heard the thunder of the

173

guns and saw them blaze forth and smelled the brimstone blown by the stiff wind into their midst: then did they quake in terror and flee: and many fell prostrate upon the ground, believing the sulphurous smoke to be the foul breath of evil spirits.

And our Captain-General ordered us to use no extremity, but only to frighten and stay them: for by good policy he hoped to pacify them and to lure them quietly to amity.

Thus we did: and when we entered their town, Balboa caused many of the captives we had taken to be loosed, willing them to go search for their lord and to bring him hither. With them he sent Albitez and a force of twelve men, taking gifts of scissors, combs, hatchets, and a colored shirt for the cacique. Likewise, to reassure them, he sent certain of the guides who had come with us from Querequá.

The cacique Chiapes, being persuaded by all these means, returned to his seat the day following, accompanied by all his vassals who had been hiding in the hills. He brought to Balboa (as a token of his friendship) one fat pig and eighty marcos of fine, wrought gold. And the love and friendship the said Chiapes came to feel toward our Captain-General was the greatest ever seen in these Indies. And at that time when we departed upon our return journey to Antigua, Chiapes was loath to let him go: and with many tears and embracings he entreated him to remain there and to take his—the king's—house and to dwell in it.

Vasco Núñez sent for the guides and laborers which had come with us from Querequá, leading us to the mountaintop whereon we had first taken our view of the sea: and after rewarding them liberally, he dismissed them with hearty thanks, willing them to return to their lord.

Shortly afterward our Captain-General called together twenty-seven of us: and under the conduct of the cacique Chiapes and certain of his retinue, we set forth toward the shores of the new sea.

And on September 29th, that being the feast day of San Miguel the archangel, we came to the edge of that wide bay or gulf which we had seen from afar off. Even at that place, the great sea seemed yet to retreat from us, for the surf did not approach the strand, but was to be reached only across a great space of muddy sand.

Our Captain-General assembled all his men together upon the

dry shore, saying: "Let us stop here." Whereupon, with some surprise, Pizarro asked him whether it was his intent to go alone to the water's edge, as he had gone alone to the hilltop.

And Balboa, with a smile: "No, *hombre*. But do you not see those two canoes, near at hand?"

"Yes: they are of the Indians."

"Why do you believe them beached so far from the water?"

Pizarro then earnestly considered the two boats, which were large craft, too heavy to be carried back and forth so great a distance. "Ha! [cried he] The tide! *Purísima*. It goes out a quarter league!"

"It does indeed [Balboa answered]: and it will return with great suddenness, if I am not deceived. Let us here await its pleasure rather than invite its peril."

We took our repose, therefore, in the shade, until the water without warning rose exceedingly in the sight of all.

Then bidding the companions to await his signal on the shore, Vasco Núñez seized the ensign, which bore upon one side the likeness of the Blessed Virgin and Child and upon the other the royal arms of Castile and León.

Holding that standard aloft in his right hand, and with his unsheathed sword in his left, he strode resolutely into the surf: and the water that splashed from his heels in shining sheets was bright in the sun as his armor which he had burnished to gleaming silver. A soft wind played in the scarlet plumes of his morion as he walked, his eyes fixed upon the great white clouds along the sea's far rim. And thus he began the act of possession, that he had engraved upon his memory like a prayer:

"Long live the most high and mighty monarchs, Don Fernando and Doña Juana, Sovereigns of Castile, of León, of Aragon, in whose names and for the royal Crown of Castile, I take real and corporeal and actual possession of these austral seas, and lands, and coasts, and ports, and islands, and everything annexed to them: and of the kingdoms and provinces which appertain to them in whatever manner or by whatever reason or title might or could exist, in times past, present, or yet to be, without any contradiction.

"And if any other Prince or Captain, Christian or infidel, of whatever law or sect or condition he may be, pretend to any right to these lands and seas, I am ready and prepared to deny him and to defend them in the names of the Castilian Sovereigns, present and future, whose is the empire and dominion over these Indies, islands, and Tierra Firme, to the north and south, with all their seas, both at the Arctic and Antarctic poles, on both sides of the equinoctial line, whether within or without the Tropics of Cancer and Capricorn—so that each thing and part of it belong and appertain most completely to Their Highnesses and to their successors, as I declare more at length by writ, setting forth all that may be said or can be said and alleged in behalf of their royal patrimony, both now and in all time to come, so long as the world endures, and until the final day of judgement of all mankind."

Having thus addicted to the dominion of Spain that wide sea with all the lands adjacent thereunto, Balboa (who now stood with the glittering waves lapping around his knees) beckoned to us to enter the water.

And all of us with loud cries rushed panting into that alluring sea: and we plunged our hands into the spilling flood as something new: and wetting our lips, we tasted salt: whereupon we hopped about, splashing fistfulls of the frothy brine into each other's faces, and giving thanks that we had reached our longed-for goal.

For who were we to be the first Christians to step foot into that infinite blue at the world's far end? Consider how we were men of but small wit and knowledge: among us were no noblemen, no bachellors of law, no royal chamberlains, no commanders of Alcantara or Calatrava. No: there was Pizarro, the bastard swineherd: Padre Andrés, a humble friar: Baracaldo, the Biscayan carpenter: Beas, the half-breed: Morales, a common soldier: and I, Juan of Toledo, of small credit and acompt.

"Gentlemen of Spain," Vasco Núñez addressed us, still holding the banner aloft, "I call upon you to witness and to give your oaths. Do you here acknowledge and attest that the Serene Monarchs of Castile have absolute dominion over this and every other part of these Indies, discovered or yet to be discovered?"

And in one voice, as though replying to a catechist, we answered: "We so swear."

"Are you prepared, by your word and by your honor, to defend these lands against any arms, Christian or infidel, who may threaten from any quarter whatsoever?"

"We are ready."

"Then let Valderrábano set down your names and your oaths."

When we returned to land, Vasco Núñez drew a dagger from his belt and with it cut a cross in the trunk of a tree growing on the shore. Into the cruciform incision, he then dashed a handful of water from the sea, to dedicate and confirm the possession he had taken of it. He repeated the ceremony with two other trees, so that there should be three in honor of the Holy Trinity.

Then all the companions who were there carved many crosses in other trees, while darting birds among the branches sang with great sweetness, affirming with us that glorious act of possession.

And all that we did that day is deserving of eternal memory.

Chapter II ∼∼∼∼∼∼∼∼∼∼∼∼∼∼∼∼∼∼∼∼∼∼∼∼∼∼

In those regions of that austral sea, the fury of the North and South winds was to be feared at that time of the year: and, associate with mighty rolling thunder and the quick flaring up of great lightnings, hindered our passage along those coasts and among the islands.

The two Indian lords of those lands (Chiapes and Tumaca) exhorted Balboa to defer his enterprise until a more quiet season. And after considering the speech of these caciques and weighing the matter, he resolved to wait until the coming of Spring or Summer to build ships wherewith we might embark upon the new sea.

We therefore went forward with our journey back to Darien: and our Captain-General determined to return by another way than we had taken hither. And here do I overpass many marvellous and tragic things which we endured, lest I should be tedious in relating them.

Neverless, I cannot forbear to mention the great commodity which by our exploit chanced to the whole Christian world: nor by what skill and knowledge Vasco Núñez pacified and brought to loyalty and friendship, every Indian domain traversed by our company. And all the Kings thereof did him much honor, willingly laying before him in tribute princely treasures of gold and orient pearls (some of them as big as beans and olives).

And though we endured much perilous labor and great jeopardies, marching thither in the season of raging storms, not one of the companions was lost to misadventure or to the weapons of hostile Indians. No other Captain who ever came out to these Indies (nor indeed will ever come) has done as well.

When we arrived at the seat of the lord Ponca, we met in that town four Castilians from Antigua: and from them we had the news that two ships had newly arrived from Española, laden with provisions and men desirous to be enrolled with Balboa's forces.

Upon receiving this information, Vasco Núñez hastened his journey as much as he might: and having come to the town of Careta, he there embarked upon the brigantine we had left in that port.

So did we come to anchor in the estuary of Darien on Friday, January 19th, of the year 1514.

Upon our return to the loyal and Spanish city of Santa Maria de la Antigua there was proclaimed a day of public rejoicing. And all who inhabited that place (Indians and Castilians alike) danced, feasted, and sang with sweet delight to celebrate the great triumph of our discovery.

We put away our murderous swords and with shouts and laughter seized in our brawny arms the young girls with their bare breasts and scented hair. Awkwardly we stamped our feet and clapped our hands to the measure of their flutes and drums: and our hearts throbbed: and all of us turned loose our joy as guests at a wedding banquet.

The whole fiesta was sweetened by the division of spoils. Our Captain-General had the goods and treasure of our conquest brought to the town square and there displayed to the sight of all: the great mound of lustrous pearls, such as Cleopatra might have envied: and divers other things esteemed by us: as well as the large quantity of gleaming gold which amounted to forty thousand pesos.

These profits and avails were all equitably divided among the compañeros, with a just share given to those who had been sick or remained behind at the General's order. It was Balboa's desire that, beside the royal fifth, we also set apart as a gift to the King two hundred of the finest and largest pearls that he might the more favor our future conquest of the lands we had already added to his dominion by our discovery of the main sea.

180

And so it was affirmed by the general voice and consent of the multitude.

Then our Captain-General spoke to us of all we had accomplished in these new lands, and of what yet remained for us to do. And he recalled to us how he had said to the dying and defeated men of San Sebastián that here on the western side of the gulf was a great river and good land: how they had answered him with the heart-sick cry: "To Darien! To Darien!"

That here we had with wonderful speed and skill raised up a good town, being set in orderly streets of reasonable length: and the whole villa cast into grounds of gardening and orchards.

Further (said he) there was peace in these parts. A Christian might walk alone into the forest and return with no wound save the scratches of briars. Thirty caciques, great and small, paid tribute from the wilderness regions, their people trafficking with us and dwelling among us with easy hearts by reason of our using them with all kindness and favor.

That we had accomplished a thing of infinite difficulty in our *entrada* and great discovery just past: and would continue and expand that great enterprise in the days to come. And he held it to be certain that our gracious Sovereign would reward us with many honorable gifts and privileges for those high deeds.

Then with one accord we lauded and amplified his name and honor: and we proclaimed him not only a great and valorous Captain, but also a master shepherd who had saved us from the wolves.

And the Indians also (who were present) gladly crowned him with a diadem of cane and bright feathers: and, with a great noise of drums and rattles, named him Elder Brother and Warrior of the Sun. (I say) no laureled Caesar of ancient Rome ever had more pomp and homage at men's hands.

Shortly after we had thus celebrated our good fortune and done our devoir to our gallant leader, a caraval arrived at Darien, bearing thither a certain *visitador* named Pedro de Arbolancha. And the said official had been sent by the King to determine the exact state of affairs in Tierra Firme. For the Bachelor Enciso and the villainous Colmenares had greatly stirred the wrath of our Sovereign by their false reports concerning Balboa (whom they had se-

181

cretly vowed to ruin), saying that he had ravaged the country like a wolf.

Upon hearing these great lies, His Highness had resolved to establish a new government in Darien: and to that end he had appointed as Governor that Pedro Arias de Ávila, of whom Martín de Zamudio had informed us in his letter.

The *cédula* which Arbolancha brought was not addressed (as before) to "Vasco Núñez de Balboa, our Governor and Captain," but to "The squires and worthy men, our vassals who are in the settlement of Darien and in whatever other part of the provinces of Urabá and Veragua."

And, after making known his will that we continue in our conquest of the new lands, the King wrote: "I will very shortly send an illustrious personage who will have charge of the government of that land, with whom will go such an armada and supplies for you that the pacification of those regions may be carried out as will be conducive to God's service and to ours, and to the good of the people there."

Enlarging upon the information contained in the *cédula*, Arbolancha made known to us the size of the aforesaid armada: perhaps two score ships, carrying two thousand new settlers.

We were also given to understand that the royal officials who would govern in the future had already been named: that they were one and all persons of account, who had good connections, to be sent out from Spain with the same Pedro Arias. In all likelihood, not a single important office would be held by any of the old settlers—we who had taken the land by fire and blood, and had brought to success our great enterprises by perilous and chargeable labors.

Hearing this, the *vecinos* began to grumble among themselves: and we forcefully made known to the *visitador* our misliking of the way matters stood.

And he (being a man who had been trafficking in these Indies above ten years) signified to us that he was fully in accord with our opinion. For (he said) he had heard very good reports of Balboa, in both Española and Cuba before coming hither to Darien. He put us in good comfort and promised that when he returned to Spain, his report to the King would enlarge the ears of His Highness and gladden his heart to hear of the merits and services of Balboa and of us as loyal vassals and worthy men.

It was now too late (he said) to petition the King to withdraw the appointments he had already made for the *gobernación* of Darien: for it was very likely that the armada had already sailed from Castile. Nevertheless, the great exploit of discovery which our Captain-General had brought to a happy conclusion had laid upon the King an obligation to favor him and to reward him. Therefore we ought to beg of His Highness that he create a new government in the lands adjoint to the new-found sea, over which he should give authority to Vasco Núñez as being justly his due as discoverer.

This we did: and when Valderrábano had written down the said petition (in which we certified the King how greatly Vasco Núñez had served His Highness and the ability he had to serve better than anyone else) all the *vecinos* set their names or marks thereto.

And Arbolancha thought well of it, wherefore he then and there turned over to Vasco Núñez the full cargo of his ship, the *Buen Jesús*, to be sold and the profits therefrom to be used for our South Sea enterprise.

Then the said Arbolancha hoisted up his sails and set forward on his voyage to Española and thence to Spain, carrying a map and full account of our great discovery: the royal quinto and gift of pearls: as well as our petition for a new *gobernación*.

Our Captain-General commanded that all necessary things be done to put our villa in good order and appearance, against the coming to Darien of the King's armada and the new governor, Pedro Arias.

And Balboa himself, ready as always to do that which he had required of us, set to work with his own hands to help certain Indian laborers repair the roof of his house.

He was thus engaged when he beheld coming through the principal plaza toward him a young officer in plumed morion and burnished bright mail, escorted by Valderrábano and two other *vecinos*. In the fiery sun of these lands, the skin of the newly arrived captain looked marvellously pink and tender.

Having come to Balboa's house, Valderrábano pointed to

Vasco Núñez (who was apparelled in cotton shirt and drawers, with hempen sandals on his feet) among the Indian workers on the roof.

And the aforesaid Captain looked up, wrinkling his nose and squinting in the bright sunlight: "Eh, where? I do not see him."

He did indeed see Vasco Núñez before him: but he could not believe that a person of that description could possibly be Vasco Núñez de Balboa, whom his enemies had pictured as a rich and pampered tyrant, battening on the wealth of the Indies.

Then, moving forward to look down upon them, Balboa said: "I am he."

The cavalier could not, even then, accept the man he there beheld as the Captain-General of Darien. Cautiously, he asked: "You are Vasco Núñez de Balboa?"

"At your orders."

The young Captain straightened to a more military stance. "I come to announce the arrival of Don Pedro de Ávila, by His Highness's grace, now Governor of Darien." And, when Balboa remained silent upon hearing this news, the Captain asked hopefully: "He is not welcome then?"

Vasco Núñez then quickly answered him: "Say to Don Pedro that he is welcome in Darien. This is a lawful town. I and those whom I govern yield ourselves to his new office."

"Ah, you are wise, señor," the Captain purred, glancing about the town with contempt. "The Governor comes with an armada of twenty-two sails and a company of eighteen hundred men."

Vasco Núñez earnestly weighed these words. Pedrarias came with the largest and best-manned armada that had ever passed over to these Indies. And in command was a man of whom Zamudio had advertised him: "It's little else than the toe of his boot he will treat you to."

"We carry a friend of yours," the Messenger-Captain was saying in his whirring voice. "It will surely please you to welcome him also."

"Of whom do you speak?"

"Of the Bachelor Martín Fernandez de Enciso." And the young officer cackled with laughter as though he had made a great jest.

Valderrábano repeated soberly: "Enciso returns?"

"Yes: and in his belt the King's writ for restitution of his goods

184

in Darien. But I go ahead of my donkey. I must return to the Governor with my report. Good day, General." And he lingered sneeringly over the title. Then he bowed to the *vecinos*, turned, and started back down the street with light, jaunty steps.

The *vecinos* (companions of hunger and miseries: veterans of a hundred battles in the hills and evil swamps of these new lands) stood in silence, looking after the glittering figure of the departing officer. And they turned their gaze upon one another, remarking the shabby doublets and dull, warped boots each wore. Then speechlessly they raised their eyes to our valiant Captain.

But he, too, sat in silence, staring sadly down the empty street.

On the next day following, Don Pedro Arias de Ávila disembarked, together with all his great company of grandees, masters of orders, royal administrators, *escuderos*, and worthy men.

After coming on shore they arrayed themselves in very good order, so that it was a thing worth seeing, which looked well in every part.

Thus prepared for their march from the estuary to the villa of Santa Maria, they set forth.

Leading the stately and magnificent procession was Don Pedro, seated regally upon a richly caparisoned sable charger whose housings were made of satin, lined with taffeta. His Highness had exempted the Governor and his wife from our sumptuary laws, granting them all privileges in dress. Accordingly, Pedrarias entered his territory apparelled like a monarch: for he wore a cape of gold over scarlet, with galooned border: satin breeches and velvet doublet: and at his side swung an elegant sword in a jewelled scabbard.

His wife, Doña Isabel de Bobadilla y Peñalosa, who rode beside him, was no less splendidly turned out. Her gold-embroidered gown, brocade bodice, flashing jewels, and pearl-encrusted gloves were all of a quality that the Queen herself could have been proud to wear.

Following them came the ecclesiastical entourage: the new Bishop of Darien in his bright purple and gold vestments, flanked by priests, seculars, friars, and a crucifer bearing aloft a massive silver crucifix.

Next in order of rank came the Crown officials: treasurer, *conta-*

dor, factor, chief justice, *veedor, alguacil mayor.* And all of them very gallant, with silk upon silk, and many pinkings and cuts.

They were closely followed by their assistants and lesser functionaries, also attired in similar braveries: and vying with each other to present a splendid spectacle, the like of which had never been seen in these vaporous forests of the Indies.

The cavalry in their bright armor and shiny casques, the well-ordered ranks of infantry, bearing new weapons of the latest design: the rows of burnished halberds in the sun: the drum and trumpet corps: the great banners of brilliant damask in all colors, and the armorial pennants of noble houses: who could behold these things and not feel the imperial power of our Sovereign close at hand?

In diminishing importance at the end of the procession came the ship's officers, mariners, merchants, mistresses, camp followers, and slaves.

As for ourselves, we of Santa Maria de la Antigua, we made a good array behind Vasco Núñez and marched forth to welcome those who had come to usurp our places. We were a shabby power in our rusted cuirasses, stained doublets, and worn-out apparel. Balboa's order was to go unarmed. So did we pass forward as soldiers stayed for some crime or disarmed in defeat.

And as we went, our Captain spoke to me in a quiet sort thus: "It appears that Malpartida had reason: that wild bird which called *'Ya acabó!'* had for us an evil prophecy, which has now shown itself to be of very truth. Here before your eyes, Juanito, you see the forces that will crush the nations of these regions. They will swarm over them, leaving behind a bare, unfruitful earth. Crazed with greed, they will sack every village, murder every cacique, burn every cornfield. Having thus ravished all the new lands, they will turn and cross swords with each other."

When we had come to the main plaza, we there awaited the arrival of Pedrarias and his troupe. And when they were come, Vasco Núñez made a brief oration of greeting.

Though the Governor responded with a bow and the grace of a cavalier, there were flints of malice in his eyes. (For his messenger had already informed him that Balboa had discovered the Other Sea.)

Don Pedro's page helped him to dismount. And the great Royal Standard having been planted in the square, he presented the other officials who, with him, were to have at their command all things in Darien.

"The very reverend Father in Christ, Juan de Quevedo . . . Don Alonso de la Puente, treasurer: Don Diego Marquez, *contador*: Juan de Tavira, factor: Licentiate Gaspar de Espinosa, chief judge: the Bachelor Martín Fernandez de Enciso, whom you all know: he is to be *alguacil mayor.*"

The mellowness of Enciso's sneer was altogether courtly. He had, as he had said, returned to Santa Maria to avenge himself of the injustice he claimed had been done him. And on that day he did in truth appear to be a personage of importance: his doublet decorated with thread of pure gold and neatly padded to widen the shoulder: and cut low at the neck and laced over a patterned stomacher.

Don Pedro waved to the heralds. They raised their trumpets (whose gonfalons were of crimson damask, adorned by the celebrated artist, Cristobal de Morales): and they sounded a loud, clear flourish. Silence fell over the multitude.

Gaspar de Espinosa then took from his belt the royal letter-patent, which he read to all there assembled. It charged us "to receive Don Pedro Arias de Ávila as Governor of Castilla de Oro (for so had the King now re-named Tierra Firme), forasmuch as the said Pedro Arias was empowered by royal decree and with the consent of the Council of Indies, to administer, govern, control, command. . . ."

Vasco Núñez de Balboa was once again a common soldier.

Being schooled in the most subtle deceits of the court in Castile, Pedrarias did not judge it meet to inform Vasco Núñez that His Highness (pricked on by the false reports of Enciso and others) had ordered an official inquiry into all his acts since the time of his taking office in Darien.

The said *residencia* was to last for the space of sixty days: and any complaint against Balboa was to be given proper credence: that is to say, his property could be seized and turned over to any of his enemies who asked for it.

"When the sixty days of *residencia* are completed [the *cédula* continued], send the aforesaid to us with all the information you have obtained as to the manner in which the said Vasco Núñez de

187

Balboa, together with other officials, have used and exercised their respective offices. If they have done unjust injury to anyone, let the plaintiffs be given full justice, and repay the injured for what they have suffered, using for such purpose the chattels of those who have injured them. Make redress and render judgement. Arrest the guilty and place them in chains: and well-guarded at their own expense, send them to us, together with the findings against them."

But Don Pedro was a cunning man. He spoke many sweet words to our Captain, praising his accomplishments and promising friendship.

"For you see, my friend [said he], I require more than aught else the help of a predecessor as skilled in governing as you have shown yourself to be. Also, there remains that great enterprise of the Sea of the South, which you have so gloriously begun. In this it is my desire to favor you as I know it to be also the King's will and pleasure."

To these fair words Vasco Núñez answered doubtfully: "His Highness is not displeased with me then?"

"Displeased? Troth, Captain: the reports to him swell with a surfeit of your good services and merit."

"But I have received notices that Enciso won a case against me at court: and that I have been cried down as a usurper: and that he inflamed the Council against me."

"*Vaya!* [says Pedrarias, his foxy smile spread across his countenance] Your proven facts give an ugly face to his complaints. His Highness gave him a big ear because he does not relish malcontents at court. An empty honor for Enciso, a job for young Espinosa to boast about in letters to Salamanca. But what is more harmless? As for you and me, we will pay them no more heed than they were gypsies."

So spoke he with the Devil's own craft, as one speaks who is a falsifier of measures or a seducer of women, sliding the words out as easily as an adder's tongue from the shadows.

And our Captain: "You are truly of a mind to facilitate us and to give us favor and help in our enterprise?"

"Can you doubt it, *Señor*? [asks Don Pedro, knitting his heavy brows in surprise] "In whatever will be of service to the King our lord, count me your warmest confidant. Now . . . if you will sub-

188

mit to me a complete account of your plans, and a report of that country that lies between here and the other sea. I do assure I will run all hazards to have your designs carried out to the ultimate completion."

And Vasco Núñez, who had for so long a time treated with the Indians (whose promises were kept): and because there was no guile in him, perceived not the treachery of the Governor, but was persuaded by his good discourse.

So he prepared a true and full account of all that had happened in Darien and the lands beyond: and he set down other secrets of the country which only he knew, such as gold-bearing streams: the villages where victuals and rest would be provided to Christians by friendly caciques: maps of the ways to be followed to the austral sea: and many other things that were needful for discovery and pacification of the unknown territories.

The said report required two days for the writing down thereof: and, when it was complete, Vasco Núñez took it to Pedrarias and gave it to him.

Then (such was the villainous and scheming nature of the man) as soon as he possessed the memorial aforesaid, he ordered Balboa taken and lodged in jail to await the conclusion of his *residencia*.

Chapter 12 ～～～～～～～～～～～～～～～

Vasco Núñez, by reason of the *residencia* ordered by the King and prolonged by his enemies, was reduced to grievous penury and despair.

Pedro Arias, one of the chief benefactors of the iniquity thus imposed, had taken for his own Balboa's house: and had conveyed himself into it three days after his arrival in Darien, together with his large retinue of servitors, retainers, and family.

The remainder of the Captain-General's property was seized in the King's name and his money disbursed to any of his accusers who put an official claim against it.

As for the demands of Enciso, they were so excessive as to become impossible to entertain.

"To honor the Bachelor's claims declared Chief Judge Espinosa] it would scarcely suffice to hand over to him the whole territory. And even if all the inhabitants, Indian and Christian, were likewise given to him as slaves, he would not yet be fully recompensed, according to his demands."

Concerning the charges against Vasco Núñez that he was responsible for the death of Diego de Nicuesa, the Chief Judge ruled that all the *vecinos* were of equal guilt in that affair. And, as it would be both rash and calamitous for the settlement, to imprison every *baquiano* in Darien, his decision was to dismiss the case.

Pedrarias, Enciso, and the Bachelor Corral greatly misliked this judgement and loudly proclaimed against it (for they had hoped devoutly for a death sentence or at the very least that Vasco Núñez would be returned to Castile).

Whereupon, Espinosa asked Pedrarias never to forget the will and commandment of the King, to wit, that the Chief Judge was to have sole authority in all judicial matters in Tierra Firme, and that he, Pedrarias, had been strictly enjoined from meddling in any *proceso* of whatever kind or intent.

He required the Governor, therefore, to deliver into his hands the memorandum of a certain *pesquisa* or secret investigation which had been conducted into the affairs of the former Captain-General.

Moved by a desire to render justice (a virtue which was lost to him afterward), and by the constant intercessions of Bishop Quevedo and even of Doña Isabel de Bobadilla on Balboa's behalf, Espinosa released our Captain from prison. He could not, however, restore to him his lands and dwelling.

And while he was thus made to find shelter in one of the poorest houses in Antigua, that which he had foreseen on the day of flags and trumpets, the rapacious men of Pedrarias had brought to pass in the land: the cruelties, the destruction, the many deaths.

In time, their vicious deeds and excesses will be known to all the world. Alas, it will be too late.

The men who had come over with high hopes of easy gain, fell under the fatal blights of this country, against which they were in no wise prepared to resist. Plague and famine took many: still they died, more than twenty a day. And it was a thing of sore distress, for their graves were dug in the shape of huge holes, to contain a score of dead Christians at one burial.

The storerooms were almost empty, the fields left barren. The ships had sprung leaks for want of proper care, and many of them would sail upon the ocean sea no more.

As for the Indians, they were all hostile: for they had been stirred up by the gross inhumanities of the Captains Ayora and Morales and Enciso, whom Pedrarias had sent forth upon *entradas*, following Balboa's charges in all save their wretched treatment of the indigenes.

Five such *entradas* were carried out without delay, in the expectation of immediate gain and because Pedrarias wished beforehand to deny to Vasco Núñez whatever grace might be granted to him by the King when he had news of our great discovery: for the Governor hoped to oppose such favors by arguing that Balboa had only seen the other coasts, whereas he—Pedro Arias—had explored and settled them.

Yet such was the greed and cruelties of him and of the men he sent out, that nothing was garnered in all those enterprises save a small amount of gold and the eternal hatred of the Indians. For the ties of friendship with the natural inhabitants of those regions, which our General had been at great pains to form and make to flourish, had been severed forever in the space of three months.

The most notorious of all the spoilers (for they were nothing more) that Pedrarias had unleashed upon the Indians, was a certain Juan de Ayora, the Governor's own lieutenant.

Ayora led a company of two hundred men-at-arms into the province of Comogra. There Panquiaco (now cacique, for his father had died) who had first informed us of the Other Sea, greeted the Castilians with gifts and words of amity.

Nevertheless, being a man of wonderful judgement, the aforesaid Panquiaco presently perceived that the beast-like Ayora (despite his sweet words) did not come from the same litter as Vasco Núñez. And he did so declare, saying that the new lord did not much resemble the great Tiba, who was his friend and elder brother.

And indeed, he was shortly shown how true his estimation was. For when the Spaniards had eaten their fill at a feast provided by the Indians for the Christians, Captain Ayora arose, stretched his limbs, belched, and ordered his men to seize Panquiaco and his guard.

After these Indians had thus been bound, Ayora told Panquiaco he must produce a great quantity of gold, or he would be thrown to the dogs.

In a great tumult and fury, the men of Comogra then set upon the Spaniards without care for their own lives. They were quickly subdued in a battle of blood and fire, but in the confusion and fighting Panquiaco escaped.

But such was the will of God, the unfortunate youth, who fled into the territory of his father's old enemy Pocorosa, was captured by the Indians of that region and cruelly put to death.

Of those Indians who fell into Ayora's hands, some were slowly roasted alive: others were thrown to the dogs, who tore them to pieces: and still others were put to torture in a vain effort to make them reveal the hiding place of more gold.

Captain Ayora spared only a few men for slaves, and a certain number of lusty young girls, whom he took for the pastime and pleasure of his men.

From the territory of Comogra, he passed into that of Pocorosa. There, after laying waste to the land, and killing the inhabitants who resisted his advance, he seized the cacique and put him in chains.

He then directed his course to Tubanamá. And being himself mounted upon a spirited charger, he amused himself along the way by riding at great speed toward the Indian porters, who, terrified by the plunging hooves, took flight. And as they ran for their lives, he urged his horse forward and impaled them upon his lance, in the manner of one riding in a joust.

After almost three months of this kind of bloody ravage and treachery, Ayora returned to Darien. There, before any division of gains could be made, he and a band of his familiars set sail secretly at night in a stolen caravel for Spain, taking with them most of the loot from their monstrous enterprises.

Greed, cruelties, crimes, bad faith, failures—a great extravagance of much suffering and little profit. Can such be God's will, or is it the work of Satan?

And, whereas the Indians were formerly like lambs, they now became like fierce lions, and were driven to such daring that, where in times before they were wont to come out to Balboa and his men with gifts, they now lay in ambush for all Christians. Where one Castilian might formerly walk alone and unarmed in the forest, two score could not go now, though they carried all manner of weapons.

Even in his treatment of the Castilians, whom he ruled, Pedrarias and his officials manifested a heartless severity that would shame the most barbarous nations.

While Christians dropped dead of starvation in the streets, the royal factor, Juan de Tavira, kept under heavy guard in the official storehouses a great abundance of cassaba meal, pork, corn, oil, onions, garlic, and other victuals.

And the said Tavira had turned away the famished and dying

194

men of his own land with the cold words: "I am not permitted to give away Crown property."

Thus, the officials of the *gobernación*, not lacking food for themselves, had no pity on the others.

And when a fire had destroyed a large depository in Antigua, a rumor ran through the settlement that Tavira had put the torch to it with his own hand to conceal shortages of Crown goods, which he had sold for his personal gain.

Yet, while crimes and injustices thus went unpunished in high places, the iniquities of the low-born or penniless were treated with great severity.

Thus, the shameful proceedings against one Diego de Cuenca, a common soldier, found guilty of stealing from a royal storehouse a cotton jacket worth little more than one ducat.

When the offense was made known to him, Pedrarias said that he would enquire into the matter himself. And when he found that none of his own following was guilty of it, he meted out the death sentence to the offender, saying that too many months had passed without an execution and that his lenity had given some persons the stomach to mischief.

The harsh sentence was carried out publicly before a large assembly in the plaza "as a just recompense for his evil acts [said Pedro Arias] and that the said Cuenca might give example and fear to others so they may be deterred to do the like."

And with the special consent and good liking of his officers and the Chief Judge, the Governor ordered that his surgeon, Dr. Rodrigo de Barreda, after the execution should perform a public autopsy on the body of the aforesaid unfortunate Cuenca.

When the surgery chest was brought to the principal plaza and opened in full view of the assembled company, they pressed closer to examine the strange assortment of implements, buzzing with wonder and curiosity.

Dr. Barreda, who was pleased to demonstrate his skill with his tools and his knowledge of anatomy, began with a learned discourse upon disease, the bones, nerves, veins, and arteries.

"I hold it to be well assured [he said with confidence, the razor held expertly in his hand, ready to execute his task] that when I discover to you the body's cavity, it will be found to hold much sanious humor, which causes corruption in the whole body by reason of the vapors that rise from it and are carried to the heart, muscles, and other parts. These fuliginous vapors arise from impure and even poisonous food which, it is clearly apparent, the deceased was wont to ingest. . . ."

But death and dismemberment were of scant novelty to us who thought too often of the companions that had perished in an ugly and lamentable way, with their bowels breaking forth from their bellies.

So we turned from that throng of cruel and evil people, who twisted their necks like vultures surrounding carrion: and we cried out to the Holy Mother of God for the shame of it.

In December of that year there came to Darien letters from our King, which greatly advantaged Balboa, but forever sealed the hatred which Pedrarias secretly had for him.

One of the letters, which was sent to Balboa by our Sovereign, praised him for his high deeds and promised him many honorable and friendly parts. And here follows the said epistle:

"*The King*: To Vasco Núñez de Balboa.

"Miguel de Pasamonte, our Treasurer General of the Indies, has sent forward to me copies of two letters you sent him, saying that they are duplicates of those you wrote to me on March 12th of this year, and which are being brought to me by Arbolancha.

"Because Arbolancha has not yet arrived, and I am awaiting his coming to take the proper steps with respect to what is necessary to be done for that region, as well as for what concerns you, this will serve only to tell you how greatly I was rejoiced to read your letters and to learn of the things you discovered in those regions of Tierra Nueva de la Mar del Sur and the Gulf of San Miguel, for which I give our Lord much thanks in the hope that it will all be in His service. I am grateful to you and I deeply appreciate your labor in achieving what you have done, as that of a most true and loyal servitor. And I also hold in service all those who went with you on that journey, and the hardships and hunger and suffering you and they endured. And since it has been so great a service to God and to us, and to the welfare and profit of these realms, you may certainly expect that you and they will be well rewarded and remunerated, and that I will always hold in mind your services and theirs, with the result that you will receive favors. And concerning yourself, I will so dispose that you be honored and your services recompensed, for in truth I well comprehend that in everything you have undertaken, you have done very well.

"It has also been pleasing to me to know how you treated the Indian caciques on that march with kindness and good will, leaving them well disposed, since that will cause them, and others elsewhere, to do that which will be in our service.

"When your letters came Pedrarias had already departed with the armada I had ordered sent to that land of Castilla del Oro, to which he goes as our Captain-General and Governor. Now I am writing to him to look after your interests and to favor you and to treat you as a person whom I greatly desire to please, and who has greatly served and is serving me: and I am certain that he will do so.

"You, as a service to me, until such time as I send orders as to how you shall further serve me (which, if it please God, will be soon), help him and counsel him in what he should do, with that good will and disposition that you have shown till now and as I expect of you. And even if he does not ask you about everything, be vigilant yourself to advise and counsel him in what you think should be done. And in the matter of fortifications and other things that you feel should be done, including roads and the like, we will hold it in service that you make your ideas known to Pedrarias: because I am writing him to the effect that whatever you think best, should be done there.

"Valladolid, the nineteenth of August
one thousand five hundred and fourteen. I, THE KING."

And to Pedro Arias, the Governor, the King wrote another letter, commanding him to consult with Vasco Núñez concerning all decisions he might make touching upon the government in Darien.

His Highness yielded for reason that our Captain, because of his great experience in things of the Indies, could not fail to hit the mark in everything he undertook.

"As you already know (wrote the Catholic King) Vasco Núñez has served us very well in what he has discovered as well as in everything else he has undertaken: and I regard him as a very good servitor and wish to favor him and to recompense him as his serv-

197

ices merit. Therefore, I command and charge you to use him very well and to favor him in all things that concern him."

After the King had thus informed Pedro Arias that he would judge the Governor's will to serve him by the good he did Vasco Núñez, he was evermore maliciously minded against Balboa: and his hostility grew apace until it was an all-consuming fire.

Considering this state of affairs, it will not seem strange that, when two caravels arrived from Spain on March 20th of 1515, bringing the King's promised reward for Vasco Núñez, Pedrarias intercepted it and sought to conceal it.

The said armada also carried provisions in a most plentiful manner, which His Highness had appointed to supply Balboa's pretended expedition to the new sea: but the Governor retained possession of these things, which he used to furnish the ravaging and useless *entradas* of his own Captains.

As for the two royal *cédulas* which the King had sent to Balboa (as it was afterward disclosed) they were brevets bestowing upon him the title of Adelantado of the South Sea (which he had discovered): and appointing him Governor of the provinces of Panamá and Coiba.

These decrees Don Pedro hid among certain other papers in his house: but it was a weak policy in him that he could not conceal any secret for a very great space of time. And when the Bishop (who was Balboa's good friend and constant advocate) was privily informed of how matters stood, he was very instant with Pedrarias that he deliver the King's *cédulas* forthwith. And from the pulpit he predicated upon the great iniquity—yes, and peril—of countermanding any judgement of our Sovereign. For (said he) such an act was not only treason against the Crown, but also a threat to the liberty of every free vassal in Darien.

Whereat, the people began to talk of it among themselves and to ask what black conjuration of that rotting boar Pedrarias (such were their own words) had moved the Bishop to sermonize upon it.

And when the Governor could no longer still the sundry conjectures and the bruit and muttering of the matter, he summoned his officials to meet in council, saying that he would there resolve the whole affair with their consent and good liking (for he well knew that those who sat in council with him, save for the Bishop, were of the same mind as he).

He then laid bare the writs of ennoblement by which our gracious King had rewarded Balboa for his most remarkable deeds: and he asked each member of the Council to give his opinion, which they all did in the manner following:

Alonso de la Puente, Treasurer: "It seems to me, gentlemen, that His Highness would be best served, and for that, spared the certain embarrassment of having too hastily conferred this honor, if we withhold the writ until that time His Highness has in his hands the complete findings against this Vasco Núñez de Balboa."

Diego Marquez, Accountant-General: "Puente has said it well. Never have I known His Highness, who is a just monarch, to reward treason such as that we have found in the acts of Balboa, with lands and titles. Let the brevet be withheld, say I."

Gaspar de Espinosa, Chief Judge: "The law for common warrants—and is this document more than a warrant, *señores?*—is that prisoners held incommunicado are to receive only direct reprieves, and all other *cédulas* are to be withheld until said prisoner's release or trial. Is the matter not clear, then? Not only do we have past violations by this man, Balboa: he is, at this moment, a just prisoner, held incommunicado for a late act of conspiracy. Only a reprieve requires immediate delivery. This writ would be subject to deferment."

Juan de Tavira, Factor: "By your leave, caballeros, I dare venture no opinion. I am unlearned in pronouncements of the law. Therefore, as you, schooled in the neat interpretation of what is and is not legal, are meet arbiters, I throw my opinion with yours. If you say the decree be withheld, I will not contradict."

Martín Fernandez de Enciso, Alguacil Mayor: "As I understand this commission, *señores*, it gives to Balboa the best and richest portion of Golden Castile. Set this excellent award against the wretched perfidies we have listed from his *residencia*, and you will be of the strong mind to save His Highness the most deplorable blunder ever in the history of Spain."

The Bishop Quevedo suffered them all thus to speak, albeit not without looking upon them the while with a lion's countenance. And when they had said their say, he rose up before them in his

199

black clerical robe like a wrathful Jehovah (for he is a man of great stature and has long, thick hair and heavy brows).

And in a loud voice he asked God to forgive him the murderous thoughts which stirred his soul when he beheld that base treachery and thieving insolence to our Sovereign. "You who sit in judgement upon His Highness! [cried he] You who have suddenly become the self-appointed Regents of Spain! Upon my soul, if I did not know of a certainty that, by my own ceaseless effort, this gross treason shall be avenged: did I not rest assured that, even though all of you were to escape that earthly punishment by death this moment, you would yet come before the tribunal of heaven—I would so far debase myself as to disconnect your heads with one of your own blades.

"And you! You—! [and here the Bishop pointed a quivering finger of accusal at Pedrarias, who shrank back, blinking] Do you think to be saved by reason of agreement from these spongy toadies whom you've shored up to multiply your opinions? Ha! It is little enough they will share of the ultimate blame, which will be yours: yours alone, Pedro Arias. Finer heads than yours have been lost for grave offence to the Crown. But let the vote be taken. I do feel myself sweating for want of clean air. Vote, vote!"

Then Pedrarias, fearing that (as the Bishop had said) he might be charged and punished for intercepting a royal *cédula*, addressed the Council, saying that they made much of nothing: "Let us deliver the documents to Balboa, for that will alter nothing. He is already Adelantado by very reason of the writ, whether he read it or no. More: there is one condition set forth in the commission that yet prevents this rotten-timbered jack from the high hand, and it is this: His Highness has wisely enjoined that all Balboa's enterprises remain subject to my approval. Let us make a good face of the matter, then, and let that liver-mouth have the boast of honor, seeing that he can buy little else than an elegant address with it."

The vote was then taken and none was found to oppose delivering the *cédula* to Vasco Núñez the following day.

Defeated thus in his will to deprive Vasco Núñez of all honor as he had deprived him of his goods, Pedrarias took occasion that same night to write a long letter to the King, praying that His Highness reconsider the brevet and withdraw the title altogether:

for this Balboa was a disreputable rogue, who mocked at authority, blasphemed the Church, robbed his fellows, deceived Crown authorities, and thwarted royal mandates. Ample evidence and testimony to support these charges were being forwarded by the same messenger, together with findings of the said Balboa's *residencia*. From all of which it would be seen that "the aforesaid Vasco Núñez is not worthy of the honor you have done him by giving him the government of Coyba and Panama, and in making him Adelantado of the South Sea."

Further: The Governor requested an order from His Highness allowing him authority to pass sentence upon Balboa "as befits his crimes and excesses."

Such a petition was, in plainer terms, request for a death warrant.

Chapter 13 ~~~~~~~~~~~~~~~~~~~~~~~~~~~~~~~~~~~~

Having received into his hands the brevets bestowed upon him by the King, Vasco Núñez made all haste to present them to Pedrarias before a notary.

Whereupon, the Governor in a churlish manner acknowledged them: and he also answered that the said decrees did not concern him: that the carrying out of the Adelantado's undertaking was no part of his charge to be looked unto: nor did the *cédulas* order him—Pedrarias—to provide troops for an expedition to the Sea of the South, which Balboa had claimed as his discovery.

Being so cut off and prevented from the preparing and setting forth of a reasonable company, and tiring of inactivity in Darien, the Adelantado (with the loyal help of the *baquianos* who had before time resorted to him) determined to raise a force secretly and to proceed to the territories granted him by the King.

But before he could privily muster the men he needed and supply them with all that was requisite for the journey, Pedrarias by divers means persuaded him to lead an *entrada* to the province of Dabaibe, giving him in large part troops recently come from Castile.

It was the Governor's hope (they tell) that the Adelantado would be lost or killed by reason of his thus having with him men who were little experienced in things of the Indies and were not able to defend themselves. And it fell out that such was near-hand the case: for during a serious skirmish with the Indian fighting men of Abibaibe (whom certain other of the Governor's Captains had stirred to great hostility in earlier *entradas*) Balboa was gravely hurt in the head by a blow from one of their war clubs. Yet it was God's will that he soon recover.

At that time great clouds of locusts descended upon those regions, dark-shadowing the skies: and they moved as shimmering sea-billows over the land, devouring all green and leafy things. And the Devil's harvest of that gleaning multitude left the fields bare and the ripening crops a vanished dream of those who had planted and tilled them.

After this happened, seeing in what hard case they found themselves for want of provisions (by reason of the great ravage of the locusts), the Adelantado conferred with his Captains and worthy men who went with him: and with their advice and counsel, he ordered the company to turn back to Darien. For (as he said afterward) had they assayed to proceed farther, it might have happened that the troops, because of the famine, might never have survived.

After his return to Antigua from that unfortunate *entrada* to Dabaibe, the Adelantado resolved to delay no longer in establishing his *gobernación* along the South Sea. And seeing the expectation of that attempt frustrated by the perfidious Governor, he sent Andrés de Garabito in a small vessel to Cuba to obtain a force of volunteers and sufficient arms to make the expedition.

And when the aforesaid Garabito returned to Antigua with sixty men and such provisions as were expedient for the march, he anchored in a small bay a distance of six leagues from Santa Maria (for the Governor had no knowledge of it) and sent word secretly to the Adelantado that they were in readiness to proceed.

But Balboa's luck was that the ship's arrival was disclosed to Pedrarias by one of the Adelantado's enemies. And the Governor, being greatly passioned, ordered Balboa seized: and fearing that the Adelantado's men would enter the jail by force of arms and free him, the Governor had a cage built in his own house, wherein he imprisoned Vasco Núñez on charges of conspiracy and rebellion.

When those who had enrolled themselves in the Adelantado's enterprise (as well as we who had been the companions of his long march to the new sea) heard of his being mewed up in the house of Pedrarias, there was a great tumult and disorder tending to mutiny. And there can be no doubt, that odious act of the Governor had cost him dear if there had not happened at that time certain marvellous things which led to the Adelantado's being set free.

The things aforesaid occurred in this sort:

During the Adelantado's abode in the keep which Pedrarias had made for him, there passed divers courtesies between him and Doña Isabel de Bobadilla y Peñalosa, the Governor's wife, who from the day of her arrival in Darien, had had him in great admiration and favor. And she, together with Bishop Quevedo, determined to help him in his present extremity.

Pedrarias (so it has been told), being acquainted with the way his wife behaved toward the man he most despised in all the world, reproached her thus: "I have well known it, that you have been on the best of terms with that mordacious hypocrite since the time we arrived on these plaguy shores. And knowing the while that the stinking scoundrel is plotting daily to devour my gains, undo my efforts, and, the Devil willing, to have me recalled to Castile in disgrace. I ask, are you my wife or some evil vampire of Quevedo's purgatory?"

To which Doña Isabel answered: "You well know, Pedro, that I should do nothing, absolutely nothing, which I thought harmful to you or to your public good. Unfortunately, I do not see how the persecution of a man who had the ill fortune to be your predecessor, is going to help you greatly, either here or in Castile. On the contrary, in dealing with a man such as Vasco Núñez (who, I need not remind you, is large in public favor) it seems to me politic to engage him as a friend rather than to prick him up to be a powerful enemy."

Don Pedro made a loud cracking sound with his knuckles (as with his way when vexed). "And what, my pretty lady [said he] would you that I do for this Vasco Núñez, who is the kind of squib to offer one the smile of angels even while his spiteful hand comes out with a dagger for the breast. Come, woman, you leave me blushing. For I suspect that panting dog has won his way into your affections more with gifts such as that excellent rank of pearls, than by any virtue of his character."

Doña Isabel answered him that the time had arrived when it

would serve him well not only to provide for the future of his children but, if possible, to further his own best interests thereby. "Therefore [said she] I ask you to consider what commodity and advantage might be yours if our daughter Maria were given in marriage to the Adelantado."

And Pedrarias was sore shaken by these words (which were not such as he expected). "Madre! [he cried] that you should think to fleer me with talk of my welfare, when your desire is to protect that he-goat with your cunning. Well—I am no fetch for your coggery."

Nevertheless, his wife continued with a calm voice, saying that such a union would not be a great condescension: that Balboa was from the loins of hidalgos, *de sangre limpio*, and further ennobled by the titles of Adelantado of the South Sea and Governor of Coyba and Panamá. More: that he was a man to whom above half the *vecinos* of Darien had pledged their loyalty: that there was a stirring in that town and a movement toward sedition. He ought, therefore, to keep in mind what had happened to Nicuesa.

But Pedrarias was not persuaded by these arguments: for, said he, the report of Balboa's *residencia* and the secret inquiry he had made of the Adelantado's treasonous acts were even then before the Council of the Indies and the Court of Spain: and soon sentence would be executed on him for his crimes and excesses. "And that will be the end of Vasco Núñez."

It was then that Doña Isabel gave to the Governor the final thrust, which brought him to agreement with her proposal: "Have you so soon forgotten, Don Pedro, the news we received that our Catholic King is dead? That Cardinal Cisneros is now the Regent of Spain? Must I remind you that it is little power now left to your great advocate, Bishop Fonseca?"

Pedrarias, cut adrift by the death of our King (of blessed memory) and left to drive (as it were) in the winds of change that were blowing in Castile, now thought earnestly upon what his wife had said. And those things being considered on, he said: "You speak with reason, and I consent to it. But look to it that there be no dark sleights."

"It will be done with honor, trust to it. Tomorrow I will inform the Bishop who will open the matter to the Adelantado. I do not know what Balboa will answer."

"What *he* will answer! Purísima! What could the gelded hinny answer except 'Amen'?"

When this news was made known to Balboa by the Bishop, he received it with a grave countenance and said to him: "Is not my fate evil enough that I have had to strive against the mischiefs of that huffish death's head, but you would have me yoked to his get?"

But the Bishop soothed him with such words as would make him to consider his present plight and his designs for the future: "By concord with Don Pedro, you will receive what is needful to make your long-delayed conquests into the lands given you by the Sovereign. As for the man himself, you need not be often in his presence. Don Pedro will die: Doña Isabel go back to Spain. Upon my soul, man, it makes over two years that you have sucked the thumb of idleness, while the ruin of the Indies smokes around you. Here is your opportunity. Will you take it?"

"And what of the girl—this daughter of that croaking toad?"

"The daughter of Doña Isabel," the Bishop reminded him. "She has her mother's beauty, her grace, her intelligence. Let her come when the fighting is over and these are peaceful countries. By my consecration, Vasco, I swear you will welcome her then."

After carefully weighing the matter, the Adelantado realized that what the Bishop had said was indeed the truth: he could not hope to get even a bowshot's distance from that town unless the Governor so willed it. Therefore, he at length replied: "I will do it. Though, as for trusting that hell-bred monster, Pedro Arias, I'll be a lamb only until I get within the fold."

After the agreements aforesaid, the Governor contracted marriage in the name of his daughter and gave his hand for her.

In this way the Adelantado secured his freedom and Pedrarias put down the evils which were being plotted to the hurt of the Governor and in disservice of the Crown.

After being given his liberty, and having restored to him the authority and honor justly his, Vasco Núñez prepared with all haste to lead an expedition to his new sea.

The Governor, while making a great show of help to his son-in-law, actually provided him with none of the necessary supplies, as he had furnished to his own Captains who had previously made

207

disastrous *entradas*, from which they had reaped small fruit and commodity.

Albeit, the Adelantado's fame was such that certain *vecinos* gladly provided at their charge all things requisite for the expedition, with every man of that society to share in all profits, commodities, and goods which might accrue from the enterprise.

The Adelantado believed the shortest way across the land to the new sea to be that which led from the port of Acla, the principal village of the territory of Careta. He decided, therefore, that the best course would be to fell timber along the coast, shape the pieces for the brigantines, and assemble them after they had been carried across the intervening land.

Accordingly, the Adelantado embarked for Acla on the 24th of August, with a force of eighty men. And as soon as they had arrived at that place, he ordered his company to rebuild with all haste the strong place which had there been destroyed by Indians who fought against Lope de Olano.

Balboa laid out a new town and, after looking to the planting of sufficient crops to sustain his people, he ordered trees to be felled for lumber with which ships could be constructed after it had been carried over the mountains to the other sea. And in all this work, the Adelantado labored with his own hands beside the meanest of his company: and he took the hardest tasks for himself.

Seeing what difficulties yet faced us and being mindful of the great hardships we had endured to cross that country, Pizarro said to him: "You well remember it, Don Vasco, that with only the weight of our little flesh, we were sorely put to it to come through that plaguy pass to the other sea, and then arrived there more like dead men than conquistadores. Now—*Valgame Dios!*—you would carry also the timber of four ships, as well as anchors, rigging, pitch, cordage, and sails. I am asking, why? Are there no trees on the other side? I remember, we cut many."

To which our Adelantado replied: "The cacique Chima, whose word is good, has said that the wood of this side is strong against the shipworm. For my part, I have little desire to see our craft make a merry banquet for the *broma*, as it is said the pithy woods of that region do."

But Pizarro yet pressed his opinion, saying: "I would not gall you into doubt: but if you heed the sayings of the indigenes, you

208

may enter only the region of hard necessity. This whole country is thicker with Indian bowmen than an Arab's bed with lice, and every one of them lying in wait for Spaniards. As you well know it, these mountains are the worst in the world: the only creatures able to inhabit them are the birds, which have wings. More: in dry season, the suns are hotter than a smelter furnace and our *compañeros* resistant as lard. In the wet season, the rivers of that country will swell and come up twenty *varas* in two days. If you get the pieces of one whole ship across and in that gulf, I will affirm that you have hold of both God's hands and sometimes ride upon His back."

Then Balboa pointed toward the distant cordillera. "Look you [said he] there where that pass is seen. There we will march through and to the river called Balsas, which flows down strong and wide, to the gulf. I have sent Francisco Companon and thirty men to build a fortress beyond the summit. There we will put together a boat and perhaps a *fusta*. We will also take what canoes may be there. And so direct our course down to the sea. Then you will see what can be done."

When all the timbers had been cut and shaped to their intended use, and the cordage, pitch, sails, anchors, and tackle for ships were in readiness, we departed from Acla. And there being too few Indians to serve as porters, the *compañeros* were required to carry upon their backs the things we had to convey to that place where the brigantines were to be built. In this great labor (concerning which there were many complaints) the Adelantado was foremost. The burden he bore was a heavy plank or timber for a ship's side.

So did we go forward by great pains and much fatigue, honed against the sharp stones of those mountain passes: our brains baked under the fiery oven of those heavens: our faces clawed by the violent rains: in peril often, and suffering all manner of ill-savors and bad fare. And if I should tell you all the particulars and the troublesome affairs of that passage, I should never make an end.

Having come to Las Balbas, where the ships were to be built, it was found that a greater part of the timber was already rotted and useless. An Indian of Careta, who had made canoes for the cacique Chima, gave it as his opinion that our wood had been taken from trees felled in the wrong season of the moon, wherefore it had decayed in the sun and rain.

Of all that we had struggled so mightily to bring thither (our shipwrights said) only enough sound timber remained to build two brigantines.

Nevertheless, the Adelantado ordered that a clearing be made at a place where the river flowed deep and wide between its banks: and that cane shelters be built, as well as scaffolds and ways for the building of the ships.

Pedrarias (with his accustomed and natural cunning) had permitted us only eight months wherein to build the ships and have them upon the Sea of the South. Yet seven months had already been overpassed in our difficult undertaking. Thus did we have but one month remaining during which time we were to bring from Acla all things still requisite to our enterprise.

Forasmuch as it was impossible to do all that was necessary in that space of time, the Adelantado sent Hernando de Argüello, the notary, to Antigua with a letter to Pedrarias, earnestly beseeching him for more time.

Then Vasco Núñez returned with all speed to Acla to spur forward the supplies. And to that port returned Arguello whom the Adelantado had sent to Antigua to petition the Governor that he consent to a greater time wherein we might complete our ships and launch them upon that austral sea.

In answer, Pedrarias said we might pursue our endeavor, but only until the feast day of St. John, when if we had not fulfilled our part, the undertaking would be placed in other hands.

Upon receiving this news, Balboa gave orders to gather together the materials of Acla and to depart at once for Las Balsas: for, said he, that wily old devil (the Governor) was weaving a web once again wherein Vasco Núñez would be caught, while Pedrarias devoured his substance.

At the very instant of his leavetaking, Maria, Balboa's Indian wife (the daughter of Chima) came to him and, after embracing him, asked: "My lord, you have not given me away?"

And Vasco Núñez, greatly perplexed at such a question, replied: "At no hand would I lose you, *palomita*. But I have been much preoccupied with the ships."

"Then you did not send that Captain to me?"

"Which Captain? Who came to you and what did he say?"

"Captain Andrés. He came twice: once in the day and one time by night. He has said, 'Your lord is done with you, Cacica. But patience, girl, you have fallen to a man who will last you a deal longer, and with more frequent flashes of merriment, by my troth.' "

"And then?"

"Then I sent him away. I said Vasco is my lord forever. He was angry. He said when he returned I would not speak to him in that way."

"You should have sent Leoncico to him for some merry sport," Vasco said.

"But Leoncico is dead."

The Adelantado was saddened by these tidings. "Dead? But, yes, he was old for a war dog, and he had passed through many battles."

Then Maria answered and said to him: "He not die because old. He die to the poison."

"Poison? Who would give Leoncico poison?"

"Not an Indian! A Castilian."

"You wish to say, it was Andrés?"

The girl did not answer him, for it is likely she had been told of this by the Devil, who speaks through certain of their idols, which they call *zemes*, and whom they consult on divers occasions.

Perceiving that she was much troubled of the spirit, Balboa said to her: "Have no fear. He will not molest you again. I will heat his ears with sure warning. Also, I will take him with me to Las Balsas. Now—I must get me to the trail. Watch for my return. And receive it from me as truth, as I swear it before God, that I will not be quit of you."

So we advanced upon the trail in the direction of Las Balsas, where the ships were a-building. And when we had made camp on the first night, Balboa sent for Andrés de Garabito, whom he took aside and said to him: "Do you think that Maria is of such a kind as to consort with any jack in service?"

And Garabito, seeing no remedy but a show of penitence, answered: "I swear to you that I had no intent against your house or honor. I thought that perhaps having married Don Pedro's daughter—well, in the Bishop's sermon— Forgive me, I did not know the Indian held rank with your Christian wife."

Understanding Garabito's words to mean contention or disrespect, the Adelantado grew hot upon it and said angrily: "Don't preoccupy yourself with my affairs. And hear me well: and I discover you in one more act of mongering, you will invite my blade —a surer blade, I swear, than that of Cortez."

Whereas Garabito's ire also rose, for Vasco Núñez had recalled the wound he—Garabito—had received from Hernan Cortez in Española for a similar offence. But, fearing Balboa's wrath, he said (with false contrition): "I pledge you loyalty in this matter as in all things. What I did was through no bad intent, but ignorance. And transgression in a fool is not sin, but folly."

Thereupon, the Adelantado's anger slowed apace: for Garabito had been faithful in all else save this. And (as everyone knew) his great weakness was women. Wherefore, Vasco Núñez told him: "Let us purge it from our memory, then. You are an excellent soldier, Andrés. Look to it that you are a cavalier as well."

Thus did Balboa conclude the affair in his own mind. Not so, Garabito, who had begun to desire the Indian girl with a consuming passion. Secretly, he now hated the Adelantado who was an obstacle to his desire. Secretly, also he determined to remove that obstacle.

Immediately we had arrived in Las Balsas, therefore, Garabito concealed himself and composed a hasty letter to Pedrarias. He then entrusted it to one of his Negro slaves, whom he directed to take it covertly to the Governor in Antigua. He had written:

"Excellency—
A certain important person here at Las Balsas is plotting against His Majesty's lawful authorities: and he intends to overthrow your government in Darien and, peradventure, to have your head in the bargain. In good faith, I must warn you to deal at once with this conspirator, before you are undone and a tyrant once more rules in Tierra Firme. I make this revelation out of service to the Crown. . . ."

The construction and final work upon the ships went forward at Las Balsas with a haste begotten of Balboa's desperate fear that

Don Pedro's extension of time would expire before we actually had the vessels afloat. Once we had launched the ships and set sail, the Governor's order to complete the voyage by June would have no more importance than a bird's cry from the thickets.

But the dry season was at an end, and the rains set in. Great jagged spurts of water tumbled out of the sky in ceaseless torrents. Soon the shipyard was knee-deep in water and slime: and the work ceased.

Balboa lay in his hammock above the muddy floor of his temporary quarters, shivering with the chill dampness. From time to time, during a lull in the downpours, he climbed down and splashed through the muck to look at the river. It was rising rapidly: already the stream had overrun its banks and was edging toward the cradles where the unfinished bergantines lay.

The supply of food was giving out: and our stores of cassaba were wet and mouldy. Daily more men came down with fever. We could not find dry fuel for fires, for everything was soaked. Rain, rain, rain.

At night the Adelantado could not sleep. He lay in the wet darkness listening to the sounds of the water: the rain stroking the thatched roof: the gurgle of the river, rising higher and higher: the bubbling cataracts down the stony slope behind the hut. The night became one long, liquid spasm pouring itself out forever in the blackness, yet never reaching completion.

Near the breaking of the day one morning the rain lightened, and Balboa heard two of his men slopping through the mud toward his hut. They entered and called out his name: and he answered them with a deep grunt from the depths of his hammock.

They said: "The river has carried away the ships, Señor Adelantado. Gone: all gone."

He did not answer them: and presently they went away. Soon afterward the day appeared, dead gray, through the matting across the doorway. Balboa clenched his hands: and buried his face in his arms and wept with anguish.

When Valderrábano came with a scanty ration of food, Balboa feigned sleep. After a moment of indecision, he heard the little man go out, his bare feet sucking noisily in the mud. A stiff, cold languor, like death, now spread through his limbs: and he lay very

213

still and thought of nothing. For the first time in his life, Vasco Núñez was unmoved by any desire whatever. Time swept by him with a raging sound of the river. And as the river had swept from him seemingly the means of realizing his dreams, so now the rushing tide of timeless dark tore from their moorings the dreams themselves, and carried them away toward the sea of oblivion.

The rains ceased at last, but famine remained with us like an unbidden guest. Balboa grubbed with his men for edible roots and seeds: and as soon as the waters had subsided, he sent out a small party under the command of Andrés Garabito to forage for food.

They soon returned, laden with supplies they had taken from an Indian settlement not far distant. They brought with them also a number of captives who could be used to help with work, if it was the Adelantado's will to try again.

Vasco Núñez called together his confederates who had employed money in the enterprise and asked of them if they wished to renounce our undertaking which now held so little promise of good success. And when he found that all of them were minded to continue, he commanded the men to return with all speed to their labor.

So the tools were dug from the deep slime and new timber was felled. Huge fires were built, and by their light night crews continued the work even during the hours of darkness. The companions worked in heavy rain: they spread a great sailcloth over their pots of pitch and kept the fires going.

The two brigantines were thus completed and rigged in shorter time than even the Adelantado ventured to hope.

Once the vessels had been set upon the breast of the river, it required but two days to sail them to the gulf. On the passage down, the river proved too shallow in certain places to permit safe going. Then the Adelantado leaped into the water with his men and helped to dredge the soft bottom.

And when we at length entered the waters of the gulf, Vasco Núñez (who stood in the leading ship) ordered the masts of our brigantines dressed with flags: and he commanded the trumpeter to sound a flourish.

And as this was done, the companions (greatly moved by the

sight of the new sea) began to leap about and to shout wildly through their tears.

The wind freshened and we set our course upon the great sea toward the Pearl Islands, which lie seven leagues from the entrance to that Gulf of San Miguel.

And to Martín de los Reyes, our chief pilot, Balboa said: "From those islands, when we have all things in readiness, we will take our voyage southward to the unknown lands beyond, where great fortune awaits us."

Yet (for such is the mystery and sorrow of all our lives) the gains of that great enterprise he had so gloriously begun were not to be his. For, though his spirit then soared like a bird across the wide sea he had taken for Castile (as it has been well said), the wings of man's life are plumed with the feathers of death.

Chapter 14 〰〰〰〰〰〰〰〰〰〰〰〰〰〰〰

We had sailed only a few leagues upon the new ocean when a mariner aboard the flagship climbed with all haste from the forward hold to report serious leaks below.

These proved to be the borings of the much-feared *broma*. In our fever to get the ships finished, we had cut trees too near the water. Careful inspection of the vessel now revealed it to be honeycombed with shipworms.

When the Adelantado was told of what state our brigantine was in, he said to the pilot: "Tell me now, according to your judgement, how far we may fare before we sink."

And Reyes answered him: "With God's hand to bear us up and our own quick arms with the buckets, I would hazard four leagues more. But even now, my bowels in their wisdom say less."

At Balboa's order, therefore, they hoisted full sail and we ran for it, steering for Isla Rica, which was the land nearest us on the port tack. And they signalled the smaller brigantine to follow.

Before we had sailed a distance of two leagues, water had risen perilously in the ship, and we had slowed to a speed of not more than two knots.

When they raised the island, however, the men found new strength in their arms, and we passed the buckets from hand to hand with lightning swing, and with great shouts of encouragement.

Thus crowding sail and in a blind frenzy, we made a landfall under the lee of that island, and there thanked God with tears of joy that He had spared our lives.

With much labor, the brigantines were hauled on shore and careened in the sand. Their condition made it clear that they could not be safely used for a long voyage of discovery.

The Adelantado decided then to build two new brigantines on the island: and he immediately told off a company of men to fell new timber.

Said he: "Spare neither yourselves nor the Indians who go with you. I feel trouble nearing its hour: and necessity has no law how far life is to be esteemed."

In the meanwhile, the worm-ravaged *San Cristobal* was chocked and tarred and refloated. She was placed under the command of Valderrábano, who sailed with thirty men for the mainland. His orders were to proceed over the mountains to Acla, where he would dispatch pitch and cordage for the new ships being built.

This done, he was to continue to Antigua with a certain amount of gold and pearls, which would be handed over to Pedrarias, together with a good account of our enterprise and an entreaty for more time to complete it.

Valderrábano returned from his mission to Antigua within six weeks, bringing disturbing news: "There is no scant of rumors and bad omens in that town. The Governor received us as though we came with pestilence. And his word was, 'Tell the Adelantado I have shown him already much favor. Say to him that matters do not stand still here, and it is time for him to show his mettle. But let him proceed with his undertaking, and I will make plain my will and judgement in the coming days.'

"Later we came to know the cause of his grieved mind and misery, and it was this: it is now commonly known in Darien that the Crown intends to send forth a new Governor to serve in his stead. More: even the identity of the said hidalgo is on every tongue. He is by name Don Lope de Sosa, Governor of the Canaries. So Pedrarias is like a pig on the eve of St. Martin's day. He is loath to face the coming *residencia*, for all his follies, crimes, and excesses wait to condemn him."

Balboa was also deeply troubled at the knowledge that a new Governor was soon to take over the *gobernación* in Darien. He,

218

too, being an official, would be recalled to Antigua to face another *residencia*. That would mean more ruinous delay, more struggle against the private ambitions of another lord paramount, eager to establish his own rule in the Indies. Balboa's men would be taken from him (or would leave in desperation) and be pressed into new *entradas*. His own ill-starred expedition to the lands of the South would go to pieces like a caravel splintering on a reef.

These thoughts being heavy upon his mind, Vasco Núñez that same evening summoned to his *bohio* those captains and worthy men who were in his closest confidence. They were Father Perez, the archdeacon: Andrés de Valderrábano, the notary: Hernando Muñoz, Andrés de Garabito, and Luis Botello.

"*Compañeros* [he addressed them], Valderrábano has brought a rumor from Antigua which gives the bite of uncertainty to our en- terprise and our fortunes. It is this: that Don Lope de Sosa may be sent over as Governor in the stead of Pedrarias. The meaning of that, as regards our own affairs, is clear. But if we act quickly, we may yet save our chickens from the fox.

"I propose that you, caballeros, go forthwith to Darien to verify the truth of the rumor and to see whether the new Governor has already arrived. When you are come to Acla, tarry a league or two outside the town while you, Botello, proceed alone into the vil- lage. Go secretly to my house. There you will find my woman, Maria. Tell her that I sent you, and give as truth of your mission the word '*Huimaca*' from her tongue. Learn from her what passes in Antigua, and whether Sosa has come. When you have done this, go back darkly, without foreslowing, to the others. If Pedro Arias still has the reign in Darien, proceed—all of you—to Santa Maria. There petition the Governor for succor and supplies."

As he spoke to them thus, a huge burst of thunder crashed over- head, and a sudden rainstorm rattled among the palm leaves out- side the hut. After a moment, Balboa continued: "But if Sosa now governs in Darien, bargain secretly with Antonio del Campo for what supplies may be had in Acla, and have them sent after you. You, Muñoz, remain to see to it. The rest of you return here quickly. We will finish the two brigantines with all haste and set sail. Thus will we leave Sosa our empty cradles, much to his dis- may, but to our own great glory afterward. What say to this, gen- tlemen?"

Answering for all, Andrés de Garabito said: "So be it." And they prepared forthwith to take their leave.

The artisans and shipwrights who labored at the making of our vessels had learned with marvellous skill to use such materials as that country yields: and so each day they wonderfully carried forward their work.

And it happened that, often when evening came, the Adelantado would climb about the unfinished ships, praising the builders for being so well-practiced in those parts.

On a certain night as we squatted upon a deck of an uncompleted ship, conversing in our accustomed sort, Balboa (who had been silently looking up at the brilliance of the stars) suddenly descried a greenish bright orb which the astrologer Micer Codro had affirmed to be near his own star of destiny.

(The aforesaid Micer Codro was an astrologer of Venice and a man of great learning, wise and experienced in natural things, and who carried a commission from our King to search out the secrets of the Indies. But of his own tragic end, I will here forbear to tell.)

Sighting his star near the green one, the Adelantado exclaimed: "Behold, *compañeros*, my star of destiny! There—the lemon-colored one. You see what mumps men are to be colted by the augurs of astrologers like that Micer Codro. As he would have it, when I beheld my star in that place, I was to be in deadly peril. Yet, look you. This butt is hardly in danger of going down—"

Whereat, we all laughed. And he continued: "We have these two sturdy bottoms almost ready for the ruffles, with cordage to come, and sails. And you, *señores*, do me the honor of pressing for a voyage under my hand. I ask you: does that not put the lie to Micer Codro's quibble?"

"It does, Señor Adelantado: he's a bag of slights, no more," one of the men rumbled from the shadows on the starboard side.

"But hold!" Vasco went on, as an afterthought. "Perhaps I do the man wrong. He also said: 'If you pass those perilous days in safety, you will become one of the greatest and richest Captains in the Indies.' Faith, and that is a prediction I won't gleek at."

But even as Balboa thus spoke, his enemies were preparing his death.

220

For (as it was later known) as soon as Botello entered Acla, as Balboa had ordered him, he was taken by the guard as a gray cat with no lawful business in the town.

He was brought forthwith before the *alcalde*, who was none other than Francisco Benitez, whom Vasco Núñez had ordered beaten during Nicuesa's trial.

When Benitez discovered (by torturing Valderrábano) that his companions awaited his return outside the town, he sent an armed guard to arrest the entire company. They were placed in irons, and report of the affair was dispatched to Pedrarias, who still governed in Antigua until the arrival of Lope de Sosa.

Then did Andrés de Garabito (in whom was the very spirit of Judas Iscariot) on the day following falsely speak of the Adelantado, throwing out great lies concerning what designs he had for setting himself up as a king or emperor in his domain along the South Sea.

Knowing nought of all that had thus passed with his men, Balboa (being himself without fraud or guile) gave credence to the words of certain messengers who came over to us from the Governor and who told that Valderrábano and the others had remained in Acla to conclude their business of obtaining supplies.

The said emissaries brought to Balboa a letter from Pedrarias (that familiar of the Devil!), wherein he wrote: "Esteemed Son: Your men have brought news of your needs, and a good report of your venture. It grieves me to hear that you have some doubts of my continued favor to the enterprise. My dear son, you will be supplied in full measure with all that you require. My former admonitions with respect to time were but for the appeasement of the treasurer Puente, who would otherwise push a bad quill against me in his reports to the Crown.

"Please come at once to Acla, and I myself will pass over thence to meet you and to see that you are given all you deserve for your services to God and to the King."

And Balboa, being himself blameless of any wrongdoing, did not suspect treachery on the part of Pedrarias (who, in truth, had never given him anything else). Therefore, leaving the company under the charge of Francisco Companon, he departed at once for Acla, being accompanied with Bartolomé Hurtado and the Governor's men, who had brought the letter from Pedrarias.

221

As they were going thence, the aforesaid couriers whom Pedrarias had sent to Balboa with the mendacious letter, perceiving that he was innocent of any crime, advertised him of the Governor's base design.

But the Adelantado put aside this counsel which those men had given him at their own great hazard, declaring that he would come to full concord with the Governor.

Yet, as they descended the mountain toward Acla, there came out to meet them an armed force under the conduct of Francisco Pizarro, who had been sent out to make stay of Vasco Núñez. And as they drew near, the bastard swineherd advanced and, drawing his sword, said to the Adelantado: "Yield yourself, for you are the King's prisoner."

And Balboa, greatly astonished at that behavior, answered him: "How is this, Francisco? You were not wont to greet me in this manner formerly."

But Pizarro did not respond, for he was a man who thought only of his own private lucre, gain, and profit: and he had secretly conceived a burning desire to achieve some notable thing. Taking the Adelantado's sword from him, therefore, he said: "Forward!"

In that town of Acla, the Adelantado was confined under heavy watch in the house of the pilot Juan de Castaneda. There Don Pedro came to talk with him, hoping to have from him (by many false words and friendly signs) certain secrets touching the South Sea exploration, which Balboa had not disclosed to any other person.

Accordingly, with his foxy smile, he said: "Do not preoccupy, son Vasco. This trial is for the satisfaction of that breed-pate, Puente. It will serve to free you once for all of the bad accusations made against you by your enemies, and will make your service to Spain the more conspicuous."

But Vasco Núñez was no longer deceived, for he perceived the iniquity and malice in the old man's eyes. And he turned from him without speaking a word.

Albeit, Pedrarias returned afterward a second time, full of fair words and false promises, saying that Balboa could count him his intercessor and friend. Whereupon the Adelantado grew angry. And he spoke into the Governor's face, thus: "It has been well said that a barren sow was never good to pigs. Being weak, you despise strength: crooked in the back, you loathe the feat. Your sight is thick, your carcass ready for the worms, your beard white with winter. Yet, being thus fully addressed to God's tribunal, you continue to bear malice and to give ready ear to false reports. A friend? I would sooner pack with the Devil!"

Hearing which, Pedrarias turned pale with ire. "Hitherto [said he] I have treated you as my own son because I believed you loyal to the Crown, and faithful to me. Though I have in my own hands, written documents showing your treason, I had hoped to prove them false. Now I see too well that they are true. Henceforth you will be treated as my enemy. Therefore, expect nothing from me save this, which I now declare."

And he left that place in great haste, crying: "More irons! More irons for Vasco Núñez!"

The false and unjust *proceso* wherein our Adelantado was tried and condemned to death turned upon the spiteful perjuries of his enemies. These were, besides the Governor Pedrarias: the Bachelor Corral: the Treasurer Puente: the Chief Judge Espinosa (who already had made a secret pact to possess Balboa's ships and property after he had been killed): Garabito the lecher: and a certain sentry (a simpleton) who testified of hearing treasonous words as he sought protection from the rain under the eaves of the Adelantado's house in Acla.

Thus was he charged with the crimes and abuses of usurpation, rebellion against the lawful authorities, and high treason against the Crown.

The Adelantado defended his cause with the best reasons. And the case provoked so great a scandal that men of good calling and degree as well as those of the common sort made suit to the Governor to release him because no one believed that he was guilty.

To all these entreaties, Pedrarias replied: "No, no, no! I would rather die myself than that he be spared. Since he has transgressed, let him die for it."

Thus, in the greatest crime ever committed in these Indies, the venomous Governor not only ordered the execution of the Adelantado, but also that of his closest confederates: Valderrábano, Muñoz, Botello, Father Perez, and Arguello.

223

Seeing that Pedrarias had no writ or right to impose the extreme penalty, and fearing that he might be brought to justice for his part in the evil deed, the Chief Justice Espinosa summoned the Governor before the notary and witnesses and required him to declare his will concerning the defendants. Thereby he sought to place the blame for their vile act at the Governor's door. So he wrote in the document as follows:

"In order to be able to pass definitive sentence, His Lordship must consider whether he order that at least the case concerning the Adelantado Vasco Núñez in particular be remitted to Their Highnesses or to the members of their most high Council, in view of the quality and title and eminence of his person: or, if he order that the *Alcalde Mayor* consider it and determine in all things according to the findings of the court, without making the said remand: or, what it be that he order with regard to the aforesaid."

Yet so great was the hatred that Pedrarias held for Vasco Núñez that he there under oath ordered Espinosa with all haste and without any delay whatsoever to sentence Balboa and the companions accused with him to the extreme rigor of the law: and that having so sentenced them, "that you carry it to due effect and actual execution."

And in the week following, that unjust and beastly sentence was carried out, save for the clerigo Fabian Perez, who was put in chains and sent to Castile.

Even the heavens frowned that sad day: the sky dark with clouds: the sun a sanguine streak, edged with cold blue, like a wound.

With great heaviness of heart, the people assembled in the plaza, where the old and ugly block had been set up. And when the Adelantado appeared in fetters between his guards, walking valorous and serene, we wept for it.

The town crier went before him, proclaiming in a loud voice: "This is the justice which our lord the King and Pedrarias his lieutenant in his name commands to be done upon this man as a traitor and a usurper of the lands subject to the Crown!"

At the first utterance of this proclamation, Balboa cried after him: "Lies! I have with all my strength served the King and I have increased his domain! Behold my reward!"

And the second time: "Let heaven be my judge."

224

And the third time: "God will avenge this wrong."

As for Pedrarias, he concealed himself in a *bohio* near the plaza, where in evil solitude he might behold with devilish joy the executions (which he viewed through the spaces between the canes of the house's wall).

When Vasco Núñez came to the place of execution, he knelt before Padre Andrés, from whose hands he received the Blessed Sacrament, after which he arose with a look of composure and strength.

And on a sudden, the voice of an unknown man among the crowd cried out dismally: "O Balboa, who can behold the injustice of thy fate and not shed tears of bitterness?"

Our great Captain and most noble Adelantado then embraced his Indian wife and saluted the Indians who mourned for him there. And he took leave of the companions, persuading them to unity, obedience, and good faith. This done, he said in a loud voice: "Padre, commend my soul to God and my substance to Pedrarias, who watches secretly from that house."

After this he knelt once more and in very quiet and reverent sort, laid his head upon the block, and there ended his life.

HISTORICAL DOCUMENTS

Documents 〰〰〰〰〰〰〰〰〰〰〰〰〰〰〰〰

I

Papal Bull of Donation

When Columbus returned from his first voyage, to report to the Spanish sovereigns that he had discovered new lands beyond the Ocean Sea, Ferdinand and Isabel immediately submitted to Pope Alexander VI a request that he, as Vicar of God, to whom belonged the entire earth, confirm their claim and title to all heathen territory beyond a line of demarcation 100 leagues west of the Cape Verde Islands.

Following is a translation of the Bull of Donation, issued by the Pontiff on the fourth day of the nones of May, 1493. (The following year, after Portugal had objected to the bull because it infringed her established right to the west coast of Africa, it was agreed that the line be moved to a meridian 370 leagues west of the Cape Verde Islands.)

The original document, written in Latin, has been preserved in the Archives of the Indies in Seville.

"Alexander, Bishop: the Servant of the Servants of God: to our most dear beloved Son in Christ, King Fernando: and to our dear beloved Daughter in Christ, Elizabeth, Queen of Castile, Legion, Arragon, Sicilie, and Granata: most noble Princes, greeting and Apostolical benediction.

"Among other works acceptable to the Divine Majesty, and according to our hearts' desire, this certainly is the chief: that the Catholic Faith and the Christian Religion, specially in this our time, may in all places be exalted, amplified and enlarged, whereby the health of Souls may be procured, and the barbarous Nations subdued and brought to the Faith. And therefore, whereas by the favor of God's Clemency (although not without equal deserts) we are called to this holy Seat of Peter: and understanding you to be true Catholic Princes, as we have ever known you, and as your noble and worthy Facts have declared in manner to the whole World, in that with all your study, diligence, and industry, you have spared no Travails, Charges, or Perils, adventuring even the shedding of your own Blood, with applying your whole Minds and Endeavors hereunto, as your Noble Expeditions achieved in recovering the Kingdom of Granata from the Tyranny of the Saracens in those days, do plainly declare your Facts, with so great Glory of the Divine Name.

"For the which, as we think you worthy, so ought we of our own free will favorably to grant you all things whereby you may daily, with more fervent minds, to the honor of God and enlarging the Christian Empire, prosecute your devout and laudable Purpose, most acceptable to the Immortal God. We are credibly informed that, whereas of late you were determined to seek and find certain Islands and Firm Lands, far remote and unknown (and not heretofore found by any other) to the intent to bring the Inhabitants of the same to honor our Redeemer and to profess the Catholic Faith, you have hitherto been much occupied in the expugnation and recovery of the Kingdom of Granata, by reason whereof you could not bring your said laudable Purpose to the end desired.

"Nevertheless, as it hath pleased Almighty God, the foresaid Kingdom being recovered, willing to accomplish your said Desire, you have, not without great Labor, Perils, and Charges appointed our well-beloved Son Christopher Colonus (a man certes well commended, as most worthy and apt for so great a Matter) well furnished with Men and Ships, and other Necessaries, to seek (by the Sea, where hitherto no man has sailed) such firm Lands and Islands far remote and hitherto unknown, who (by God's help) making diligent search in the Ocean Sea, have found certain remote Islands and firm Lands, which were not heretofore found by any other: in the which (as is said) many Nations inhabit, living peaceably, and going naked, not accustomed to eat Flesh: and as far as your Messengers can conjecture, the Nations inhabiting the aforesaid Lands and Islands believe that there is one God, Creator in Heaven, and seem apt to be brought to the embracing of the Catholic Faith, and to be endued with good Manners: by reason whereof, we may hope, that if they be well instructed, they may easily be induced to receive the Name of our Savior Jesus Christ.

"We are further advertised that the forenamed Christopher has now builded and erected a Fortress, with good Munition, in one of the aforesaid principal Islands, in which he has placed a Garrison of certain of the Christian men that went thither with him, as well to the intent to defend the same as also to search other Islands and firm Lands far remote, and yet unknown. We also understand that in these Lands and Islands lately found is a great plenty of Gold and Spices, with divers and many other precious things, of sundry kinds and qualities. Therefore, all things diligently considered (especially the amplifying and enlarging of the Catholic Faith, as it behooves Catholic Princes, following the examples of your Noble Progenitors, of famous memory) you have determined, by favor of Almighty God, to subject unto you the firm Lands and Islands aforesaid, and the Dwellers and Inhabitants thereof, and to bring them to the Catholic Faith.

"We, greatly commending this your godly and laudable purpose in our Lord, and desirous to have the same brought to a due end, and the Name of our Savior to be known in those parts, do exhort you in our Lord, and by the receiving of your holy Baptism whereby you are bound to Apostolical Obedience, and earnestly require you by the Bowels of Mercy of our Lord Jesus Christ, that when you intend, for the zeal of the Catholic Faith, to prosecute the said Expedition to reduce the People of the aforesaid Lands and Islands to the Christian Religion, you shall spare no Labors at any time, or be deterred with any Perils, conceiving firm hope and confidence that the Omnipotent God will give good success to your godly Attempts. And that being authorized by the Privilege of the Apostolic Grace, you may the more freely and boldly take upon you the Enterprise of so great a matter, we of our own motion and not either at your request, or at the instant petition of any other persons, but of our own mere liberality and certain

231

science, and by the fullness of Apostolical power, do grant, give, and design to you, your heirs and successors, all the firm Lands and Islands found or to be found, discovered or to be discovered, toward the West and South, drawing a Line from the Pole Arctic to the Pole Antarctic (that is) from the North to the South: containing in this Donation whatsoever firm Lands or Islands are found, or to be found, toward India or toward any other part whatsoever it be, being distant from, or without the aforesaid Line, drawn a hundred leagues toward the West, and South, from any of the Islands which are commonly called De los Azores and Capo Verde.

"All the Islands, therefore, and firm Lands found and to be found, discovered and to be discovered, from the Line toward the West and South, such as have not actually been heretofore possessed by any other Christian King or Prince, until the day of the Nativity of our Lord Jesus Christ last past, from which begins the present year, being the year of our Lord one thousand four hundred and ninety-three, whensoever any such shall be found by your Messengers and Captains, we by the Authority of Almighty God, granted unto us in Saint Peter and by the Vicarship of Jesus Christ which we bear on earth, do forever by the tenor of these presents, give, grant, assign unto you, your heirs and successors (the Kings of Castile and Legion) all those Lands and Islands, with their Dominions, Territories, Cities, Castles, Towers, Places, and Villages, with all the Rights and Jurisdictions thereunto appertaining; constituting, assigning, and deputing you, your heirs and successors, the Lords thereof, with full and free Power, Authority, and Jurisdiction: Decreeing nevertheless by our Donation, Grant, and Assignation, that from no Christian Prince, which actually has possessed the aforesaid Islands and firm Lands unto the day of the Nativity of our Lord before said, their Right obtained, to be understood hereby to be taken away, or that it ought to be taken away.

"Furthermore, we command you in the virtue of holy Obedience (as you have promised and as we doubt not you will do, upon mere Devotion and Princely Magnanimity) to send to the said firm Lands and Islands, honest, virtuous, and learned men, such as fear God, and are able to instruct the Inhabitants in the Catholic Faith and good Manners, applying all their possible diligence in the premises. We furthermore straitly inhibit all manner of persons of what state, degree, order, or condition whatsoever they be, although of Imperial and Regal Dignity, under the pain of the Sentence of Excommunication, which they shall incur, if they do to the contrary, that they in no case presume without special License of you, your heirs and successors, to travel for Merchandises or for any other cause, to the said Lands or Islands, found or to be found, discovered or to be discovered, toward the West and South, drawing a Line from the Pole Arctic to the Pole Antarctic, whether the firm Lands and Islands, found and to be found, be situate toward India, or toward any other part, being distant from the Line drawn a hundred Leagues toward the West, from any of the Islands commonly called De los Azores and Capo Verde: Notwithstanding Constitutions, Decrees, and Apostolical Ordinances whatsoever there are to the contrary. In him from whom Empires, Dominions, and all good things do proceed: Trusting that Almighty God, directing your Enterprises, if you follow your godly and laudable Attempts, your Labors and Travails herein, shall in short time obtain a happy end, with felicity and glory of all Christian People. But forasmuch as it should be a thing of great difficulty, these Letters to be carried to all such places as should be expedient: we will, and of like motion and knowledge do decree: That whithersoever the same shall be sent, or wheresoever they shall be received, with the subscription of a common Notary thereunto required, with the Seal of any person constitute in Ecclesiastical Court, the same faith and credit to be given thereunto in Judgment, or elsewhere, as should be exhibited to these Presents.

"Let no man therefore, whatsoever, infringe or dare rashly to contrary this Letter of our Commendation, Exhortation, Request, Donation, Grant, Assignation, Constitution, Deputation, Decree, Commandment, Inhibition, and Determination. And if any shall presume to attempt the same, let him know that he shall thereby incur the Indignation of God Almighty, and the holy Apostles, Peter and Paul.

"Given at Rome at Saint Peter's: In the year of the Incarnation of our Lord 1493. The fourth day of the Nones of May, the first year of our Papacy."

II

The Requirement (El Requirimiento)

1.

The Requirement was a face-saving document drafted in 1513 by a prominent Spanish jurist, Dr. Palacio Rubios. He was assisted by a panel of lawyers and church authorities.

The proclamation was intended to be translated into the Indian tongues and read in full to the natives of the New World before they were attacked, despoiled, and taken captive. But, in practice, the formality soon degenerated to a fast reading of the text in Castilian just outside the Indian village that was about to be plundered.

Balboa was an outstanding exception to this hypocritical sophistry, used as a pious excuse for the bloody crimes committed by the conquistadores. Unless the Indians posed an immediate threat to the safety and well-being of his men, in every instance of his dealings with them, he showed the greatest patience, sympathy, and tact.

"By command of the King, Don Fernando, and of Doña Juana his daughter, Queen of Castile and León, subduers of the barbarous nations, we their servants notify and make known to you, as best we can, that the Lord our God, One and Eternal, created the Heaven and the Earth, and one man and one woman, of whom you and we, and all the men of the world, were and are descendants, and all those who will come after us. But, on account of the multitude of generations which has sprung from this man and

235

woman in the five thousand years since the world was created, it was necessary that some men should be divided into many kingdoms and provinces, for in one alone they could not support themselves.

"Of all these nations God our Lord gave charge to one man, called St. Peter, that he should be Lord and Superior of all the men in the world: that all should obey him: and that he should be the head of the whole human race, wherever men should live, and under whatever law, sect, or belief they should be: and he gave him the world for his kingdom and jurisdiction.

"And he commanded him to place his seat in Rome, as the place most fitting from which to rule the world: but also he permitted him to have his seat in any other part of the world, and to judge and govern all Christians, Moors, Jews, Gentiles, and all other sects. This man was called Pope, as if to say, Admirable Great Father and Governor of men. The men who lived in that time obeyed that St. Peter, and took him for Lord, King, and Superior of the universe: so also they have regarded the others who after him have been elected to the pontificate, and so has it been continued even till now, and will continue till the end of the world.

"One of these Pontiffs, who succeeded that St. Peter as Lord of the world, in the dignity and seat which I have before mentioned, made donation of these isles and mainland of the Ocean Sea to the aforesaid King and Queen and to their successors, our lords, with all that there are in these territories, as is set forth in writs which passed upon the subject as aforesaid, which you can see if you wish.

"So their Highnesses are kings and lords of these islands and land of Tierra-firme by virtue of this donation: and some islands, and indeed almost all (to whom this has been notified) have received and served their Highnesses, as lords and kings, in the way that subjects ought to do, with good will, without any resistance, immediately, without delay, when they were informed of the aforesaid facts. And also they received and obeyed the friars and virtuous men whom their Highnesses sent to preach to them and to teach them our Holy Faith; and all these, of their own free will, without any reward or condition, have become Christians, and are so: and their Highnesses have joyfully and benignantly received

236

them, and also have commanded them to be treated as their subjects and vassals; and you too are held and obliged to do the same.

"Therefore, as best we can, we entreat and require you that you understand well what we have said to you, and that you take the time that shall be necessary to understand and deliberate upon it, and that you acknowledge the Church as the Ruler and Superior of the whole world, and the Supreme Pontiff called Pope, and in his name the King and Queen Doña Juana our lords, in his place, as superiors and lords and kings of these islands and this Tierra-firme by virtue of the said donation, and that you consent and give place that these religious fathers should declare and preach to you the aforesaid.

"If you do so, you will do well, and that which you are obliged to do to their Highnesses: and we in their name shall receive you in all love and charity, and shall leave you your wives, and your children, and your lands, free without servitude, that you may do with them and with yourselves freely that which you like and think best: and they shall not compel you to turn Christians, unless you yourselves, when informed of the truth, should wish to be converted to our Holy Catholic Faith, as almost all the inhabitants of the other islands have done. And, besides this, their Highnesses will award you many privileges and exemptions, and will grant you many benefits.

"But, if you do not do this, and maliciously make delay in it, I certify to you that, with the help of God, we shall powerfully invade your country, and shall make war against you in all ways and manners that we can, and shall subject you to the yoke and obedience of the Church and of their Highnesses; we shall take you and your wives and your children, and shall make slaves of them, and as such shall sell and dispose of them as their Highnesses may command: and we shall take away your goods, and shall do you all the mischief and damage that we can, as to vassals who do not obey, and refuse to receive their lord, and resist and contradict him: and we earnestly confirm that the deaths and losses which shall accrue from this will be your fault, and not that of their Highnesses, nor ours, nor of these cavaliers who come with us. And that we have said this to you and made this Requisition, we request the notary here present to give us his testimony in writing:

237

and we ask the rest who are present that they should be witnesses of this Requisition."

<h2 style="text-align:center">2.</h2>

In an account which he wrote of an abortive and disgraceful entrada led by Pedrarias the Nephew—and in which he was second in command—Bachelor Enciso tells of the Indians' response to the Requirimiento when it was explained to them *after* their town had been taken, with considerable loss of Indian life. (Enciso's implication that the colloquy took place before the battle was merely the wily lawyer's way of giving the King the impression that he had carried out the royal command.)

Says the Bachelor:

"They answered me that what I had said concerning there being only one God and that He ruled the heavens and earth and was the Lord of all things, seemed good to them: and that so should it be: but as for what I had said (that the Pope was lord of the world instead of God and that he had given that land to the King of Castile) they said that the Pope must have been drunk when he did it, forasmuch as he gave away what was not his: and that the King who had asked and had taken the donation must be some madman, because he had asked for what belonged to others: and if anyone tried to seize it, they would have his head on a pole: that they were lords of all that land and had no need of any other sovereigns.

"Again, I demanded that they submit themselves: that otherwise I would make war on them and take their possessions and kill as many as I could seize and would take them and sell them as slaves. And they answered me that they would have my head on a pole first: and they tried to do it, but they could not because we took the village by force."

238

III

Balboa's Letter of January 20, 1513

Of the five lengthy and informative letters Vasco Núñez is known to have written to the King, only the following has been preserved in its entirety. The remaining four are known from references and quotations in other documents and from summaries prepared by royal secretaries for quick perusal by the Spanish monarch.

It is unlikely that the mysterious disappearance of Balboa's other letters (as well as more than a score of reports and memoranda which he sent to various Crown authorities) was accidental. The archivists and clerks employed at the House of the Indies in Seville were outstandingly efficient and painstaking in their jobs. Certainly, they were never careless with correspondence addressed to the King.

A more reasonable explanation is that Balboa's enemies destroyed all his carefully detailed reports they could get their hands on because of what they revealed. It is clearly evident, from what Vasco Núñez has to say about Pedrarias in the present letter, for example, that he was not a man to mince words or to clothe his accusations in polite double-talk.

In the following translation, I have used punctuation and paragraphing which do not appear in Balboa's original letter, but which seem necessary to make the writer's meaning clear for English-speaking readers.

"Most Christian and most Mighty Lord:
"Some days past I wrote to your very Royal Majesty by caravel

which came to this town, making known to your most R.H. all the things that have happened in these parts: likewise I wrote by a brigantine which departed from this town for the Island Española to make known to the Admiral how we were in very urgent need: and now God has supplied us with two ships laden with provisions with which we have been relieved: and it has been the means of this land remaining inhabited: for we were in such great extremity that if the help had been delayed much longer, when it might come, it would not be necessary because it would not find anyone to succor because of the famine we endured: for by reason of the great necessity we have had, there would be lacking the three hundred men we find here, whom I have governed: Alonso de Ojeda's men from Urabá, and those from Veragua who belonged to Diego de Nicuesa, whom I with much labor have brought together as your Royal Majesty will see in another letter that I am writing to your very R.H., giving account of everything that has passed here.

"Your most R.H. sent me a command, ordering me to send for those persons who were in the settlement of Diego de Nicuesa: to bring them to this town and to do them much honor in every way possible. Your very R.H. is aware that after Diego de Nicuesa came to this town, and from here set out to go to the Island Española, I took as good care of the people he left in his settlement as if they had been in my charge and I had myself brought them from Castile by order of your most R.H.: for if I had not helped them, they would now be lost because five or six were dying of hunger every day, and by the assaults of the Indians. All the people that Diego de Nicuesa left are now here in this town with me. From the first day of their arrival here they have been treated as well as if they had been sent by order of your most Royal Highness, for there has been no difference made with them, any more than if they had come here on the first day. As soon as they arrived here, they were given their pieces of land for building and planting in very good locations, close to those occupied by the men who came with me to this town, for the land was not yet divided, and they arrived in time to receive some of the best pieces.

"I have to inform your most Royal Highness that both the governors, as well Diego de Nicuesa as Alonzo de Ojeda, performed their duties very ill, and that they were the causes of their own perdition, because they knew not how to act, and because, after they

240

arrived in these parts, they took such presumptuous fancies into their thoughts that they appeared to be lords of the land. They imagined they could rule the land and do all that was necessary from their beds: and thus they acted, believing that they had nothing further to do. But the nature of the land is such that if he who has charge of the government sleeps, he cannot awake when he wishes, for this is a land that obliges the man who governs to be very watchful. The country is difficult to travel through, on account of the numerous rivers and morasses and mountains, where many men die owing to the great labour they have to endure, for every day we are exposed to death in a thousand forms. I have thought of nothing, by day or by night, but how to support myself and the handful of men whom God has placed under my charge, and how to maintain them until your Highness sends reinforcements.

"I have taken care that the Indians of this land are not ill-treated, permitting no man to injure them, and giving them many things from Castile, whereby they may be drawn into friendship with us. This honourable treatment of the Indians has been the cause of my learning great secrets from them, through the knowledge of which large quantities of gold may be obtained, and your Highness will thus be well served. I have often wondered how it would be possible for us to sustain life, seeing that we have been as badly succoured from the island of Española as if we had not been Christians. But our Lord, by his infinite mercy, has chosen to supply us with provisions in this land, though we have often been in such straits that we expected to die of hunger: yet at the time of our greatest necessity our Lord has pointed out the means of relief.

"Your most Royal Highness must know that, after we came here, we were forced to travel from one place to another, by reason of the great scarcity, and it astonishes me how we could have endured such hardships. The things that have happened have been more by the hand of God than by the hand of men. Up to the present time I have taken care that none of my people shall go hence unless I myself go in front of them, whether it be by night or day, marching across rivers, through swamps and forests and over mountains: and your Royal Highness should not imagine that the swamps of this land are so light that they can be crossed easily, for many times we have had to go a league, and two and three leagues, through swamps and water, stripped naked, with our clothes fastened on a shield upon our heads: and when we had come to the end of one swamp we have had to enter another, and to walk in this way from two or three to ten days.

"And if the person who is entrusted with the government of this land remains in his house, and leaves the work to others, no one else he can send in his place can manage the people so well, or fail to make mistakes which may cause the destruction of himself and of all who are with him. I can say this with truth, as a person that has seen what happens: for sometimes (although they have not been above three), when I have been unable to go with the men because I have been detained by some business connected with the sowing of the crops, I have observed that those whom I have sent in my place, have not acted according to reason.

"I, my Lord, have taken care that everything that has been obtained, up to the present day, shall be properly divided, as well the gold and the pearls (the shares of your most Royal Highness being put on one side) as the clothing and eatables: but up to the present time we have valued the eatables more than the gold, for we have more gold than health, and often have I searched in various directions, desiring more to find a sack of corn than a bag of gold: and I can certify the truth of this to your most Royal Highness, for we have been more in want of food than of gold. I assure your most Royal Highness that, if I had not personally gone in front of my men, searching for food for those who went with me, as well as for those that remained in this town, there would have been no one left in the town or in the land, unless our Lord had miraculously taken pity upon us. The way I have adopted in dividing the gold that has been procured, is to give a proper share to each man who has been engaged in finding it. All receive shares of the food, although some have not gone in search of it.

"I desire to give an account to your most Royal Highness of the great secrets and marvellous riches of this land of which God has made your most Royal Highness the Lord, and me the discoverer before any other, for which I give many thanks and much praise for all the days of the world, and I hold myself to be the most fortunate man that has been born in the world, seeing that our Lord has been served at my hands rather than at those of another.

242

"As so propitious a commencement has been made, I beseech your most Royal Highness that I may be permitted to complete this great enterprise, and I am bold to make this supplication to your most Royal Highness, because I know that you will thus be well served, for I venture to say that, with the help of God, and with industry, I shall be able to conduct the enterprise in such a way that your most Royal Highness will be thereby well served. But for this purpose your most Royal Highness should order that 500 or more men be sent from the island of Española, that, united with those already here, although we have not more than 100 fit to bear arms, I may be able to march into the interior of the land, and pass over to the other sea on the south side.

"That which I, by much labor and great hardships, have had the fortune to discover, is as follows:

"In this province of Darien many very rich mines have been found, and there is gold in great quantities. Twenty rivers have been discovered, and thirty containing gold flow from a mountain about two leagues from this town, toward the south. This mountain is toward the west, and between the town and the mountain no gold-bearing rivers have been seen, but I believe they exist. Following the course of the great river of San Juan for thirty leagues on the right-hand side, one arrives at a province called Abanumaque, which contains much gold. I have certain intelligence that there are very rich rivers of gold in this province, from a son of a cacique, and from other Indian men and women whom I have taken. Thirty leagues up this great river, on the left hand, a very large and beautiful stream flows into it, and two days' journey up this stream there is a cacique called Dabaibe. He is a very great lord with a large and very populous land. He has great store of gold in his house, so much indeed that he who does not know the things of this land would be very hard of belief. I know this of a certainty. All the gold that goes forth from this gulf comes from the house of the cacique Dabaibe, as well as all that is owned by the caciques of those districts, and it is reported that they have many pieces of gold curiously worked, and very large. Many Indians who have seen them, tell me that this cacique Dabaibe has certain bags of gold, and that it takes the whole strength of a man to lift one of them onto his back.

"The cacique collects the gold, and this is the manner of his obtaining it:

"Two days' journey from his house there is a very beautiful country inhabited by a very evil Carib race, who eat as many men as they can get. They are a people without a chief, and there is no one whom they obey. They are warlike, and each man is his own master. They are lords of the mines, and these mines (according to the news I have heard) are the richest in the world. They are in a land where there is a mountain which appears to be the largest in the world, and I believe that so large a mountain has never before been seen. It rises up on the Urabá side of this gulf, somewhat inland, it may be twenty leagues from the sea. The way to it is in a southerly direction. At first the land is flat, but it gradually rises, and at last it is so high that it is covered with clouds. During two years we have only twice seen its summit, because it is continually obscured by clouds. Up to a certain point it is covered with a forest of great trees, and higher up the mountain has no trees whatever. It rises in the most beautiful and level country in the world, near the territory of this cacique Dabaibe. The very rich mines are in this land toward the rising of the sun, and it is two days' journey from the rich mines to the abode of this cacique Dabaibe.

"There are two methods of collecting the gold without any trouble. One is by waiting until the river rises in the ravines, and when the freshets pass off, the beds remain dry, and the gold is laid bare, which has been robbed from the mountains and brought down in very large lumps. The Indians describe them as being the size of oranges or of a fist, and others like flat slabs. The other way of gathering gold is by waiting until the plants on the hills are dry, which are set on fire, and when they are consumed the Indians go to search in the most likely places, and collect great quantities of very beautiful grains of gold. The Indians who gather this gold bring it in grains to be melted, and barter it with this cacique Dabaibe, in exchange for youths and boys to eat, and for women to serve them as wives, whom they do not eat. He gives them also many pigs, as well as fish, cotton cloth, and salt, and such worked pieces of gold as they want. These Indians only trade with the cacique Dabaibe, and with no one else.

"This cacique Dabaibe has a great place for melting gold in his house, and he has a hundred men continually working at the gold.

244

I know all this of a certainty, for I have never received any other account, in whatever direction I may have gone. I have heard it from many caciques and Indians, as well from natives of the territory of this cacique Dabaibe, as from those of other parts, so that I believe it to be true, because I have heard it in many forms, obtaining the information from some by torments, from others for love, and from others in exchange for things from Castile.

"I also have certain information that, after this river of San Juan is ascended for fifty leagues, there are very rich mines on both sides of the river. The means used to navigate this river is small canoes of the Indians because there are many narrow and winding branches, concealed within groves of trees: and these cannot be entered except in canoes three or four *palmos* wide. After this river has been explored, boats can be built on the model of *fustas*: eight *palmos* in width and equipped with twenty oars for rowing, because the river has a very strong current and even the Indian canoes can barely stem it. During the seasons when strong winds blow, vessels which carry up to a dozen *botas* could navigate by sail, assisted by oars at some of the turns in the river. Sometimes it is necessary to go as much as three leagues off the course and at times to deviate five and even eight leagues by land.

"One cannot travel by land on horseback up this river, so far as we have been able to discern: but horses can sometimes be embarked upon the river from certain inlets which flow into it: for at the principal river they cannot be boarded because the surrounding area is swampy. The nearest point to the river at which they may be embarked by using the inlets is half a league.

"The people who dwell along the upper reaches of this great river are evil and warlike: much cunning is necessary in dealing with them. I have news of many other things, which I will not certify until I know more about them, believing that I shall know them with the help of God.

"That which lies down this coast toward the west is a province called Careta, about twenty leagues from here: there are in it certain rivers which contain gold, according to some Indian men and women who are in this town. We have not gone there to dig for gold, in order not to stir up the country (which is at peace) until we have more men, for we are few in number.

"Farther down the coast, at a distance of forty leagues from this

245

town, and going twelve leagues inland, there is a cacique called Comogre and another called Pocorosa, both of whom live the same distance from the sea. They carry on constant warfare with each other. Each has a town inland and two others on the sea-coast, from which they supply the interior with fish. The Indians have assured me that in the territories of these two caciques there are rivers very rich in gold.

"A day's journey from the seat of this cacique Pocorosa are some mountains which are the most beautiful that have been seen in these parts. They are clear of forests, save for some groves along the *arroyos* which descend from the mountains. In those sierras are certain caciques who keep a great quantity of gold in their houses. It is said that these caciques store their gold in *barbacoas* like *maiz*, because it is so abundant they do not care to keep it in baskets. They say that all the rivers in those mountains contain gold and that there is a great store of large grains.

"The manner in which the Indians collect the gold is by picking up the nuggets when they see them in the water and placing them in their baskets. They also gather it from the ravines when they are dry. And in order that your most Royal Highness may be more fully informed concerning these parts, I am sending to you a branded Indian from that region who has collected it many times. Your most Royal Highness should not take this to be a laughing matter, for in truth I am well assured of it by many Indian person-ages and caciques.

"I, my lord, have been quite near these mountains, within a day's journey: but I did not reach them because I did not have enough men: for a man goes only as far as he can, not as far as he wishes. Beyond these mountains, the country is very flat toward the south, and the Indians say that the other sea is three days' journey from there. All the caciques and Indians of the province of Comogre tell me that there is much wrought gold in the houses of the caciques whose domains lie along the other sea: so much so that it would drive us out of our minds [to see it]. They say that in rivers along the other coast there is gold in great quantity and in very large grains. They say that Indians from the other sea come in their canoes up a river which flows past the seat of the cacique Comogre and bring much gold from the mines in large lumps to be melted. In exchange for the gold they are given cotton cloth

246

and handsome Indians, both men and women. But they do not eat them as do the people dwelling near the great river.

"They say that the Indians of the other coast are very amiable and well-behaved. They tell me that the other sea is very good for canoe navigation, for it is always smooth and never rough like the sea on this side, according to what the Indians say. I believe that there are many islands in that sea. They say there are many large pearls and that the caciques have baskets full of them, as have all the Indians, men and women, generally.

"This river runs from the territory of the cacique Comogre to the other sea: and before reaching there, it forms itself into three branches, each of which empties into the other sea. They say that the pearls are brought to the cacique Comogre for trade in canoes coming up the western branch. They say that canoes from the eastern branch bring gold from all parts, which is an incredible thing and without any comparison.

"Forasmuch as our Lord has made you ruler of such a great land, where so much treasure is, it should not be overlooked: for if your most Royal Highness will be pleased to send me troops, I will, through our Lord's goodness, discover high things, whereby may be obtained so much gold and such riches that with them might be conquered a great part of the world. And if your Royal Highness is pleased with this and will leave me in charge of the things that are necessary to do here, I have so much confidence in the mercy of our Lord that I will know how to apply such proper skill and industry as will bring it all to good estate and that your Royal Highness will be well served. And if this be not accomplished, I have nothing better to offer than my head, which I put as forfeit.

"I assure your most Royal Highness that I have worked with greater diligence in the service of your most Royal Highness than the governors who were lost here, Alonso de Ojeda and Diego de Nicuesa: for I do not remain in bed while my troops enter and explore the country. I must inform your most Royal Highness that no company has gone into any part of this land that I have not gone before them as a guide, opening the way with my own hands for those who went with me. In proof, I submit the deeds and the fruits which each one of those who has come over here has given.

"Most powerful Lord: as a person who has seen the things of

these parts and who has more knowledge of the land than anyone else hitherto has had, and because I desire that the things which I have here begun shall flourish and grow to a state that is best suited to the service of your very R.H., I wish to make known to you what is now necessary to be done and provided. Until the land is known and it is seen what is in it, the principal requirement is that a thousand men should come from the island of Española, for men who might come from Castile would not be worth much until they became accustomed to the country, and for the present would be the cause of destroying both themselves and we who are here with them.

"Your very R.H. should command that for the present this land be supplied with provisions directly by your very R.H. This behooves you in order that the land be explored and its secrets known. And thus two results will be attained: first, much money will be earned in goods: and the other and principal one is that, being provided with victuals, it will be possible to do great things and to discover vast riches, by the help of God. At the same time, it is necessary that plenty of materials for the building of small river craft be constantly available here . . . [words illegible in original]: pitch, nails, ropes, and sails. It is necessary that some master shipwrights come, who know how to build brigantines.

"Your Highness should command that two hundred crossbows be sent, made exactly to specification, having very strong stocks and fittings . . . [words illegible] very quick-shooting and not above two pounds in weight. With these, much money would be made because here everybody is happy to have a crossbow or two, since in addition to being very good weapons against the Indians, they supply those who own them with plenty of birds and game. Two dozen very good hand-guns of lightweight metal are needed, made of bronze because those of iron are soon damaged by the rains and moisture and they are eaten with rust. Your most R.H. should command that two dozen pieces of ordnance be made of bronze, because those of iron were lost. It is enough that they be twenty-five to thirty pounds in weight, and long, so that a man may carry one of them wherever it might be needed: and very good powder.

"As soon as more troops arrive, a fort must be built in the province of Dabaibe, the strongest that can be made, because the

248

country is thickly settled with evil people. Another fortress should be built among the mines of Tubanamá in the province of Comogre, likewise because that land is heavily populated. And these fortresses, most powerful Lord, at present could not be built of lime and stone or of adobe, but must be constructed of a double palisade of very strong timber, filled in the middle with earth that is mixed and packed: and around it a very secure fosse. And if they tell your most R.H. that at present fortresses of lime and stone, or of anything else, may be built in this country, it is because they who might say it have not seen the quality of the land.

"This that I say, most powerful Lord, can be put into effect when more reinforcements come, if our Lord please: and from these two seats, the one of Dabaibe and the other of the province of Comogre, the land will be explored and the secrets of it will be known: and of the other sea, which is on the south side, and everything else that is needful.

"Your very R.H. should order that master artisans come to keep the crossbows in repair, for every day they get out of order because of the heavy rains.

"In everything that I have mentioned, money will be made, and it need not cost your very R.H. anything except to give orders for providing the troops needed: for I dare, with the help of our Lord, to do everything in these parts that will be best suited to the service of your most R.H., most puissant Lord: for as I have said, I am here to serve and advise your most R.H. of all that might appear to me to be in your interest.

"And now the residents of this town send to entreat your most R.H. to grant them certain favors, the greater part of which it is best that Your Highness should concede to them, for it will be greatly to your benefit. Regarding those Indians in certain provinces who eat men, and others who dwell at the bottom of this gulf of Urabá and in the lowlands of the great river San Juan and many other swampy lands that lie around the gulf up to the entrance into the level country of the province of Dabaibe: none of them have any tillable lands, nor any other means of subsistence save only fish: and with the fish they trade for corn: they are a worthless people: and they do more, for when Christians have set sail in canoes on the great river of San Juan, they have come out in their canoes against them and they have killed some of us Chris-

249

tians: and in like manner, they sally forth from the thickets where all the Indians of the country round about congregate.

"The region where the Indians eat men is very poor and unprofitable: and can never at any time be turned to good account. Likewise, the Indians of the Caribana have well deserved death a thousand times, because they are a very wicked people who at various times have killed many Christians, including some of ours during the passage there when we lost our ship. I would not make slaves of so evil a people, but would order them to be destroyed, both old and young, that no memory may remain of such a vile race. I declare this, my Lord, in regard to the point of Caribana and as far as twenty leagues inland, the one because the people are very evil and the other for the reason that the land is very sterile and worthless. And it will serve Your Highness to give license that all these Indians be carried to the island of Española and to the other islands settled with Christians to be sold and profit from them, and with the price of them, other slaves might be brought here: for in order to hold them in these parts, it would be impossible to make use of them, even for one day, because the land is very extensive, where they can run away and hide. Thus the settlers in these parts, not having Indians secured, cannot do what is conducive to the service of Y.H., nor can any gold be taken from the mines.

"The settlers are also sending to entreat Y.H. to grant them permission to bring Indians from Veragua, from a gulf called San Blas, which is some fifty leagues from this town, down the coast. Your Highness will be well served in granting them this request, because it is a very worthless land, covered with great marshes and many mountains: and seen from the sea, all the land is flooded so that no profit whatever may be had from these Indians of Veragua and of Caribana, which are lowlands, except in this way, by bringing them to Christian settlements, whence they may be taken to Cuba, Jamaica, and other islands peopled by Christians, to exchange them for other Indian *naborias*, of which there are many in those islands, a great number of them wild. Thus, by sending the warlike Indians far from their own homeland, the natives of these parts will labor well in the islands, and those of the islands here. I counsel Your Highness thus because it will be very conducive to your service that you give them the privilege of taking Indians from the neighboring islands to this mainland. Concerning this, I must inform Your Highness that for a distance of two hundred leagues around this town, there is no inhabited island except one in Cartagena, where at present there are many natives, who well defend themselves.

"In that which concerns the gold that is collected from the Indians by barter and in warfare, it will be conducive to your service to give permission that henceforth a fifth may be given to Your Highness of all that may be obtained: and the reason it will benefit Your Highness is that, your share now being a fourth, it makes them reluctant to go forth to explore the country and to engage in war through great hardships, for, in truth, they are so excessive that it is unbearable. And they prefer rather to take gold from the mines, there being many good ones near here, than to go out to die. And this being the case, if I, or the governor who may succeed me, make the Christians go inland on expeditions of discovery, they will never go willingly: and a thing done unwillingly never can be done so well as it ought to be: while, if it be done willingly, all will be done well and according to our desire. Therefore, I certify to Your Highness that if the King's share is a fifth, the gold will be collected in much larger quantity than remaining at the fourth part: besides which, the country will be discovered, as Your Highness desires.

"With respect to the Indians' cloth and the trifles in their houses, they are matters of small account and of little value: and everything else is taken in such amounts that they cannot benefit from them, for, in truth, many times things are left with the Indians in their houses because of having no room to carry them: so it is expedient to the service of Your Highness to give all these things to the settlers free of tax.

"In regard to arms and pieces of ordnance, and supplies for constructing brigantines and master shipwrights to build them, these things are expedient above everything else, because without these no good work can be done. If Your Highness should now order them to be sent, it would be at the expense of the settlers in these parts, without any expense to Your Highness. On all that Your Highness might provide from Castile, of what I have named, much will be gained and the country provided with what is needed. Your Highness would receive all this from me as your

251

loyal servant and give faith to all of this because thus will your Highness's service be advanced. I do not desire to build air castles as did the governors whom Your Highness sent out before me, for between them both they have lost eight hundred men: and those whom I have been able to rescue, of those left shipwrecked and who escaped, amount to only fifty, and this is the truth. Your Highness will consider all that I have done and discovered and endured with these people, without any help save that I received from God, and by my own labor: and who has thus been able to sustain and support himself merely with the help of the Indians: and it will prove to Your Highness that it is I who knows how to inform him of what best suits these parts. And if I should err in something that promotes the service of Your Highness, I entreat Your Highness to at least consider my excessive wish and desire to serve Your Highness.

And though, most puissant Lord, I may not at present comprehend all that is needed for the future of this land, I can certify that I know better how to administer than all those who have come here hitherto. And that Your Highness may fully understand what this means, consider how little those governors have discovered, found out, and obtained up to now: how they all have failed and have departed, leaving these shores full of graves. And although many Christians have been buried in the ground, it is also true that many of those who died have been devoured by dogs and crows. I do not wish to enlarge upon this, except to indicate to Your Highness what each man has been able to do and has in truth done up to now.

"Most puissant Lord, in order that Your Highness may be better informed of all that has happened here, I am sending Sebastián de Campo [Ocampo]: and I entreat Your Highness to give him full credence, for he has been apprised by me of the whole truth concerning all that should be done in the service of Your Highness and of what is required in this land.

"Your Highness must know that in the days past, there were certain disagreements here because the *alcaldes* and *regidores* of this town, filled with envy and falsehood, tried to seize me: and when they failed in that, they made false charges against me, with false witnesses and in secret: of which I complain to Your Highness: for if such acts are not punished, no governor whom Your Highness sends here will be free from attacks. For I, being *alcalde mayor* for Your Highness, have been exposed to a thousand slanders: and they have acted in like manner with all those who have come to these parts. And if the justice of Your Highness is not feared, that which is best for your service will not be done.

"And because the *alcaldes* and *regidores* sent an accusation against me, which I believe Your Highness will see there, I appointed two gentlemen as my judges, that they might draw up a report of my life, and of the great and loyal services I have performed for Your Highness in these parts of the Indies, and mainland and these provinces in which we now are, which I send to Your Highness that you may see the malice of these people and because I believe Your Highness will be pleased with all that I have done in these parts for your service. I beg Your Highness to examine it all, so that favor may be shown me according to my services. I am sending also a report of what happened after they devised their wickedness.

"Most puissant Lord, I desire to ask a favor of Your Highness, for I have done much in your service: and it is that Your Highness will command that no Bachelor of Laws, or of anything else, lest it be of medicine, shall pass over to this part of Tierra Firme upon pain of heavy punishment which Your Highness shall order to be imposed. For no Bachelor comes here who is not a devil and who does not lead the life of devils. And not only are they themselves evil, but they stir up a thousand lawsuits and quarrels. This mandate will be greatly to the advantage of Your Highness's service, for the country is new.

"Most powerful Lord: by a brigantine we sent from here, aboard which were Juan de Quicedo and Rodrigo de Colmenares, I forwarded to Your Highness 500 *pesos* of gold in most beautiful grains from the mines: and forasmuch as the navigation is somewhat dangerous for small vessels, I now send to Your Highness by Sebastián del Campo, 370 *pesos* of gold from the mines. I would have sent more had it not been for the impossibility of collecting it during the short space of time the vessels were here. In all that I have said, I beg Your Highness to provide what most will promote his service.

"May Our Lord prosper the life and royal estate of Your Highness by the addition of many more kingdoms and dominions to your sacred rule: and may all that is discovered in these regions come directly under your charge, as your most R.H. may desire: for there are greater riches here than in any other part of the world.

"From the town of Santa Maria del Antigua, of the province of Darien, in the gulf of Urabá: today Thursday the 20th of January in the year 1513. The creature and servant of Your Highness, who kisses your most royal hands and feet.

Vasco Núñez de Balboa"

IV

The Companions

Andrés de Valderrábano, the King's notary and official chronicler of the expedition led by Balboa across the Isthmus, when he discovered the Pacific, listed in his journal the names of the sixty-seven "caballeros and hidalgos and worthy men who were present in the discovery of the Sea of the South with the magnificent and most noble lord captain Vasco Núñez de Balboa, governor for Their Highnesses in Tierra Firme." They were:

Andrés de Vera, priest
Francisco Pizarro
Diego Albitez
Fabian Pérez
Bernardino de Morales
Diego de Texerina
Cripstóbal Valdebuso
Bernardino de Cienfuegos
Sebastián de Grijalba
Francisco de Ávila
Johan de Espinosa
Johan de Valasco
Benito Burán
Andrés de Molina
Antonio de Baracaldo
Pedro de Escobar
Cripstóbal Daza
Francisco Pesado
Alonso de Guadalupe
Hernando Muñoz
Hernando Hidalgo
Johan Rubio de Malpartida
Alvaro de Bolaños
Alonso Ruiz
Francisco de Lucena
Martín Ruiz
Pascual Rubio de Malpartida

Francisco González de Guadacama [Guadalcanal]
Francisco Martín
Pedro Martín de Palos
Hernando Díaz
Andrés Garcia de Jaén
Luis Gutiérrez
Alonso Sebastián
Johan Vegines
Rodrigo Velásquez
Johan Camacho
Diego de Montehermoso
Johan Matheos
Maestre Alonso de Sanctiago
Gregorio Ponce
Francisco de la Tova
Miguel Crespo
Miguel Sánchez
Martín García
Cripstóbal de Robledo
Cripstóbal de León, silversmith
Johan Martínez
Valdenebro [Francisco]
Johan de Beas, Loro
Johan Ferrol
Johan Gutiérrez de Toledo
Johan de Portillo
Johan García de Jaén
Matheo Lozano
Johan de Medellín
Alonso Martín, *esturiano*
Johan García, *marinero*
Johan Gallego
Francisco de Lentín, Sicilian
Johan del Puerto
Francisco de Arias
Pedro de Orduña
Ñuflo de Olano, Negro
Pedro Fernández de Aroche

Andrés de Valderrábano, Notary